Remote Access

The Cram Sheet

This Cram Sheet contains the distilled, key facts about Remote Access Exam Cram. Review this information last thing before you enter the test room, paying special attention to those areas where you feel you need the most review. You can transfer any of these facts onto a blank sheet of paper before beginning the exam.

Many of the Cisco exams have recently gone to a fill in the blank format for some of the questions. This requires typing in the answer with the correct spelling and syntax. It is important to NOT rely on the "short cuts" that are common when entering commands. Some helpful reminders are listed here.

NEEDS

1. The Federal Communications Commission (FCC) regulates the speed to 53Kbps; hence your 56Kbps modem could run at 33.6Kbps toward the network and 53Kbps back to the modem user.

2. The technique of "bit stuffing" results in a data throughput of 56Kbps, every eigth bit is unreliable. To overcome this, a new technique was developed called "bi-polar 8 zero substitution". As the CSU (channel service unit) sees an 8-bit string of all zeros it is replaced by a substitute byte of 00011011, with two bipolar violations.

CENTRAL SITE

3. Every byte has a start bit and one or two stop bits added to the end of the byte. In today's world, the most common form of asynchronous clocking is 8-N-1 or eight bits, no parity and one stop bit. Thus for every 8 bits of information, you must transmit at least 10 bits, or 20 percent overhead.

4. The Electronic Industries Association/Telecommunications Industry Association (EIA/TIA) defines a standard for the interface between DCE and DTE devices called the EIA/TIA-232. This standard was previously referred to as the RS-232-C standard, where the RS stood for recommended standard.

5. For example, you want to set up an 8-N-1 connection to the fourth asynchronous port on a router, which has the 10.44.5.6 address assigned to its E0 port. To connect in character mode using Telnet you would issue the following command: **Telnet 10.44.5.6 2004** where 10.44.5.6 is the router's E0 port and 2004 is the Cisco reserved port number for the fourth asynchronous port on the router.

6. It should be noted that on router models with A/S ports, the serial ports default to synchronous, and the interface must be declared for asynchronous usage using the **physical-layer async** command.

7. The correct initialization string must be sent to the modem for proper operation. This can be accomplished by using a **chat-script** or the **modem autoconfigure** command. The

protocols because it is too busy handling others. Where priority queuing will handle all traffic in an upper queue before moving to a lower queue, custom queuing will handle a certain amount of bandwidth in a given queue then move on to the next queue. Custom queuing allocates traffic up to 16 queues via a queue list, 10 queues if using an IOS version prior to 11.0.

38. Use the **compress** command to configure Point-to-Point software compression for an LAPB, PPP, or HDLC link.

39. Header compression is primarily used in situations where the payload of the packet is much smaller than the header. TCP/IP header compression only works on the TCP/IP protocol and the primary usage is on packets with small payloads, such as Telnet, while crossing slow WAN links.

ACCESS NETWORKS

40. Advantages of NAT include conservation of IP addresses, elimination of renumbering requirements due to overlap or changing ISPs, and increased security. Disadvantages include processor overhead to accomplish the translation, determining what device generated what packet, and some functionality issues with certain applications.

41. To convert the configuration for simple NAT translation to overload the administrator has to be able to type the command argument "overload". Overloading an inside global address uses the same syntax but with the extra argument the router knows to track the port numbers for the translation table.

42. You may clear a single entry or the entire NAT table by using the **clear ip nat** command.

43. Authorization allows the administrator to control authorization on a one-time basis, per-service, per-user list, per-group or per-protocol. AAA lets the administrator create attributes that describe what the user is allowed to do. The attributes are compared to the database for a given user and the capabilities are returned to the AAA server.

44. Accounting allows the administrator to collect information such as start and stop times for user access, executed commands, traffic statistics, and the like for storage in the RDBMS. Accounting allows the tracking of service and resources that are "consumed" by the user. The thrust is that this information can be used for client billing, internal billing, network management, or audit trails.

45. What method will be used if a users tries to access privileged mode on the router? If no AAA methods are set, then the user must have the enable password as the IOS would demand. If AAA is being used and *no* default is set, then the user will also need the enable password for access to the privileged mode.

46. Once a user has been authenticated, they can be further restricted to what they are allowed to do. This is done using the **aaa authorization** command. These restrictions can be applied to activities or services offered on the router.

CORIOLIS
Certification Insider Press

24. In order to move Layer 3 traffic across an X.25 network, the router must be told of the association. You need to provide **x25 map** statements in order for the router to understand that to reach the IP network to which it wants to send packets, it must send those packets across an X.25 link.

25. X.25 supports up to eight circuits carrying data from a single protocol, as well as up to nine protocols sending data across a single circuit.

26. The default X.25 packet size is 128 bytes.

27. The **modulo** command tells the router that the maximum window size is one less than the number specified. A modulo of 8 indicates that the maximum window size is 7, whereas a modulo of 128 means the maximum is 127. The default is a modulo of 8 while the default window size is 2.

28. The Committed Information Rate (CIR) is the bandwidth that is guaranteed to get through. This differs in Frame Relay from the Burst Rate which is the maximum amount of data the pipe is capable of sending. You may send a T1 worth of data but only the CIR amount is guaranteed to get through.

29. The DLCI is a circuit ID for the link from the CO switch to your office. This is a value that is local to the CO switch.

30. The Local Management Interface (LMI) is a Frame Relay signaling standard between your router and the CO switch. LMI is responsible for making sure both devices know the other is there. In addition to acting as keepalives, LMI also acts as a form of Cisco Discovery Protocol (CDP). LMI can provide the router with its DLCI number and IP information regarding the device on the other side of the cloud.

31. BECNs and FECNs are messages from Frame Relay switches to you saying "don't send so much data!" When a Frame Relay device becomes congested and BECNs and FECNs are generated, this situation creates problems for you. If the router doesn't throttle back the number of packets it's sending out per second, packets over the CIR value will be dropped.

32. A floating static route allows for the existence of a static route on the router, but doesn't allow it to interfere with the normal routing process until needed. It's created just like a regular static route with the addition of Administrative Distance information at the end An example would be: **ip route 10.1.2.0 255.255.255.0 192.168.1.4 130**. The route exists in the routing table but won't be used if a routing protocol with an AD better than 130 can find a route to the destination network.

33. You can configure dial backup to activate an interface when the amount of traffic on the primary link reaches or exceeds a certain amount. Unlike many Cisco interface references, the **backup load** command doesn't use a portion of 255 in the command. The value referenced is a straight percentage of the link's capability.

34. You can configure dial backup on an interface so that another interface activates if the primary interface goes down. This is often done with an ISDN line being the backup for a T1. If the T1 drops then the ISDN line comes up. Use the **backup interface** command on the primary interface to point to the backup interface.

35. Weighted fair queuing raises the priority level of packets that are smaller above the priority level of large packets. This tends to benefit traffic generated by applications where the user will notice a lag. An example would be Telnet traffic. Telnet sends small TCP packets containing a single character.

36. Priority queuing places traffic in groups according to the configured priority of the traffic in question. It is possible to place IPX traffic in a higher priority grouping than IP and vice versa. Priority Queuing focuses on routing the most important traffic at the possible expense of traffic that is not as important. Priority Queuing queues can hold 20, 40, 60, and 80 packets by default for each of High, Medium, Normal, and Low queues.

37. Custom queuing allows the administrator to prioritize traffic so that important traffic is serviced more frequently at the same time that this queuing strategy does not ignore certain

common method of initialization is the **modem autoconfigure** command.

8. In addition to authentication, the PPP LCP allows for Callback, Compression, and Multilink.

9. PAP's major problem is passwords that cross the line in clear text.

10. Callback is designed by Cisco to aid in bill consolidation. Instead of having numerous telecommuting employees pay long distance fees that they have to expense, the router will call them back after the person has authenticated. While Cisco does not officially market callback as a security feature, many organizations use it as such.

11. PPP has four types of compression available to it: Stacker, Predictor, MPPC, and TCP Header compression.

12. Multilink allows for bundling of data circuits into a larger virtual pipe. For example, ISDN has two data channels that each support up to 64Kbps. You can use each channel separately or you can bind them together to form a virtual 128Kbps pipe. Multilink accomplishes this by load balancing across the circuits. Multilink ensures that packets do not arrive out of order by fragmenting the packets and then shooting the fragments across the multilinked bundle.

ENHANCING ON DEMAND CONNECTIVITY

13. The use of ISDN and DSL now provide the home user a digital "last mile". These technologies are replacing the existing modems for those who require a higher speed remote connection. The target markets here are the telecommuters and the SO/HO users.

14. A BRI circuit is composed of two channels of 64K each called B channels and one 64k D channel that is divided between 16k used for call set-up and 48K used for signaling.

15. Super Frame (SF) is used for some older T1 carrier configurations. Extended Super Frame (ESF) is used for T1 PRI configurations. Cyclic Redundancy Check 4 (CRC-4) is used for E1 PRI configurations. The line coding is AMI for T1, B8ZS for T1 PRI and HDB3 for E1 PRI configurations.

16. DSL uses frequencies greater than 4400 Hz up to 1 MHz to signal over existing copper pair that supplies voice communication.

17. A dialer profile separates configuration components from each other. Some items, like physical interface characteristics, reside in one type of configuration while others, like a phone number, reside in another configuration. This allows for mixing and matching of configuration components depending on the need.

18. A dialer pool is a group of physical interfaces. You need to configure each physical interface you want to be a member of the pool with a pool ID and priority information. An interface may belong to multiple pools.

19. A map class is a very useful part of a dialer profile. While they are an optional component, they can be used to specify different layer 1 characteristics for a call.

20. When you have multiple lines and only one phone number for incoming calls, you need to use a roll over or hunt group. This is the same concept that lots of companies use for customer service. Call one number and the next available person will pick up the phone. Use the same concept here except for data calls.

21. The 700 series router was originally a product offering from a company that Cisco purchased in the last three years. The purchase gave Cisco two ISDN products targeted for the Telecommuter and SOHO market.

22. Full PPP support is offered with the 700 series, which includes PAP and CHAP, Multilink PPP. Data compression can be added by purchasing an upgraded software feature set. The 700 can also function as a DHCP server or relay agent, and will perform PAT (Port Address Translation).

23. The 700 can store a maximum of 20 profiles. There can be 16 user profiles, or 16 definitions for remote connections. There are three permanent profiles called LAN, standard and internal, and the system profile to make a total of 20. The system profile is also referred to as the global profile in some Cisco documentation.

Remote Access

Craig Dennis
Eric Quinn

CCNP Remote Access Exam Cram
©2000 The Coriolis Group. All Rights Reserved.

Limits Of Liability And Disclaimer Of Warranty

Trademarks

The Coriolis Group, LLC
14455 N. Hayden Road
Suite 220
Scottsdale, Arizona 85260

480/483-0192
FAX 480/483-0193
http://www.coriolis.com

Library of Congress Cataloging-in-Publication Data
Dennis, Craig.
    CCNP remote access exam cram / by Craig Dennis and Eric Quinn.
        p.   cm.
    Includes index.
    ISBN 1-57610-437-0
    1. Electronic data processing personnel--Certification.   2. Computer networks--Examinations--Study guides.   3. Computer terminals--Remote terminals.   I. Quinn, Eric.   II. Title.
QA76.3.D465   2000
004.67--dc21

President, CEO
Keith Weiskamp

Publisher
Steve Sayre

Acquisitions Editor
Jeff Kellum

Marketing Specialist
Cynthia Caldwell

Project Editor
Tom Lamoureux

Technical Reviewer
William Wagner

Production Coordinator
Todd Halvorsen

Cover Designer
Jesse Dunn

Layout Designer
April Nielsen

Printed in the United States of America
10 9 8 7 6 5 4 3 2 1

14455 North Hayden Road • Suite 220 • Scottsdale, Arizona 85260

Coriolis: The Smartest Way To Get Certified™

To help you reach your goals, we've listened to readers like you, and we've designed our entire product line around you and the way you like to study, learn, and master challenging subjects.

In addition to our highly popular *Exam Cram* and *Exam Prep* books, we offer several other products to help you pass certification exams. Our *Practice Tests* and *Flash Cards* are designed to make your studying fun and productive. Our *Audio Reviews* have received rave reviews from our customers—and they're the perfect way to make the most of your drive time!

The newest way to get certified is the *Exam Cram Personal Trainer*—a highly interactive, personalized self-study course based on the best-selling *Exam Cram* series. It's the first certification-specific product to completely link a customizable learning tool, exclusive *Exam Cram* content, and multiple testing techniques so you can study what, how, and when you want.

Exam Cram Insider—a biweekly newsletter containing the latest in certification news, study tips, and announcements from Certification Insider Press—gives you an ongoing look at the hottest certification programs. (To subscribe, send an email to **eci@coriolis.com** and type "subscribe insider" in the body of the email.) We also sponsor the Certified Crammer Society and the Coriolis Help Center—two other resources that will help you get certified even faster!

Help us continue to provide the very best certification study materials possible. Write us or email us at **cipq@coriolis.com** and let us know how our books have helped you study. Tell us about new features that you'd like us to add. Send us a story about how we've helped you; if we use it in one of our books, we'll send you an official Coriolis shirt!

Good luck with your certification exam and your career. Thank you for allowing us to help you achieve your goals.

Keith Weiskamp
President and CEO

Look For These Other Books From The Coriolis Group:

CCNA Routing and Switching Exam Prep
by Mark Poplar, Jason Waters,
Shawn McNutt, and David Stabenaw

CCNP Switching Exam Cram
by Richard Deal

CCNA Routing and Switching Practice Tests Exam Cram
by Robert Gradante

CCNP Support Exam Cram
by Matthew Luallen

CCIE Routing and Switching Exam Cram
by Henry Benjamin and Tom Thomas

*This book is dedicated to Sandra, Jacob, Joseph and David—the "group".
I love you guys. Thank you for being quiet on those nights when daddy
had to get some stuff done. The other person that this book is dedicated to
is my wife, Sharon. Thank you dear for reading the rough drafts
at the pool and making me try to explain it better.
Also, thank you for believing in me that I could finish this project.
—Craig Dennis*

ଈ

*I'd like to dedicate my portion of this book to my wife, Carolann, and
daughter, Lee, who have supported my certification efforts through the
years as well as understood the very long weeks those of us
in the computer industry have to put in from time to time.
I'd also like to thank my mother for buying the Commodore 64
that got me started on this track so very long ago.
—Eric Quinn*

ଈ

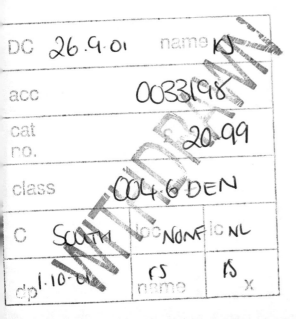

About The Authors

Craig Dennis CNE, CBE, CCNA, CCDA, CCDP, CCSI for ICRC, ACRC, CLSC, CMTD, BCRAN, CRLS, DCN CID, spent several years with Texaco working on their Research and Development facilities. He was the Network Manager for the Marine Corps National Capitol Region Network. Craig is currently an instructor for Global Knowledge, Inc.

Eric Quinn CCNP, CCDP, CCSI, CNE, MCSE, MCT, has worked as a Network Administrator for several high-tech firms, has been a consultant for manufacturing and design firms, and has designed ERP and e-commerce network infrastructure for companies nationwide. Eric is currently an instructor for a Cisco Training Partner, teaching ICND, BSCN, BCMSN, BCRAN and SNAM as well as custom security courses.

Acknowledgments

I learned many things about writing a book. Most of the words are mine. The underlying concepts are also mine. The smooth presentation to the reader comes from the dedicated efforts of the people at the Coriolis group. Syntax, style, format, bold, bullet and EXAM ALERT are things that may be the stuff of nightmares in the days to come. I have to thank Tom Lamoureux for never being 'pushy' about anything. Tom you were always a source of calm over the phone, even though I probably was a bit behind. Thanks also to Shari Jo who initially contacted me for this endeavor and always kept the big picture in the frame.

Next, I would like to thank the operator at Coriolis, Rose Yearnd, for putting up with my usual answer of 'duh'. I did manage to "remotely access" Tom and Shari Jo when necessary, even if it was with operator support.

I also want to thank my co-author, Eric, for giving me the parts that I wanted and helping with the parts that nobody wanted. I think we made a good team.

Last, but of course not least, I want to thank my parents. In so many ways they have helped me get to where I am. Their upbringing and constant dedication to their children's education is what allowed me to be able to string some words together to actually put a book together. Thanks Pearl. Thanks Rally. They now run P & R Enterprises out of Culpeper, Virginia, in case anybody out there needs some skillful woodwork or recipe information.

The author is the guy who spews out a bunch of words that make sense only to him. The publisher takes that diatribe and tries to make sense out of it. Friends never criticize and encourage the author even when the words are not coming. The family makes sacrifices so the author can spew out words. Now that I have finished this work, I can say that I can take credit for very little of the effort that the final product needed.

—*Craig Dennis*

I'd like to thank Tres Paxton and Bob Pape for inspiring future studies. Thanks also go out to Vick Tagawa and his future RFC on "Transporting IP packets via a dimpled spheriod."

—*Eric Quinn*

Contents At A Glance

Table Of Contents

Introduction

Welcome to the *CCNP Remote Access Exam Cram*! This book aims to help you get ready to take—and pass—the Cisco career certification test 640-505, "Remote Access." This Introduction explains Cisco's certification programs in general and talks about how the *Exam Cram* series can help you prepare for Cisco's career certification exams.

Exam Cram books help you understand and appreciate the subjects and materials you need to pass Cisco career certification exams. *Exam Crams* are aimed strictly at test preparation and review. They do not teach you everything you need to know about a topic (like the reasons for dial-backup or electing interesting packet types). Instead, we present and dissect the questions and problems we've found that you're likely to encounter on a test. We've worked from Cisco's own training materials, preparation guides, and tests, and from a battery of third-party test preparation tools. Our aim is to bring together as much information as possible about Cisco certification exams.

Nevertheless, to completely prepare yourself for any Cisco test, we recommend that you begin your studies with some instructor-led classroom training. You should also pick up and read one of the many study guides available from Cisco or third-party vendors, including The Coriolis Group's *Exam Prep* series. We also strongly recommend that you install, configure, and fool around with the Internetwork Operating System (IOS) software or environment that you'll be tested on, because nothing beats hands-on experience and familiarity when it comes to understanding the questions you're likely to encounter on a certification test. Book learning is essential, but hands-on experience is the best teacher of all!

The Cisco Career Certification Program

The Cisco Career Certification program is relatively new on the internetworking scene. The best place to keep tabs on it is the Cisco Training Web site, at **www.cisco.com/certifications/**. Before Cisco developed this program, Cisco Certified Internetwork Expert (CCIE) certification was the only available Cisco certification. Although CCIE certification is still the most coveted and prestigious certification that Cisco offers (possibly the most prestigious in the internetworking industry), lower-level certifications are now available as stepping stones on the road to the CCIE. The Cisco Career Certification program includes several certifications in addition to the CCIE, each with its own acronym (see Table 1). If you're a fan of alphabet soup after your name, you'll like this program.

> *Note:* *Within the certification program, there are specific specializations. For the purposes of this book, we will focus only on the Remote Access track. Visit www.cisco.com/warp/public/10/wwtraining/certprog/index.html for information on the other specializations.*

➤ *Cisco Certified Design Associate (CCDA)*—The CCDA is a basic certification aimed at designers of high-level internetworks. The CCDA consists of a single exam (640-441) that covers information from the Designing Cisco Networks (DCN) course. You must obtain CCDA and CCNA certifications before you can move up to the CCDP certification.

➤ *Cisco Certified Network Associate (CCNA)*—The CCNA is the first career certification. It consists of a single exam (640-507) that covers information from the basic-level class, primarily Interconnecting Cisco Network Devices (ICND). You must obtain CCNA certification before you can get your CCNP and CCDP certification.

➤ *Cisco Certified Network Professional (CCNP)*—The CCNP is a more advanced certification that is not easy to obtain. To earn CCNP status, you must be a CCNA in good standing. There are two routes you can take to obtain your CCNP. For the first route, you must take four exams: Routing (640-503), Switching (640-504), Remote Access (640-505), and Support (640-506). For the second route, you must take the Foundation (640-509) and Support (640-506) exams.

Although it may seem more appealing on the surface, the second route is more difficult. The Foundation exam contains more than 130 questions and lasts almost 3 hours. In addition, it covers all the topics covered in the Routing, Switching, and Remote Access exams.

Whichever route you choose, there are four courses Cisco recommends that you take:

Table 1   Cisco CCNA, CCNP, And CCIE Requirements*

CCNA

Only 1 Exam Required	
Exam 640-507	CCNA (Cisco Certified Network Associate)

CCNP

All 5 of these are required	
Exam 640-507	CCNA (Cisco Certified Network Associate)
Exam 640-503	Routing
Exam 640-504	Switching
Exam 640-505	Remote Access
Exam 640-506	Support

CCIE

1 Written Exam and 1 Lab Exam Required	
Exam 350-001	CCIE Routing and Switching Qualification
Lab Exam	CCIE Routing and Switching Laboratory

* This is not a complete listing. We have included only those tests needed for the Routing and Switching track.

➤ *Building Scalable Cisco Networks (BSCN)*—This course corresponds to the Routing exam.

➤ *Building Cisco Multilayer Switched Networks (BCMSN)*—This course corresponds to the Switching exam.

➤ *Building Cisco Remote Access Networks (BCRAN)*—This course corresponds to the Remote Access exam.

➤ *Cisco Internetworking Troubleshooting (CIT)*—This course corresponds to the Support exam.

Once you have completed the CCNP certification, you can further your career (not to mention beef up your resume) by branching out and passing one of the CCNP specialization exams. These include:

➤ Security—Requires you to pass the Managing Cisco Network Security exam (640-422)

➤ *LAN ATM*—Requires you to pass the Cisco Campus A TM Solutions exam (640-446)

➤ *Voice Access*—Requires you to pass the Cisco Voice over Frame Relay, ATM, and IP exam (640-447).

➤ *SNA/IP Integration*—Requires you to pass the (SNA Configuration for Multiprotocol Administrators (640-445) and the SNA Foundation (640-456) exams.

➤ *Network Management*—Requires you to either pass the Managing Cisco Routed Internetworks and Managing Cisco Switched Internetworks—MCRI—and Managing Cisco Switched Internetworks—MCSI)

➤ *Cisco Certified Design Professional (CCDP)*—The CCDP is another advanced certification. It's aimed at high-level internetwork designers who must understand the intricate facets of putting together a well-laid-out network. The first step in the certification process is to obtain the CCDA and CCNA certifications (yes, both). As with the CCNP, you must pass the Foundation exam or pass the Routing, Switching, and Remote Access exams individually. Once you meet those objectives, you must pass the Cisco Internetwork Design exam (640-025) to complete the certification.

➤ *Cisco Certified Internetwork Expert (CCIE)*—The CCIE is possibly the most influential certification in the internetworking industry today. It is famous (or infamous) for its difficulty and for how easily it holds its seekers at bay. The certification requires only one written exam (350-001); passing that exam qualifies you to schedule time at a Cisco campus to demonstrate your knowledge in a two-day practical laboratory setting. You must pass the lab with a score of at least 80 percent to become a CCIE. Recent statistics have put the passing rates at roughly 20 percent for first attempts and 35 through 50 percent overall. Once you achieve CCIE certification, you must recertify every two years by passing a written exam administered by Cisco.

➤ *Certified Cisco Systems Instructor (CCSI)*—To obtain status as a CCSI, you must be employed (either permanently or by contract) by a Cisco Training Partner in good standing, such as GeoTrain Corporation. That training partner must sponsor you through Cisco's Instructor Certification Program, and you must pass the two-day program that Cisco administers at a Cisco campus. You can build on CCSI certification on a class-by-class basis. Instructors must demonstrate competency with each class they are to teach by completing the written exam that goes with each class. Cisco also requires that instructors maintain a high customer satisfaction rating, or they will face decertification.

Taking A Certification Exam

Alas, testing is not free. Each computer-based exam costs between $100 and $200, and the CCIE laboratory exam costs $1,000. If you do not pass, you must pay the testing fee each time you retake the test. In the United States and Canada, computerized tests are administered by Sylvan Prometric. Sylvan Prometric can be reached at (800) 755-3926 or (800) 204-EXAM, any time from 7:00 A.M. to 6:00 P.M., Central Time, Monday through Friday. You can also try (612) 896-7000 or (612) 820-5707. CCIE laboratory exams are administered by Cisco Systems and can be scheduled by calling the CCIE lab exam administrator for the appropriate location.

To schedule a computer-based exam, call at least one day in advance. To cancel or reschedule an exam, you must call at least 24 hours before the scheduled test time (or you may be charged regardless). When calling Sylvan Prometric, have the following information ready for the telesales staffer who handles your call:

➤ Your name, organization, and mailing address.

➤ Your Cisco Test ID. (For most U.S. citizens, this is your Social Security number. Citizens of other nations can use their taxpayer IDs or make other arrangements with the order taker.)

➤ The name and number of the exam you wish to take. For this book, the exam name is Remote Access 640-505.

➤ A method of payment. The most convenient approach is to supply a valid credit card number with sufficient available credit. Otherwise, Sylvan Prometric must receive check, money order, or purchase order payments before you can schedule a test. (If you're not paying by credit card, ask your order taker for more details.)

When you show up to take a test, try to arrive at least 15 minutes before the scheduled time slot. You must supply two forms of identification, one of which must be a photo ID.

All exams are completely closed book. In fact, you will not be permitted to take anything with you into the testing area. However, you are furnished with a blank sheet of paper and a pen. We suggest that you immediately write down on that sheet of paper all the information you've memorized for the test. Although the amount of time you have to actually take the exam is limited, the time period does not start until you're ready, so you can spend as much time as necessary writing notes on the provided paper. If you think you will need more paper than what is provided, ask the test center administrator before entering the exam room. You must return all pages prior to exiting the testing center.

In *Exam Cram* books, the information that we suggest you write down appears on the Cram Sheet inside the front cover of each book. You will have some time to compose yourself, to record this information, and even to take a sample orientation exam before you begin the real thing. We suggest you take the orientation test before taking your first exam, but because they're all more or less identical in layout, behavior, and controls, you probably won't need to do this more than once.

When you complete a Cisco certification exam, the software will tell you whether you've passed or failed. All tests are scored on a basis of 100 percent, and results are broken into several topic areas. Even if you fail, we suggest you ask for—and keep—the detailed report that the test administrator should print for you. You can use this report to help you prepare for another go-round, if needed. Once you see your score, you have the option of printing additional copies of the score report. It is a good idea to have it print twice.

If you need to retake an exam, you'll have to call Sylvan Prometric, schedule a new test date, and pay another testing fee. The first time you fail a test, you can retake the test the next day. However, if you fail a second time, you must wait 14 days before retaking that test. The 14-day waiting period is in effect for all tests after the second failure.

Tracking Cisco Certification Status

As soon as you pass any Cisco exam (congratulations!), you must complete a certification agreement. You can do so online at the Certification Tracking Web site (www.galton.com/~cisco/), or you can mail a hard copy of the agreement to Cisco's certification authority. You will not be certified until you complete a certification agreement and Cisco receives it in one of these forms.

The Certification Tracking Web site also allows you to view your certification information. Cisco will contact you via email and explain it and its use. Once you are registered into one of the career certification tracks, you will be given a login on this site, which is administered by Galton, a third-party company that has no in-depth affiliation with Cisco or its products. Galton's information comes directly from Sylvan Prometric, the exam-administration company for much of the computing industry.

Once you pass the necessary exam(s) for a particular certification and complete the certification agreement, you'll be certified. Official certification normally takes anywhere from four to six weeks, so don't expect to get your credentials overnight. When the package arrives, it will include a Welcome Kit that contains a number of elements, including:

➤ A Cisco certificate stating that you have completed the certification requirements, suitable for framing, along with a laminated Cisco Career Certification identification card with your certification number on it

➤ Promotional items, which vary based on the certification.

Many people believe that the benefits of the Cisco career certifications go well beyond the perks that Cisco provides to newly anointed members of this elite group. There seem to be more and more job listings that request or require applicants to have a CCNA, CCDA, CCNP, CCDP, and so on, and many individuals who complete the program can qualify for increases in pay or responsibility. In fact, Cisco has started to implement requirements for its Value Added Resellers: To attain and keep silver, gold, or higher status, they must maintain a certain number of CCNA, CCDA, CCNP, CCDP, and CCIE employees on staff. There's a very high demand and low supply of Cisco talent in the industry overall. As an official recognition of hard work and broad knowledge, a Cisco career certification credential is a badge of honor in many IT organizations.

How To Prepare For An Exam

Preparing for any Cisco test (including Remote Access) requires that you obtain and study materials designed to provide comprehensive information about Cisco router operation and the specific exam for which you are preparing. The following list of materials will help you study and prepare:

➤ *Instructor-led training*—There's no substitute for expert instruction and hands-on practice under professional supervision. Cisco Training Partners, such as GeoTrain Corporation, offer instructor-led training courses for all of the Cisco career certification requirements. These companies aim to help prepare network administrators to run Cisco routed and switched internetworks and pass the Cisco tests. Although such training runs upwards of $350 per day in class, most of the individuals lucky enough to partake find them to be quite worthwhile.

➤ *Cisco Connection Online*—This is the name of Cisco's Web site (**www.cisco.com**), the most current and up-to-date source of Cisco information.

➤ The CCPrep Web site—This is the most well-known Cisco certification Web site in the world. You can find it at **www.ccprep.com** (formerly known as **www.CCIEprep.com**). Here, you can find exam preparation materials, practice tests, self-assessment exams, and numerous certification questions and scenarios. In addition, professional staff is available to answer questions that you can post on the answer board.

➤ *Cisco training kits*—These are available only if you attend a Cisco class, at a certified training facility, or if a Cisco Training Partner in good standing gives you one.

➤ *Study guides*—Several publishers—including Certification Insider Press—offer study guides. The Certification Insider Press series includes:

> ➤ *The* Exam Cram *series*—These books give you information about the material you need to know to pass the tests.

> ➤ *The* Exam Prep *series*—These books provide a greater level of detail than the *Exam Cram* books and are designed to teach you everything you need to know from an exam perspective.

Together, the two series make a perfect pair.

➤ *Multimedia*—These Coriolis Group materials are designed to support learners of all types—whether you learn best by listening, reading, or doing:

> ➤ *The* Practice Tests Exam Cram *series* —Provides the most valuable test preparation material: practice exams. Each exam is followed by a complete set of answers, as well as explanations of why the right answers are right and the wrong answers are wrong. Each book comes with a CD that contains one or more interactive practice exams.

> ➤ *The* Exam Cram Flash Card *series* —Offers practice questions on handy cards you can use anywhere. The question and its possible answers appear on the front of the card, and the answer, explanation, and a valuable reference appear on the back of the card. The set also includes a CD with an electronic practice exam to give you the feel of the actual test—and more practice!

> ➤ *The* Exam Cram Audio Review *series*—Offers a concise review of key topics covered on the exam, as well as practice questions.

➤ *Other publications*—You'll find direct references to other publications and resources in this text. There's no shortage of materials available about Cisco routers and their configuration. To help you sift through some of the publications out there, we end each chapter with a "Need To Know More?" section that provides pointers to more complete and exhaustive resources covering the chapter's information. This should give you an idea of where we think you should look for further discussion.

By far, this set of required and recommended materials represents an unparalleled collection of sources and resources for Cisco routers configuration guidelines. We anticipate that you'll find that this book belongs in this company. In the next section, we explain how this book works, and give you some good reasons why this book counts as a member of the required and recommended materials list.

About This Book

Each topical *Exam Cram* chapter follows a regular structure, along with graphical cues about important or useful information. Here's the structure of a typical chapter:

➤ *Opening hotlists*—Each chapter begins with a list of the terms, tools, and techniques that you must learn and understand before you can be fully conversant with that chapter's subject matter. The hotlists are followed by one or two introductory paragraphs to set the stage for the rest of the chapter.

➤ *Topical coverage*—After the opening hotlists, each chapter covers a series of at least four topics related to the chapter's subject. Throughout this section, topics or concepts likely to appear on a test are highlighted using a special Exam Alert layout, like this:

> This is what an Exam Alert looks like. Normally, an Exam Alert stresses concepts, terms, software, or activities that are likely to relate to one or more certification test questions. For that reason, any information found offset in Exam Alert format is worthy of unusual attentiveness on your part. Indeed, most of the information that appears on the Cram Sheet appears as Exam Alerts within the text.

You'll find what appears in the meat of each chapter to be worth knowing, too, when preparing for the test. Because this book's material is very condensed, we recommend that you use this book along with other resources to achieve the maximum benefit.

In addition to the Exam Alerts, we have provided tips that will help build a better foundation for Remote Access knowledge. Although the information may not be on the exam, it is certainly related and will help you become a better test taker.

> This is how tips are formatted. Keep your eyes open for these, and you'll become a Cisco internetworking expert in no time!

➤ *Practice questions*—Although we talk about test questions and topics throughout the book, a section at the end of each chapter presents a series of mock test questions and explanations of both correct and incorrect answers. We also try to point out especially tricky questions by using a special icon, like this:

Ordinarily, this icon flags the presence of a particularly devious inquiry, if not an outright trick question. Trick questions are calculated to be answered incorrectly if not read more than once, and carefully, at that. Although they're not ubiquitous, such questions make regular appearances on the Cisco exams. That's why we say exam questions are as much about reading comprehension as they are about knowing your material inside out and backwards.

➤ *Details and resources*—Every chapter ends with a section titled "Need To Know More?" It provides direct pointers to Cisco and third-party resources offering more details on the chapter's subject. In addition, this section tries to rank or at least rate the quality and thoroughness of the topic's coverage by each resource. If you find a resource in this collection that you like, use it, but don't feel compelled to use all the resources. On the other hand, we recommend only resources we use regularly, so none of our recommendations will be a waste of your time or money (but purchasing them all at once probably represents an expense that many network administrators and would-be CCNPs might find hard to justify).

The bulk of the book follows this chapter structure slavishly, but there are a few other elements that we'd like to point out. Chapter 16 is a sample test that provides a good review of the material presented throughout the book to ensure you're ready for the exam. Chapter 17 is the answer key. In addition, you'll find a handy glossary and an index.

Finally, the tear-out Cram Sheet attached next to the inside front cover of this *Exam Cram* book represents a condensed and compiled collection of facts, figures, and tips that we think you should memorize before taking the test. Because you can dump this information out of your head onto a piece of paper before answering any exam questions, you can master this information by brute force—you need to remember it only long enough to write it down when you walk into the test room. You might even want to look at it in the car (not while driving) or in the lobby of the testing center just before you walk in to take the test.

How To Use This Book

If you're prepping for a first-time test, we've structured the topics in this book to build on one another. Therefore, some topics in later chapters make more sense after you've read earlier chapters. That's why we suggest you read this book from front to back for your initial test preparation. If you need to brush up on a topic or you have to bone up for a second try, use the index or table of contents to go straight to the topics and questions that you need to study. Beyond the tests, we think you'll find this book useful as a tightly focused reference to some of the most important aspects of Remote Access.

Given all the book's elements and its specialized focus, we've tried to create a tool that will help you prepare for—and pass—Cisco Career Certification Exam 640-505, "Remote Access." Please share your feedback on the book with us, especially if you have ideas about how we can improve it for future test-takers. We'll consider everything you say carefully, and we'll respond to all suggestions.

Please send your questions or comments to us at **cipq@coriolis.com**. Please remember to include the title of the book in your message; otherwise, we'll be forced to guess which book you're writing about. Also, be sure to check out the Web pages at **www.coriolis.com**, where you'll find information updates, commentary, and clarifications on documents for each book that you can either read online or download for use later on.

Thanks, and enjoy the book!

Self-Assessment

The reason we included a Self-Assessment in this Exam Cram is to help you evaluate your readiness to tackle CCNP certification. It should also help you understand what you need to master the topic of this book—namely, Exam 640-405, "Configuring, Monitoring and Troubleshooting Dialup Services" and Exam 640-505 "Remote Access." But before you tackle this Self-Assessment, let's talk about concerns you may face when pursuing a CCNP, and what an ideal CCNP candidate might look like.

CCNPs In The Real World

In the next section, we describe an ideal CCNP candidate, knowing full well that only a few real candidates will meet this ideal. In fact, the description of that ideal candidate might seem downright scary. But take heart: Although the requirements to obtain a CCNP may seem pretty formidable, they are by no means impossible to meet. However, you should be keenly aware that it does take time and requires some expense and substantial effort to get through the process.

The first thing to understand is that the CCNP is an attainable goal. You can get all the real-world motivation you need from knowing that many others have gone before, so you will be able to follow in their footsteps. If you're willing to tackle the process seriously and do what it takes to obtain the necessary experience and knowledge, you can take—and pass—all the certification tests involved in obtaining a CCNP. In fact, we've designed these Exam Crams, and the companion Exam Preps, to make it as easy on you as possible to prepare for these exams. But prepare you must!

The same, of course, is true for other Cisco career certifications, including:

➤ CCNA, which is the first step on the road to the CCNP certification. It is a single exam that covers information from Cisco's Introduction to Cisco Router Configuration (ICRC) class and the Cisco LAN Switch Configuration (CLSC) class. Cisco also has developed a class that is geared to CCNA certification, known as Cisco Routing and LAN Switching (CRLS).

➤ CCDA, which is the first step on the road to the CCDP certification. It also is a single exam that covers the basics of design theory. To prepare for it, you should attend the Designing Cisco Networks (DCN) class and/or the Cisco Internetwork Design (CID) class.

➤ CCDP, which is an advanced certification regarding internetwork design. It consists of multiple exams. There are two ways to go about attaining the CCDP. You could pass the individual exams for ACRC, CLSC, CMTD, and CIT. However, if you're not one for taking a lot of exams, you can take the Foundation Routing/Switching exam and the CIT exam. Either combination will complete the requirements.

➤ CCIE, which is commonly referred to as the "black belt" of internetworking. It is considered the single most difficult certification to attain in the internetworking industry. First you must take a qualification exam. Once you pass the exam, the real fun begins. You will need to schedule a two-day practical lab exam to be held at a Cisco campus, where you will undergo a "trial by fire" of sorts. Your ability to configure, document, and troubleshoot Cisco equipment will be tested to its limits. Do not underestimate this lab exam.

The Ideal CCNP Candidate

Just to give you some idea of what an ideal CCNP candidate is like, here are some relevant statistics about the background and experience such an individual might have. Don't worry if you don't meet these qualifications, or don't come that close—this is a far from ideal world, and where you fall short is simply where you'll have more work to do.

➤ Academic or professional training in network theory, concepts, and operations. This includes everything from networking media and transmission techniques through network operating systems, services, and applications.

➤ Three-plus years of professional networking experience, including experience with Ethernet, token ring, modems, and other networking media. This must include installation, configuration, upgrade, and troubleshooting experience.

➤ Two-plus years in a networked environment that includes hands-on experience with Cisco routers, switches, and other related equipment. A solid understanding of each system's architecture, installation, configuration, maintenance, and troubleshooting is also essential.

➤ A thorough understanding of key networking protocols, addressing, and name resolution, including TCP/IP, IPX/SPX, and AppleTalk.

➤ Familiarity with key TCP/IP-based services, including ARP, BOOTP, DNS, FTP, SNMP, SMTP, Telnet, TFTP, and other relevant services for your internetwork deployment.

Fundamentally, this boils down to a bachelor's degree in computer science, plus three years of work experience in a technical position involving network design, installation, configuration, and maintenance. We believe that well under half of all certification candidates meet these requirements; in fact, most meet less than half of these requirements—at least, when they begin the certification process. But because thousands of people have survived this ordeal, you can survive it too—especially if you heed what our Self-Assessment can tell you about what you already know and what you need to learn.

Put Yourself To The Test

The following series of questions and observations is designed to help you figure out how much work you must do to pursue Cisco career certification and what kinds of resources you should consult on your quest. Be absolutely honest in your answers, or you'll end up wasting money on exams you're not yet ready to take. There are no right or wrong answers, only steps along the path to certification. Only you can decide where you really belong in the broad spectrum of aspiring candidates.

Two things should be clear from the outset, however:

➤ Even a modest background in computer science will be helpful.

➤ Extensive hands-on experience with Cisco products and technologies is an essential ingredient to certification success.

1. Have you ever taken any computer-related classes? [Yes or No]

    If Yes, proceed to question 2; if No, proceed to question 4.

2. Have you taken any classes included in Cisco's curriculum? [Yes or No]

    If Yes, you will probably be able to handle Cisco's architecture and system component discussions. If you're rusty, brush up on basic WAN technologies, such as ISDN, Frame Relay and analog. You'll also want to brush up on the basics of dialup networking, especially encapsulation types, PPP CHAP and PAP, access lists, and dialer maps.

    If No, consider some extensive reading in this area. We strongly recommend instructor-led training offered by a Cisco Training Partner.

However, you may want to check out a good general advanced routing technology book, such as *Cisco CCIE Fundamentals: Network Design and Cast Studies* by Andrea Cheek, H. Kim Lew, and Kathleen Wallace (Cisco Press. ISBN: 1-57870-066-3). Another good book is: *ISDN and Broadband ISDN With Frame Relay and ATM* by William Stallings (Prentice-Hall Engineering/Science/Mathematics. ISBN: 0-02415-513-6.) This may be a bit high level, but gives a good foundation for ISDN and Frame; these are two main topics in the course. If these titles don't appeal to you, check out reviews for other, similar titles at your favorite online bookstore.

3. Have you taken any networking concepts or technologies classes? [Yes or No]

If Yes, you will probably be able to handle Cisco's internetworking terminology, concepts, and technologies. If you're rusty, brush up on basic internetworking concepts and terminology, especially networking media, transmission types, the OSI Reference model, and networking technologies such as Ethernet, and WAN links, with an emphasis on ISDN and Frame

If No, you might want to read one or two books in this topic area. Check out the "Need To Know More?" section at the end of each chapter for a selection of resources that will give you additional background on the topics covered in this book.

4. Have you done any reading on routing protocols and/or routed protocols (IP, IPX, AppleTalk, etc.)? [Yes or No]

If Yes, review the requirements stated in the first paragraphs after Questions 2 and 3. If you meet those requirements, move on to the next question.

If No, consult the recommended reading for both topics. A strong background will help you prepare for the Cisco exams better than just about anything else.

The most important key to success on all of the Cisco tests is hands-on experience with Cisco routers and related equipment. If we leave you with only one realization after taking this Self-Assessment, it should be that there's no substitute for time spent installing, configuring, and using the various Cisco products upon which you'll be tested repeatedly and in depth. It cannot be stressed enough that quality instructor-led training will benefit you greatly and give you additional hands-on configuration experience with the technologies upon which you are to be tested.

5. Have you installed, configured, and worked with Cisco routers? [Yes or No]

If Yes, make sure you understand basic concepts as covered in the classes Introduction to Cisco Router Configuration (ICRC), Advanced Cisco Router Configuration (ACRC), and Building Cisco Remote Access Networks (BCRAN), before progressing into the materials covered here, because this book expands on the basic topics taught there.

 You can download objectives and other information about Cisco exams from the company's Training and Certification page on the Web at **www.cisco.com/training**.

If No, you will need to find a way to get a good amount of instruction on the intricacies of configuring Cisco equipment. You need a broad background to get through any of Cisco's career certification. You will also need to have hands-on experience with the equipment and technologies on which you'll be tested.

 If you have the funds, or your employer will pay your way, consider taking a class at a Cisco Training Partner (preferably one with "distinguished" status for the highest quality possible). In addition to classroom exposure to the topic of your choice, you get a good view of the technologies being widely deployed and will be able to take part in hands-on lab scenarios with those technologies.

Before you even think about taking any Cisco exam, make sure you've spent enough time with the related software to understand how it may be installed and configured, how to maintain such an installation, and how to troubleshoot that software when things go wrong. This will help you in the exam, and in real life!

Whether you attend a formal class on a specific topic to get ready for an exam or use written materials to study on your own, some preparation for the Cisco career certification exams is essential. At $100 to $200 (depending on the exam) a try, pass or fail, you want to do everything you can to pass on your first try. That's where studying comes in.

6. Have you taken a practice exam on your chosen test subject? [Yes or No]

If Yes, and you scored 70 percent or better, you're probably ready to tackle the real thing. If your score isn't above that crucial threshold, keep at it until you break that barrier.

If No, obtain all the free and low-budget practice tests you can find (see the list above) and get to work. Keep at it until you can break the passing threshold comfortably.

We have included a practice exam in this book, so you can test yourself on the information and techniques you've learned. If you don't hit a score of at least 70 percent after this test, you'll want to investigate the other practice test resources we mention in this section.

For any given subject, consider taking a class if you've tackled self-study materials, taken the test, and failed anyway. The opportunity to interact with an instructor and fellow students can make all the difference in the world, if you can afford that privilege. For information about Cisco classes, visit the Training and Certification page at **www.cisco.com/training** or **www.geotrain.com** (use the "Locate a Course" link).

If you can't afford to take a class, visit the Training and Certification page anyway, because it also includes pointers to additional resources and self-study tools. And even if you can't afford to spend much at all, you should still invest in some low-cost practice exams from commercial vendors, because they can help you assess your readiness to pass a test better than any other tool. The following Web sites offer some practice exams online:

➤ CCPrep.com at **www.ccprep.com** (requires membership)

➤ Network Study Guides at **www.networkstudyguides.com** (pay as you go)

 When it comes to assessing your test readiness, there is no better way than to take a good-quality practice exam and pass with a score of 70 percent or better. When we're preparing ourselves, we shoot for 80-plus percent, just to leave room for the "weirdness factor" that sometimes shows up on Cisco exams.

Assessing Readiness For Exam 640-505

In addition to the general exam-readiness information in the previous section, there are several things you can do to prepare for the Remote Access exam. You will find a great source of questions and related information at the CCprep Web site at **www.ccprep.com**. This is a good place to ask questions and get good answers, or simply to watch the questions that others ask (along with the answers, of course).

You should also cruise the Web looking for "braindumps" (recollections of test topics and experiences recorded by others) to help you anticipate topics you're likely to encounter on the test.

When using any braindump, it's OK to pay attention to information about questions. But you can't always be sure that a braindump's author will also be able to provide correct answers. Thus, use the questions to guide your studies, but don't rely on the answers in a braindump to lead you to the truth. Double-check everything you find in any braindump.

For Remote Access preparation in particular, we'd also like to recommend that you check out one or more of these resources as you prepare to take Exam 640-505:

➤ Cisco Connection Online (CCO) Documentation (**www.cisco.com/ univercd/home/home.htm**). From the CCO Documentation home page you can select a variety of topics, including but not limited to Troubleshooting Internetwork Systems and Internetwork Troubleshooting guides, as well as Internetwork Technologies Overviews and Design Guides.

➤ Cisco Systems, Inc. *Cisco IOS Dial Solutions*. Cisco Press. ISBN 1-57870-055-8.

➤ Hardwick, Steve: *ISDN Design, A Practical Approach. Academic Press, Inc.* Harcourt Brace Jovanovich, Publishers. ISBN 0-12-324970-8.

➤ Held,Gilbert. *The Complete Modem Reference: The Technicians Guide to Installation, Testing, and Trouble-Free Communications.* John Wiley & Sons. ISBN 0-47-115457-1.

Stop by the Cisco home page, your favorite bookstore, or an online bookseller to check out one or more of these resources. We believe CCO Documentation provides a wealth of great material. The Cisco Press Series, which can be found at most large bookstores, provides both specific information on individual topics like Dialup or Design, as well as more encompassing topics about routing and switching. Many of the large bookstores now feature coffee shops where books can be "test driven" before purchased. Considering the cost of some the more technical books on digital telephony and dial plans, test driving makes good sense.

One last note: Hopefully, it makes sense to stress the importance of hands-on experience in the context of the Remote Access exam. As you review the material for that exam, you'll realize that hands-on experience with the Cisco IOS with various technologies and configurations is invaluable. There are a plethora of commands needed to enable dial-up communications on an asynchronous port that can only be reinforced through experience.

Onward, Through The Fog!

Once you've assessed your readiness, undertaken the right background studies, obtained the hands-on experience that will help you understand the products and technologies at work, and reviewed the many sources of information to help you prepare for a test, you'll be ready to take a round of practice tests. When your scores come back positive enough to get you through the exam, you're ready to go after the real thing. If you follow our assessment regime, you'll not only know what you need to study, but when you're ready to make a test date at Sylvan Prometric. Good luck!

Cisco Certification Exams

Terms you'll need to understand:

√ Radio button

√ Checkbox

√ Exhibit

√ Multiple-choice question formats

√ Careful reading

√ Process of elimination

Techniques you'll need to master:

√ Preparing to take a certification exam

√ Practicing (to make perfect)

√ Making the best use of the testing software

√ Budgeting your time

√ Guessing (as a last resort)

√ Breathing deeply to calm frustration

Exam taking is not something that most people anticipate eagerly, no matter how well prepared they may be. In most cases, familiarity helps ameliorate test anxiety. In plain English, this means you probably will not be as nervous when you take your fourth or fifth Cisco certification exam, as you will be when you take your first one.

Whether it is your first exam or your tenth, understanding the details of exam taking (how much time to spend on questions, the environment you'll be in, and so on) and the exam software will help you concentrate on the material rather than on the setting. Likewise, mastering a few basic exam-taking skills should help you recognize—and perhaps even outfox—some of the tricks and gotchas you're bound to find in some of the exam questions.

This chapter, besides explaining the exam environment and software, describes some proven exam-taking strategies that you should be able to use to your advantage.

The Exam Situation

When you arrive at the testing center where you scheduled your exam, you will need to sign in with an exam coordinator. He or she will ask you to show two forms of identification, one of which must be a photo ID. After you have signed in and your time slot arrives, you will be asked to deposit any books, bags, or other items you brought with you. Then, you will be escorted into a closed room. Typically, the room will be furnished with anywhere from one to half a dozen computers, and each workstation will be separated from the others by dividers designed to keep you from seeing what is happening on someone else's computer.

You will be furnished with a pen or pencil and a blank sheet of paper, or, in some cases, an erasable plastic sheet and an erasable felt-tip pen. You are allowed to write down any information you want on both sides of this sheet. Before the exam, you should memorize as much of the material that appears on The Cram Sheet (inside the front cover of this book) as you can so you can write that information on the blank sheet as soon as you are seated in front of the computer. You can refer to your rendition of The Cram Sheet anytime you like during the test, but you will have to surrender the sheet when you leave the room.

Most test rooms feature a wall with a large picture window. This permits the exam coordinator standing behind it to monitor the room, to prevent exam takers from talking to one another, and to observe anything out of the ordinary that might go on. The exam coordinator will have preloaded the appropriate Cisco certification exam—for this book, that's Exam 640-505—and you will be permitted to start as soon as you are seated in front of the computer.

All Cisco certification exams allow a certain maximum amount of time in which to complete your work (this time is indicated on the exam by an onscreen counter/clock, so you can check the time remaining whenever you like). Exam 640-505 consists of 62 randomly selected questions. You may take up to 90 minutes to complete the exam and you need a score of 706 points our of 1000 to pass. All Cisco certification exams are computer-generated and use a multiple-choice format. From time to time you may be prompted to enter actual configuration commands as if you were at the command-line interface. It is important not to abbreviate the commands in any way when this type of question is posed. Although this may sound quite simple, the questions are constructed not only to check your mastery of basic facts and figures about Cisco remote access methods, technology, and configuration of a router to that end, but they also require you to evaluate one or more sets of circumstances or requirements. Often, you will be asked to give more than one answer to a question. Likewise, you might be asked to select the best or most effective solution to a problem from a range of choices, all of which technically are correct. Taking the exam is quite an adventure, and it involves real thinking. This book shows you what to expect and how to deal with the potential problems, puzzles, and predicaments.

Exam Layout And Design

Some exam questions require you to select a single answer, whereas others ask you to select multiple correct answers or fill in the blank with a code command. The following multiple-choice question requires you to select a single correct answer. Following the question is a brief summary of each potential answer and why it is either right or wrong.

Question 1

What is the key piece of information on which routing decisions are based?

○ a. Source network-layer address

○ b. Destination network-layer address

○ c. Source MAC address

○ d. Destination MAC address

Answer b is correct. The destination network layer (or layer 3) address is the protocol-specific address to which this piece of data is to be delivered. The source network-layer address is the originating host and plays no role in getting the information to the destination. Therefore, answer a is incorrect. The source and destination MAC addresses are necessary for getting the data to the router, or the next hop address. However, they are not used in pathing decisions. Therefore, answers c and d are incorrect.

This sample question format corresponds closely to the Cisco certification exam format—the only difference on the exam is that questions are not followed by answer keys. To select an answer, position the cursor over the radio button next to the answer. Then, click the mouse button to select the answer.

Let's examine a question that requires choosing multiple answers. This type of question provides checkboxes rather than radio buttons for marking all appropriate selections.

Question 2

> Which of the following are possible encapsulations for an ISDN-capable interface? [Choose the four best answers]
>
> ❏ a. Frame Relay
>
> ❏ b. LAPB
>
> ❏ c. PPP
>
> ❏ d. HDLC
>
> ❏ e. ATM

Answers a, b, c, and d are correct. ISDN is also capable of supporting X.25 encapsulation. Answer e is incorrect because Basic Rate Interfaces are not capable of providing Asynchronous Transfer Mode (ATM) services. Specialized ATM interfaces are required for utilization of that technology.

For this type of question, more than one answer is required. Cisco does not give partial credit for partially correct answers when the test is scored. For Question 2, you have to check the boxes next to items a, b, c, and d to obtain credit for a correct answer. Notice that picking the right answers also means knowing why the other answers are wrong!

Question 3

Enter the command to display information regarding custom queuing operations. [Fill in the blank]

"Show queuing custom" is the answer. You will have to know the exact command. Unfortunately for most of us, you cannot abbreviate the commands in
the blank as if you were actually at the command-line interface. You must
know the exact syntax and command variables of the question to get credit.

Although these three basic types of questions can appear in many forms, they
constitute the foundation on which all the Cisco certification exam questions
rest. More complex questions include so-called exhibits, which are usually network scenarios, screenshots of output from the router, or even pictures from
the course materials. For some of these questions, you will be asked to make a
selection by clicking on a checkbox or radio button on the screenshot itself. For
others, you will be expected to use the information displayed therein to guide
your answer to the question. Familiarity with the underlying utility is your key
to choosing the correct answer(s).

Other questions involving exhibits use charts or network diagrams to help
document a workplace scenario that you will be asked to troubleshoot or configure. Careful attention to such exhibits is the key to success. Be prepared to
toggle frequently between the exhibit and the question as you work.

Using Cisco's Exam
Software Effectively

Work on the questions until you know you will run out of time. If questions
remain unanswered, you will want to zip through them and guess. Not answering a question guarantees you won't receive credit for it, but a guess has at least
a chance of being correct.

At the very end of your exam period, you are better off guessing than leaving questions unanswered.

Exam-Taking Basics

The most important advice about taking any exam is this: Read each question carefully. Some questions are deliberately ambiguous, some use double negatives, and others use terminology in incredibly precise ways. The authors have taken numerous exams—both practice and live—and in nearly every one have missed at least one question because they did not read it closely or carefully enough.

Here are some suggestions on how to deal with the tendency to jump to an answer too quickly:

➤ Make sure you read every word in the question. If you find yourself jumping ahead impatiently, go back and start over.

➤ As you read, try to restate the question in your own terms. If you can do this, you should be able to pick the correct answer(s) much more easily.

➤ Try to articulate to yourself what you do not understand about the question, why the answers do not appear to make sense, or what appears to be missing. If you chew on the subject for awhile, your subconscious might provide the details that are lacking or you might notice a "trick" that will point to the right answer.

➤ Breathe. Deep rhythmic breathing is a stress reliever. Breathe in for a count of 4, hold it for 2, and then exhale for a count of 4. You will be surprised how this can clear your mind of the frustration that clouds it and allow you to regain focus.

Above all, try to deal with each question by thinking through what you know about Cisco remote access methods and technologies—the characteristics, behaviors, facts, and figures involved. By reviewing what you know (and what you have written down on your information sheet), you will often recall or understand things sufficiently to determine the answer to the question. It is important to keep the Cisco perspective in mind when trying to understand a tricky question. Most questions are geared to test a specific concept or idea. Most often, your first inclination is correct when two answers seem equally correct. If your first thought is answer b and you have to spend 30 or 40 seconds convincing yourself why answer c is better, you should probably stick with b. This is not to say "don't think", but don't *over* think a question.

Question-Handling Strategies

Based on exams the authors have taken, some interesting trends have become apparent. For those questions that take only a single answer, usually two or three of the answers will be obviously incorrect, and two of the answers will be plausible—of course, only one can be correct. Unless the answer leaps out at you (if it does, reread the question to look for a trick; sometimes, those are the ones you are most likely to get wrong), begin the process of answering by eliminating those answers that are most obviously wrong.

Things to look for in obviously wrong answers include spurious menu choices or utility names, nonexistent software options, and terminology you have never seen. If you have done your homework for an exam, no valid information should be completely new to you. In that case, unfamiliar or bizarre terminology probably indicates a totally bogus answer.

Numerous questions assume that the default behavior of a particular utility is in effect. If you know the defaults and understand what they mean, this knowledge will help you cut through many Gordian knots.

As you work your way through the exam, another counter that Cisco thankfully provides will come in handy—the number of questions completed and questions outstanding. Budget your time by making sure that you have completed one-quarter of the questions one-quarter of the way through the exam period (or the first 16 questions in the first 22 minutes) and three-quarters of them three-quarters of the way through (48 questions in the first 66 minutes).

If you are not finished when 85 minutes have elapsed, use the last 5 minutes to guess your way through the remaining questions. Remember, guessing is potentially more valuable than not answering, because blank answers are always wrong, but a guess may turn out to be right. If you do not have a clue about any of the remaining questions, pick answers at random, or choose all a's, b's, and so on. The important thing is to submit an exam for scoring that has an answer for every question.

Mastering The Inner Game

In the final analysis, knowledge breeds confidence, and confidence breeds success. If you study the materials in this book carefully and review all the practice questions at the end of each chapter, you should become aware of those areas where additional learning and study are required.

Next, follow up by reading some or all of the materials recommended in the "Need To Know More?" section at the end of each chapter. The idea is to become familiar enough with the concepts and situations you find in the sample questions that you can reason your way through similar situations on a real exam. If you know the material, you have every right to be confident that you can pass the exam.

After you have worked your way through the book, take the sample test in Chapter 16. This will provide a reality check and help you identify areas you need to study further. Make sure you follow up and review materials related to the questions you miss on the practice exam before scheduling a real exam. Only when you have covered all the ground and feel comfortable with the whole scope of the practice exam should you take a real one.

 If you take the sample test and do not score at least 75 percent correct, you will want to practice further.

Armed with the information in this book and with the determination to augment your knowledge, you should be able to pass the certification exam. However, you need to work at it; otherwise, you'll spend the exam fee more than once before you finally pass. If you prepare seriously, you should do well. Good luck!

Additional Resources

A good source of information about Cisco certification exams comes from Cisco itself. Because its products and technologies—and the exams that go with them—change frequently, the best place to go for exam-related information is online.

If you haven't already visited the Cisco Certified Professional site, do so right now. The Cisco Career Certifications home page (shown in Figure 1.1) resides at **www.cisco.com/warp/public/10/wwtraining/certprog/index.html**.

Note: This page might not be there by the time you read this, or it might have been replaced by something new and different, because things change regularly on the Cisco site. Should this happen, please read the sidebar titled "Coping With Change On The Web."

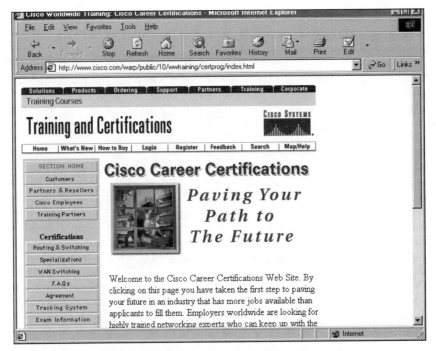

Figure 1.1   The Cisco Career Certifications home page.

The menu options in the left column of the home page point to the most important sources of information in the Career Certification pages. Here's what to check out:

➤ *Routing and Switching*—Use this entry to explore the CCIE certification track for routing and switching.

➤ *Specializations*—Use this entry to explore different CCNP specialization options.

➤ *WAN Switching*—Use this entry to explore the CCIE certification track for WAN Switching.

➤ *FAQs*—Use this entry to access the most commonly asked questions regarding any Cisco Career Certification.

➤ *Agreement*—Prior to certification, all candidates must complete the certification agreement or Cisco will not recognize them as certified professionals.

➤ *Tracking System*—Once you have registered with Sylvan Prometric, and taken any Cisco exam, you will automatically be added to a living certification tracking system so that you can keep up with your progress.

➤ *Exam Information*—This entry actually points to a class locator. It should be noted that no book is an adequate replacement for instructor-led, Cisco-authorized training. This entry will assist your efforts to find a class that meets your scheduling needs.

These are just the high points of what's available in the Cisco Certified Professional pages. As you browse through them—and we strongly recommend that you do—you will probably find other informational tidbits mentioned that are every bit as interesting and compelling.

Coping With Change On The Web

Sooner or later, all the information we have shared with you about the Cisco Certified Professional pages and the other Web-based resources mentioned throughout the rest of this book will go stale or be replaced by newer information. In some cases, the URLs you find here might lead you to their replacements; in other cases, the URLs will go nowhere, leaving you with the dreaded "404 File not found" error message. When that happens, do not give up.

There's always a way to find what you want on the Web if you are willing to invest some time and energy. Most large or complex Web sites—and Cisco's qualifies on both counts—offer a search engine. As long as you can get to Cisco's site (it should stay at **www.cisco.com** for a long while yet), you can use this tool to help you find what you need.

The more focused you can make a search request, the more likely the results will include information you can use. For example, you can search for the string "training and certification" to produce a lot of data about the subject in general, but if you are looking for the preparation guide for Exam 640-505, "Remote Access" you will be more likely to get there quickly if you use a search string similar to the following:

```
"Exam 640-505" AND "preparation guide"
```

Finally, feel free to use general search tools—such as **www.search.com**, **www.altavista.com**, and **www.excite.com**—to search for related information. The bottom line is this: If you can't find something where the book says it lives, start looking around. If worst comes to worst, you can always email us. We just might have a clue.

If there's one principle that applies to taking the Remote Access exam, it could be summed up as "Get it right the first time." You cannot elect to skip a question and move on to the next one when taking this exam. Nor can you return to a question once you've moved on, because the software gives you only one chance to answer the question. If you encounter a question that you can't answer, you must guess an answer before the testing software will allow you to move on to the next question.

The Selection Of Remote Access Hardware

Terms you'll need to understand:

√ Availability

√ Reliability

√ Access control

√ Leased line

√ Frame Relay

√ ISDN

√ Central office

√ Branch office

√ Remote office/home office

Techniques you'll need to master:

√ Understanding the Product Selection Tool

√ Determining the site description

√ Understanding the selection criteria for a WAN connection

√ Recommending a router series for a given design

The selection of a hardware product for remote access usage is quite simple. The research prior to making the connection is the difficult part. The information you must obtain is the same as that taught in high school writing class: who, what, when, where, how, and how much (OK, the last one is an addition). The *who* pertains to what vendors are in the area and *what* services they offer now or in the future (*when*). Once the decision has been made on the technology that will be put in place, the question of *how* is answered by selecting a product with that specification. Cisco has a wide product line that can be positioned for any *what*. The last question is *how much*, and the cost of the service is generally the driving factor.

If you're positioning home access to the Internet, the first question (*who*) is easy. Who are the Internet Service Providers in the area? What are their offerings? When can it be hooked up? How do I have to connect? If these were the only questions, I would soon come to the conclusion that the company BigInternetProvider can supply a dedicated T3 link to my house, and I need a router that will handle a T3 circuit. Done deal. If the question *how much* comes into play at this point, a certain amount of rethinking may occur unless I have just won the lottery.

The *how much* generally drives all decisions for RAS connectivity. This is the hardest question to put into perspective. Prices are going down, and speeds are going up. New technologies are being developed each day. The key issue is to select the hardware based on the technology that will be supported.

Factors That Affect Hardware Selection

Regardless of the speeds, prices, and technologies, the questions we mentioned earlier revolve around the following factors:

➤ *Availability*—Concisely put, can I get this type of access in my area? What are the geographic restrictions to this technology, and will it become available in my area? Metropolitan Area Networking (MAN) is generally available in most major cities (New York, Washington D.C., Atlanta, and so on). Can I predict that it will be available in Cody, Wyoming? The answer is doubtful.

➤ *Bandwidth*—Another term for this item is *speed*. How much information will I be getting, and how long will it take? Determining the usage is a critical issue.

➤ *Cost*—WAN costs are submitted every month. This parameter is the driving force behind most decisions. A critical feature to Cisco is Dial-on-Demand Routing (DDR). This feature allows for the WAN link to be present only when traffic warrants. The key issue is that the administrator or customer must establish what is *interesting* traffic.

➤ *Ease of management*—Any solution must be palatable to the customer. If the administrative overhead of a solution outweighs the viability of the solution, it may be more costly. What is the cost of ignorance? The answer to this question isn't simple. Any value-added reseller (VAR) that continually charges a customer to tweak a system will eventually go bankrupt because recurring costs will be too high. Any VAR that consistently puts in a system that is free from management worries will eventually go bankrupt because installation costs will be too high. The dilemma is to offer the right management solution for each situation.

➤ *Application traffic*—What type of traffic will be carried on the link? Is it primarily used for file transfer or email? What are the packet sizes? What type of delay is acceptable? In the case of email, delay may not be a critical issue. If the email gets there 10 seconds or 10 minutes after it has been sent, the delay may be acceptable. In the case of file transfer or other user interactive requests, however, the difference between 10 seconds and 10 minutes is definitely a cause for alarm.

➤ *Reliability and quality of service*—Will voice or video be added at a later time? How critical is the traffic? If the user is a brokerage house, the aspect of reliability may override all other factors. If it's Joe-Bob's Tire Shop, the criticality of the connections may be minor. Yes, Joe and Bob want communication; but in the event of a major outage due to hurricane or snowstorm, they may be willing to accept a loss of connectivity. (Not many people buy tires during a hurricane.) Are backup links needed? In this age of communication, if the local Frame Relay access point goes out, will Joe and Bob require a sufficiently reliable alternative?

➤ *Access control*—Today, many companies are embracing the idea of e-commerce. Consumers, customers, and outsiders are given access to some part of the corporate network. What type of control is in place or can be put in place to protect the internal network, and how much will that type of control cost? A small bio-technical research firm whose only asset is the information on the network may be willing to spend much money and effort to ensure protection. Joe and Bob, on the other hand, may be willing to spend only a small amount. (If lots of people find out that Joe and Bob have an excess of steel-belted radials in stock, customers may line up knowing that the tires they need won't be on back order.)

Much of this information could be considered common sense; however, many consumers of Wide Area Network (WAN) technology buy a big router because it's better than a small router. The cost of any networking equipment is tiny compared to the monthly cost to maintain the WAN service. The decision process should be divorced from the hardware and focus strictly on the usage and needs. In a global sense, the cost of the router will be a small fraction of the cost. The brunt of the cost will be borne each month for access charges to the telephone company network. Bigger in this case may be better, in order to eliminate "upgrade" charges that might result from heavier demand later in the life of the project.

> The selection of equipment should be based upon need using the following criteria:
>
> ➤ Availability
>
> ➤ Bandwidth
>
> ➤ Cost
>
> ➤ Ease of management
>
> ➤ Applications and traffic patterns supported
>
> ➤ Quality of service and need for backup
>
> ➤ Control of access to the shared network

WAN Connection Selection

The issues discussed in the previous section force the consumer to look critically at the information that will be required to put the resource into place. The next milestone is to select the carrier technology to support the functions that are identified. For remote access, the choices are as follows (in descending order of speed and control):

➤ *Leased line*—A leased line gives the consumer complete control of the facility in terms of what data is to be put on it. The customer effectively owns the bandwidth of this link. This arrangement offers a great deal of security and control to the customer; however, this is probably the highest-cost solution available. Lease facilities can be obtained at very high data rates. The question is how much bandwidth the consumer is willing to select and at what cost. Speeds can range up to multiple megabit transfer rates.

➤ *Frame Relay*—Frame service probably carries the majority of business circuits in the United States. The customer has some control over what resources are being used by specifying a Committed Information Rate (CIR) or guaranteed rate of delivery; however, the Frame provider controls the latency or delay through the network. The question of cost is lessened with Frame Relay because many companies share the circuits, but the speed is a function of the offering of the local provider. Speeds can range up to multiple megabit transfer rates, but they're generally positioned up to T1 (1.544Mbps) speeds.

➤ *Integrated Services Digital Network (ISDN)*—ISDN offers more bandwidth than a simple dial-up link; however, it's a circuit-switched connection and is subject to availability of the remote end. The control of the circuit given over to the provider. Speed for ISDN is limited from the remote user's perspective, using a Basic Rate Interface (BRI) up to 128Kbps of data.

➤ *Asynchronous Dialup*—Simple modem connectivity is sometimes all that is needed for communication. Speeds are limited to 53Kbps or slower, depending on the type of connection and the modem being used. Dialup is the least expensive of all communication methods, and is available almost everywhere.

Once you've answered the questions of what has to be done and how it can be done, the next question is where the hardware will be positioned or installed.

Site Requirements

Growth potential is a factor in determining what type of site is important. In general, each company site can be placed into one of three categories: central, branch, or remote. A central site by definition requires more hardware than a branch, which by definition requires more hardware than a remote. Considerations for each type of site are discussed in the following sections.

Central Site

If the installation will be taking place in a central site, it's generally assumed that room for growth should be a driving factor. The central site is sometimes referred to as an *enterprise site* or *headquarters*. The key issue here is that other remote or branch sites may be added or deleted over time; the hardware platform should be flexible, so that a fork-lift upgrade isn't needed every time a corporate direction change occurs.

Considerations at the central site would include what *speeds and feeds* are needed. The speeds should be sufficient to aggregate the information flows from the branch and remote sites. The cost is a major consideration, because the recurring WAN charges will be the dominant cost factor. Access control is another major central site issue because the corporate information base is maintained there.

Branch Office

If the installation is to be done in a branch office, there is less need for flexibility than at the central site. This doesn't mean that a fixed configuration device is acceptable; however, it may be more palatable if it contains enough ports to allow for expansion. A branch office is smaller than a central site and gives a presence to the company in a specific region. Branch office support generally includes access to smaller single-function remote offices or remote users.

Considerations at the branch office include the WAN connection type with an eye on the per-month charges, as at the Central Office (CO). In addition, the branch office must be able to authenticate itself to the CO. The issue of availability is another critical factor in the branch: How often and how long will a connection be needed? Is a backup necessary? The CO will generally use links that are always available or highly reliable, whereas the branch may not want to pay for that security.

Remote Office Or Home Office

An installation at a remote office (RO) or home office (HO) location is likely to be a fixed-function device with cost as a main factor. Once the access method is chosen, it's unlikely to change in the near term. The traffic or data that exits the RO or HO can usually be categorized very neatly. An example would be a remote salesperson who must gain access to the corporate catalogue of information on pricing and upload sales data and email.

The overriding consideration at these offices is generally cost. In addition, the remote office must maintain a method for authentication to the branch or CO and justify the connection time to a central or branch office. In general, these offices would use a dial-on-demand methodology to minimize WAN charges.

 The concepts of Home, Small, Branch, and Central Office can be viewed with a certain overlap of function; however, the Remote Access exam used the terms in a precise manner as describe here. If a scenario were presented for a Telecommuter using ISDN, the likely candidate would be the 700 series product. Care should be taken to answer any question regarding the positioning of equipment in relation to the definition of the location.

Hardware Selection

Once the what, how, and where have been satisfied, you can make the final decision about hardware. Cisco is continually making deletions and additions to the product line available for any WAN situation, including the Remote Access Services (RAS) scenario. The thrust of the discussion in this chapter isn't to review the entire product line, but to present the portion of the product line that is usually associated with remote access. The product families that could be used in a remote scenario are as follows:

➤ *Cisco 700 Series*—This family of routers supports Internet Protocol (IP) and Internetwork Packet Exchange (IPX) routing over ISDN. It has no scalability to add additional ports and was designed for a home office or telecommuter. The 700 is positioned as an inexpensive ISDN access device.

➤ *Cisco 800 Series*—This family of routers is the lowest priced, entry-level router that runs the IOS software. Because the base operating system is the same as the higher-end router platforms, it's positioned to benefit the small office or corporate home user. This platform offers the ability for the corporate staff to use the same language to configure the remote device. The WAN options are the same as for the 700 series.

➤ *Cisco 1000 Series*—One of the older devices, this family of routers provides either ISDN or serial connections for the branch or remote office. This router could be used for X.25 or Frame Relay. It's sometimes called an *end-node router*. The key issue is that this router provides an expanded set of WAN options. It's a fixed configuration router; hence the selection of the WAN option must be made prior to purchase.

➤ *Cisco 1600 Series*—This series is relatively new and offers a modular construction, allowing the WAN interfaces to be changed by the customer as needs change. The WAN cards that can be used in the 1600 can be shared with the 2600 and 3600 router series, allowing for a small set of *hot-spare* boards. The 1600 uses the trademark IOS and is generally positioned at a branch office site and not a remote or home use location.

➤ *Cisco 2500 Series*—The 2500 router series is the oldest router platform mentioned so far. It's a fixed-configuration router that offers a wide range of options for the branch or central office. This router series isn't modular. If a different port configuration is needed, a new 2500 would be required to replace the existing device.

➤ *Cisco 2600 Series*—This router series is replacing the current 2500 router due to its flexibility with the WAN card design. The 2600 can support many different hardware configurations in a single chassis. The customer can mix and match both LAN and WAN resources simply by changing boards on the chassis. The positioning of the 2600 is a branch office site or a small central facility.

➤ *Cisco 3600 Series*—This series provides two, four, or six module slots, whereas the 2600 provides only two. The device is considered a piece of CO equipment because the flexibility and port density are so high.

➤ *Cisco 4500 and 4700 Series*—Both of these router models are being eclipsed by the 3600; however, they are not end-of-life products. The 4500/4700 series provides a modular design similar to the 3600 and is intended for large regional offices and CO facilities that require a high rate of throughput.

➤ *Cisco AS5000 Series*—The 5200 and 5300 routers provide a very high port density typically found at an Internet Service Provider (ISP) point of presence (POP). This chassis incorporates the functions of modems, switches, routers, and channel banks into a single platform. In addition, the AS5000 series can support serial, digital, ISDN, and asynchronous access through a single physical interface. This support of a mixed-media requirement makes this series a very useful fit for the CO environment that must support many different branch and remote offices.

➤ *Cisco 7200 Series*—The use of this device in a RAS environment is mentioned for completeness. The 7200 series can provide a CO with a high density of high-speed interfaces when many branch offices are being aggregated.

 The 700 and 800 series routers are considered Telecommuter devices. The 1600 and 2600 are, according to the above definitions, Branch Office equipment. The 3600 series and above constitute Central Office equipment. The reader should be able to position this equipment based on case study information during the exam.

The previous router descriptions represent much of the Cisco product line. We recommend that to properly position this equipment, you visit **www.cisco.com** to gain the most up-to-date information.

It isn't impossible to review the entire suite of Cisco products before making a decision on product selection for every installation. It would, however, be time consuming. Cisco provides some tools to make the selection process much faster.

The Cisco Product Selection Tool can be obtained on CD-ROM or used on the Web site. This tool allows you to quickly narrow the selection to a small handful of router platforms by clicking on the options required for the application. As the options are selected, the Product Selection Tool pares down the

Cisco product line so that only the router platforms that match the search criteria are displayed.

In addition to using the product search engine, the customer or consumer can simply provide the requirements to a Cisco certified VAR or to a Cisco sales engineer and ask what products will satisfy the requirements. Doing so may sound a bit trite, but Cisco has been focused on ensuring that the right solution is provided for the right scenario in every instance in which their product is used. The emphasis that Cisco has placed on the certification process for their VARs is evidence of this commitment.

The BCRAN courseware was more focused on the how, what, when, and where questions than on particular product line model numbers and interface specifications. Questions *will* concern the interface and model specifications, however the reader should not focus on these *alone*.

Practice Questions

Question 1

> The following are considerations for selecting the WAN technology: [Choose the three best answers]
>
> ❑ a. Cost
>
> ❑ b. Availability
>
> ❑ c. Available router interfaces
>
> ❑ d. Management ease
>
> ❑ e. Corporate policy

Answers a, b, and d are correct. Answer c is incorrect because the selection of a hardware device comes after the selection of the technology. Basing a design decision on an available router is an arbitrary consideration. Answer e, corporate policy, may come into play; however, from a purely technical standpoint, it's also irrelevant.

Question 2

> Which WAN method offers the most control by the customer?
>
> ○ a. Frame Relay
>
> ○ b. Leased line
>
> ○ c. Asynchronous modem connection
>
> ○ d. ISDN

Answer b is correct. A leased line will carry only the customer's traffic. Answers a and d, Frame Relay and ISDN, are switched networks that can become congested based upon the other users of the service. Answer c, an asynchronous modem connection, is incorrect because the customer has control over the modem but not the carrier system. If the line is busy, the customer can't unbusy the line, but must wait for the receiver or trunk to become available. The idea behind "control" is not based on the end user determining *when* to make the call.

Question 3

Which router series would be considered an entry-level device that runs the IOS software?

○ a. 1600 series

○ b. 2500 series

○ c. 800 series

○ d. 700 series

Answer c is correct. The 800 series router is an entry-level device that supports ISDN connectivity. Answers a and b, the 1600 and 2500 routers, are not entry-level devices. Both series offer many port configuration options. Answer d is incorrect because the 700 series is an entry-level device, but it doesn't run the standard IOS.

Question 4

What additional consideration must be addressed at a branch site that is not addressed at the central office?

○ a. Recurring WAN costs

○ b. Availability

○ c. Authentication

○ d. Port density

Answer c is correct. Authentication of the branch must be planned for. The methodology of authentication can be a factor in the selection of the WAN link. Along the same vein, you must consider the security of the WAN technology. You must also consider the question of what traffic will flow and how sensitive that traffic is. Answer a is true for the branch, central, and remote offices—cost is a factor for any WAN technology. Answers b and d, availability and port density, are factors that will affect the decision at both a branch and central installation. Some degree of flexibility is needed at both the central and branch offices. The key here is to recognize that once a communication link is being established to a branch or remote office, it's incumbent upon the branch or remote to plan for authentication.

Question 5

Where would you find the most up-to-date information concerning router products?

- ○ a. **www.cisco.com**
- ○ b. Cisco product catalog
- ○ c. Product Selection Tool CD-ROM
- ○ d. Local Cisco sales office

Answer a is correct. Each answer will give you information about Cisco product offerings. However, the Cisco Web site is the most current and up-to-date repository of information. Answers b and c are products that are produced from the Web information and are out of date the day after publication. The local sales offices get their information the same way others do: from the Cisco Web-site. If answer d was "Local Cisco sales office—after you have signed a non-disclosure agreement" then it might be better than going to **www.cisco.com**. In all honesty, even after you sign a non-disclosure, the Web is probably still the best bet.

Need To Know More?

 Cisco Systems. *Product Catalog.* This book is the standard documentation set that lists the products and part numbers for all the current Cisco products. The key word, however, is *current.* It's current when printed, and it's generally out of date very shortly thereafter when it comes to new features and products. The catalog can be a handy reference, but you should consult the Web site to verify the book's contents.

 Cisco Systems. *Documentation CD.* Any recent version of the CD has much background information on the various technologies discussed here. The search engine will allow you to look specifically at white paper information in lieu of a command search. The CD will contain what was known about the router product line at the time the CD was burned.

 Cisco Systems. *Product Selection Tools or Sales Tools CD.* This CD has changed over time to reflect the different products and options available for the Cisco product line. The name and contents of the CD seem to change with each release of the CD. This is a CD version of the current Web-based search and selection tools. As the Web-based tools evolve, so does the CD.

 Visit the official Cisco Web site at **www.cisco.com** for information and links relating to all technologies employed by Cisco. This is by far the best source for hardware features and functionality. Any other source or document will, by necessity, lag behind the Web-based information about Cisco products.

Wide Area Network Connectivity

3

Terms you'll need to understand:

√ Wide Area Network (WAN)

√ Hertz

√ Last mile

√ Digital transmission

√ Analog transmission

√ Channelized

√ Nonchannelized

√ T1

√ DS0

√ T3

√ Carrier network

Techniques you'll need to master:

√ Defining T1 channel speeds

√ Describing digital transmission

√ Describing analog transmission

√ Understanding signaling methods

√ Defining channelized and non-channelized signaling

The concept of Wide Area Networking (WAN) may seem like a recent phenomenon with data networks. However, the early telephone networks were actually WANs for voice communications.

The use of the term WAN grew when small Local Area Networks (LANs) were connected over a telephone or carrier network. The groundwork was laid then for the number of bits per byte, the 64Kbps channel, the framing of packets, and the general transmission of information. Such groundwork formed the foundation for how people would talk on the phone or exchange verbal data bytes from human workstations.

Today, the term WAN is most suited to the usage of telecommunication links to carry both voice and data. But even in today's fast-paced world—with its cell phones, pagers, video conferencing, and general information overload—it's good to review where it all started—and wonder if we should have gone down this path in the first place.

The first thing to look at is the basic signaling systems that are used. Then, we'll build on that discussion until we reach today's ultra-fast information highways.

 Cisco certification is valuable to prove that a level of knowledge has been obtained, but the history of telecommunications is needed to provide a basis for that knowledge. The tests, which are designed to test more than facts, require a basic understanding of the technology presented.

Physical Signaling

Physical signaling is nothing more than electrically quantifying the change of pressure waves created by a person's voice box. When speaking, you generate sound waves. The diaphragm in your ear interprets these waves as it vibrates with the pressure changes. The human voice is capable of creating from 100 to 5,000 cycles of information per second. Each cycle is called a *hertz*. (It was originally called an *avis*, but that term slipped to number two.) The human ear is capable of receiving and understanding from 25 to 22,000 hertz. However, these physical limits don't take into consideration the selective hearing phenomena found in many teenagers. For instance, when you say to a 15-year-old "take out the trash," it may appear that the youth is incapable of receiving and processing the signal.

A hertz (Hz) is a simple sine wave, as you can see in Figure 3.1. The human voice sends out a waveform that is constantly changing in amplitude and frequency. The *amplitude* change is the strength of the signal. The *frequency* of the signal is the number of rotations around the baseline in a period of time. The

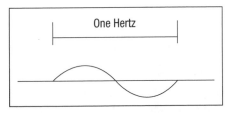

Figure 3.1   A sinusoidal wave oscillates around a baseline. A single oscillation is one hertz.

higher the amplitude, the louder the signal; the greater the number of cycles, the higher the pitch. For example, you could use a large number of tuning forks, each capable of producing a specific frequency, to re-create a human voice. If you wanted the trash removed, you might need to increase the amplitude of the signal and maintain a low frequency. This approach would give you a low (short frequency) booming (high amplitude) voice, which has proven to be the optimum communication parameter for teenagers.

The telephone companies could pass all frequency and amplitude changes over the entire range of the analog spectrum; however, they don't have to because a phone conversation uses only a subset of the range. A typical conversation uses 300 to 3,300 Hz. Because it would be expensive for a telephone company (telco) to pass the entire range of frequencies, the telco uses a filter on the circuit to send the conversation frequencies only. When you yell at someone over the phone, your voice doesn't have the same impact as if you were in his face. The telco dampens the high amplitude; hence, the recipient of your wrath is insulated.

Analog Transmission

In its pre-digital days (digital is coming up in the next section), the telco needed to push the analog signal down the wire so that the recipient's ear diaphragm would be able to oscillate correctly to understand the sender. Whenever a signal is transmitted down a wire, impedance to the signal results in *attenuation*, or signal loss. So, the telco needed to put amplifiers every 15,000 to 18,000 feet to boost the signal back to an understandable waveform. The amplifiers offered both an advantage and a disadvantage. The advantage was the obvious extension of the distances that sound could travel. The disadvantage was that the amplifiers amplified the entire signal, including any noise that was picked up due to electrical interference (lightning, sunspots or, of course, Death Star transmissions searching for the rebel base).

However, analog transmissions over long-distance amplification wouldn't allow for a global network of communication. To make a global network possible, the telcos migrated to a digital form of communication.

The Conversion To Digital Technologies

By converting an analog signal to a digital signal, the noise can be eliminated from the call. By replacing the amplifiers with repeaters, the digital 1s and 0s can be repeated to the receiving end and converted back to a simulated analog signal. When the repeater receives a signal, it must distinguish if it's a 1 or 0 and then repeat it. Because the repeater regenerates (not just amplifies) the digital 1s and 0s, the signal doesn't suffer from noise added between repeaters. Figure 3.2 shows the resulting digital signal when it's converted back to a sine wave at the far end, re-creating the voice pattern.

The issue was how to convert the analog waveform to an understandable series of 1s and 0s. A theorem presented by Nyquist states that the sample rate should be at least two times the maximum frequency of the line. Because the maximum frequency passed by the filters is 3,300 Hz, the sample rate should be at least 6,600 Hz. The samples-per-second rate selected by the telco was 8,000 Hz. Each sample taken is 8 bits; hence, a number between 0 and 255 represents the amplitude (or distance from the baseline). This value then allows for the receiving end to re-create the analog waveform, as shown in Figure 3.3.

This technique is similar to a child's connect-the-dot picture. The closer the dots, the more exacting the picture. It's possible that some various nuances of a voice pattern would be lost in this digitized transmission; however, the human ear isn't sensitive enough to discern the lost precision. Additionally, if some of the transmission is distorted or lost at a very high frequency or amplitude, the receiver can always say, "Huh?" This was fine for voice communication, but as we move into the digital age even a small loss of precision can't be tolerated.

Sampling at 8,000 samples per second, with each sample represented as an octet (or 8 bits), it's necessary to transmit 64,000 bits per second to carry a voice signal. This digital signal is referred to as a *DS0*—the bandwidth required for a voice call. The development of voice technology provided the basis for communication and yet, at the same time, produced today's limits on data communication.

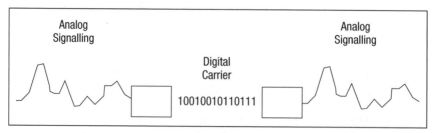

Figure 3.2   The analog wave is converted or digitized to a series of 1s and 0s that are then transmitted to the far end, where the analog wave form is re-created.

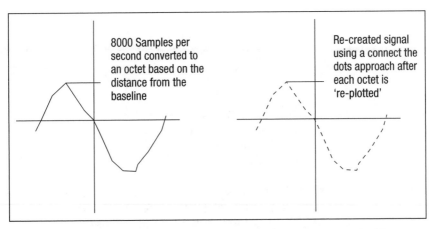

8000 Samples per second converted to an octet based on the distance from the baseline

Re-created signal using a connect the dots approach after each octet is 're-plotted'

Figure 3.3   The re-creation of an analog waveform is represented by a series of plotted points based on the sampled value of the input analog signal.

Mixing Analog And Digital

In the current world, the telco's infrastructure is primarily digital. The last mile or local loop, however, remains analog. Hence, home users are faced with using modems when using their PCs to communicate with the rest of the world. The *last mile* or *local loop* refers to the wiring that exists from the Central Office (CO) facility to the customer premises. The customer premises would be the home in the case of a home-office. This same wiring would be in place to any small business that has typical analog phone service. The modem functions as the digital (from the PC) to analog (the local loop) converter and vice versa. When you're connecting to your office using your PC from home, a minimum of four digital/analog conversions occur:

➤ At your home, from the PC (digital) to the last mile (analog)

➤ At the central office (CO), from analog to digital to be carried across the telco network

➤ At the CO that services your destination, from digital to analog to cross the last mile

➤ At the receiving modem, from analog to digital again

This process is illustrated in Figure 3.4.

The premise of remote access is directed and built around the local or home user. The earlier statement that the last-mile would be generally analog is true in this context. However, many larger corporations have a much wider arsenal

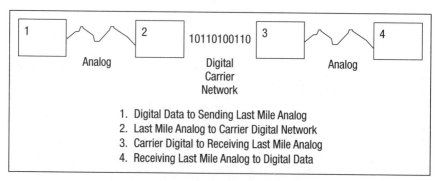

1. Digital Data to Sending Last Mile Analog
2. Last Mile Analog to Carrier Digital Network
3. Carrier Digital to Receiving Last Mile Analog
4. Receiving Last Mile Analog to Digital Data

Figure 3.4   The digital PC transmission is encoded by the modem to be transmitted across the digital network. The transmission is delivered to the last mile at the far end for another digital/analog conversion.

of options available because the telcos will position faster speed technologies at the premises for large corporations or business complexes under the assumption that they will be used. From the small business/home use perspective it is unlikely that the telcos will position a T1 circuit at every home on the block with the hope that many homeowners will opt for a faster circuit.

The recent standardization of 56Kbps modem technology (cleverly called V.90) eliminates the need for the analog/digital conversion at the head or receiving site. The connection to an Internet service provider (ISP) or corporate entity that has a digital connection to the telco for the last mile eliminates the need for the analog/digital conversion at the receiving end. Hence, with V.90 it's conceivable for the home user to receive at 56Kbps; however, transmitting is still limited to 33.6Kbps due to the initial analog/digital conversion.

The Federal Communications Commission (FCC) regulates the speed to 53Kbps. Hence, your 56Kbps modem could run at 33.6Kbps toward the network and 53Kbps back to the modem user, but *upload* and *download* speeds are not equal with V.90 service.

The Next Generation Of Digital Transmissions

The world is moving toward digital transmissions, as telecommuting, Web surfing, and video teleconferencing become the norm in today's data-hungry society. *Viva la revolucion.* The last step to providing high-speed connectivity to the home is the digitizing of the last mile. This digitization is available today with Integrated Services Digital Network (ISDN) and Digital Subscriber Loop (DSL) technologies for home users.

In the mid-1960s, the Bell system introduced to the network the T1, a digital carrier system. The older analog systems used analog multiplexing devices to supply 24 voice channels. The T1 is a true digital system that carries 24 DS0s, allowing for global digital representation of voice and eliminating the noise in long-distance communications. The aggregated rate is defined at 1.544Mbps. Each DS0 is 64Kbps and can carry a separate voice call. The 24 channels are time-division multiplexed (TDM). The concept of TDM is that each discrete channel gets a "shot" at the line for a time segment. TDM contrasts with Frequency Multiplexing, where each frequency is a sample on a "round-robin" basis and Statistical Multiplexing (Statmux) where, using statistics, the longer talker or higher volume channel is serviced more often.

TDM is a very simple algorithm that allows all the channels the same transmission time over the multiplexed channel. Even if a channel has nothing to say it can say "nothing". Frequency multiplexing is effectively the same; however, discrete frequencies are sampled. Statmuxess rely on software to determine which channels or frequencies have the "most to say" and service those on a higher proportional basis than the other channels or frequencies. In general, statmuxes conform to channel demand better but require a higher overhead. TDM requires less overhead but can be inefficient in a selected installation. However, given the number of circuits and the arbitrary use of circuits, TDM provides a good method to allocate bandwidth.

TDM can be thought of as a mother. Mothers nurture all their children the same and treat them all equally. Statmuxes generally are like professional football coaches. They tend to treat their money players better than they treat the down-linemen. Most telcos are mothers. No pun intended.

With TDM, one sample (8 bits) from each time slot (24) plus a framing bit (1) make up a *frame*; hence a frame is 193 bits. This results in the addition of 8Kbps of overhead for the transmission and results in the 1.544Mbps rate. Unfortunately, T1 digital service isn't generally positioned for home use (naturally).

In the United States, the T1 system is used where the resultant transmission rate is 1.544bps. In Europe, the bundling of channels is done differently; however, the underlying concepts are the same. The European E1 has 32 64-Kbps circuits (versus the T1's 24) and uses an entire channel to provide the signaling for the circuits. Hence, the E1 system has 31 64-Kbps user data channels and one 64-Kbps channel to provide the multiplexing. The E1 transmission rates are 2.048-Mbps.

Western Electric and Northern Telecom developed high-speed switching systems to allow the telcos to build large integrated digital switch systems. Within the United States, these two switch manufacturers still supply all the switches to the carriers. The switch types are the Electronic Switching System #5 (5ESS) from Western Electric and the DMS100 from Northern Telecom.

Timing Is The Critical Issue

The most critical issue with these high-speed digital circuits is timing. The timing is maintained in band by the 1 bits. The receivers and transmitters synchronize on the pulses within the eight-bit samples. Because a 0 is a non-pulse, sending a string of 0s might cause the receivers and transmitters to lose timing or *slip*. To fix this problem, the *1s density rule* was established: The most common implementation, set by AT&T, requires 1 pulse or 1 bit in every 8 bits of transmitted data.

Originally this requirement was met by *bit stuffing*, a technique that marks or makes every eighth bit a 1. Doing so doesn't create a problem with voice transmissions because you're correct 50 percent of the time, and the loss of one bit every so often may not be noticed by the human ear. However, being unsure of every eighth bit in a data stream could mean the difference between hitting the reactor exhaust vent and destroying the Death Star or being reduced to space jelly.

The technique of bit stuffing results in a data throughput of 56Kbps, because every eighth bit is unreliable. To overcome this problem, a new technique was developed: *bipolar 8 zero substitution* (B8ZS). When the channel service unit (CSU) sees an eight-bit string of all 0s, that string is replaced by a substitute byte of 00011011, with two bipolar violations. A *bipolar violation* is generated when two successive 1 bits are in the same electrical direction, as shown in Figure 3.5. This double violation indicates to the receiver, which is also configured for B8ZS, that a substitution has occurred and to reset the bits to an all-0 pattern. In this fashion, all bits are significant and the 1s density is maintained for clocking purposes.

 This B8ZS mechanism allows for *clear channel signaling*, or the use of the entire 64Kbps.

It's incumbent upon the administrator to encode the line for the local telco settings. In all of the router settings for Wide Area Networking (WAN), the customer is using the telco network and therefore must code to its settings. It's imperative to match the provider network to ensure proper data transfer.

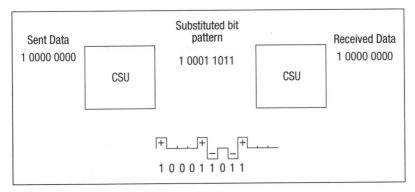

Figure 3.5   The last real 1 bit was marked positive. The two bipolar violations indicate to the receiving station that the true meaning of the octet is eight 0s.

Channelized Vs. Nonchannelized

The *channelization* of the DS0s made it possible for the provider to position multiplex voice signals over a single link or channel. As the need for faster uses was developed, it became necessary to use some of the DS0s in an aggregated fashion.

The new revolution calls for larger pipes to transmit video and support telecommuting. Instead of using the DS0s as discrete channels, they can be aggregated (or *nonchannelized*) to provide a larger pathway for data. For this technique to work, it's imperative that the subscriber (or customer) and the carrier (or provider) agree on the configuration. As with any good design, you must aggregate bandwidth as you near the backbone of the network.

As higher-speed technology is placed into the home, the carriers' infrastructure must grow to support the information flow. Home Web surfers and telecommuters are constantly looking for a faster modem. However, as we approach the limit of modem technologies, the end user is finding more attractive methods to gain access to the world of data, such as ISDN and DSL.

The DS0 was the building block on which the digital signaling 1 (DS1) was established. DS1 is the multiplexing of 24 DS0s. DS3 is the aggregated multiplexed signal of 672 DS0s. Often, the terms T1 and T3 are used interchangeably with the DS1 and DS3 designations; the true meaning of the *T* is the designation of the original specification of the T carrier system. The E1 uses the same building blocks with larger overall transmission signaling. The European system uses 32 DS0s for a DS1.

The provisioning (or configuration) of a T carrier line can be channelized as multiple 64Kbps circuits or as an aggregation of circuits. The key issue is that both the subscriber and the carrier must agree on the use.

The basis for all communications has been evolution. Today, as we move into newer technologies, it's important to remember where it all began. The move from analog to digital gave humans the ability to communicate over longer distances more clearly. The aggregation of the digital channels to nonchannelized communication gave rise to higher bandwidths needed for today's applications.

Modem technologies have grown to allow for transfer rates unheard of when Alexander Graham Bell said, "Mr. Watson, come here, I want you!" ISDN gave rise to the extension of the digital infrastructure to the consumer, and DSL is evolving as the next step to providing real-time data transfer to the home.

Practice Questions

Question 1

What hertz range is used by the telephone company for human speech?

○ a. 25 Hz through 22,000 Hz

○ b. 0 Hz through 3,000 Hz

○ c. 300 Hz through 3,300 Hz

○ d. 1,000 Hz through 10,000 Hz

Answer c is correct. The human voice uses a range from 100 Hz through 5,000 Hz, but most conversations only use between 300 and 3,300 Hz. The telephone companies elected to use only a subset of the voice range for transmission, leaving out the whisper and the scream. The human ear is capable of receiving between 25 and 22,000 Hz, but because the telephone companies' goal was to deliver voice, the very low and very high ends were not considered. Answer b is the correct absolute range, but not the correct starting and ending number of hertz. Answer a is the range that the human ear can detect, but not what the telephone company will send, hence the high and low end distortions. Answer d is simply incorrect from all perspectives.

Question 2

What physical equipment do the telephone companies use to propagate a digital signal over long distances?

○ a. Amplifiers

○ b. Repeaters

○ c. Multiplexers

○ d. Band-pass filters

Answer b is correct. The telco uses repeaters to receive and then repeat the signal as a one or zero. Amplifiers, answer a, were used in the early days of the phone companies; however, extraneous "noise" was amplified with the signal that was being sent. Answers c and d are incorrect because although multiplexers and band-pass filters are telco equipment, they have nothing to do with repeating a signal.

Question 3

With 56Kbps technology, it's possible to achieve which of the following?
[Choose the two best answers]

- ❏ a. 56Kbps downloads
- ❏ b. V.90 compatibility
- ❏ c. 56Kbps uploads
- ❏ d. 33.6Kbps uploads
- ❏ e. 56Kbps bidirectional
- ❏ f. 53Kbps upload

Answers a and d are correct. The key word is *possible*. A user can't get 56Kbps because the FCC limits the transmission speed to 53Kbps. Answer b, V.90 compatibility, is wrong because it does not ensure backward compatibility to other 56Kbps technologies. Answer c is wrong because the maximum upload speed is limited by the analog-to-digital conversion. 56Kbps bi-directional, answer e, is wrong for the same reason that answer c is wrong. Answer f could be technically correct if the answer were stated as 53Kbps download, but since it is upload and the limit is 33.6Kbps it is clearly wrong. This question points out the need to understand what can be done and what is possible.

Question 4

A T1 circuit has how many DS0s?

- ○ a. 12
- ○ b. 16
- ○ c. 24
- ○ d. 32

Answer c is correct. There are 24 DS0s in a T1. There are 32 DS0s in an E1 circuit, hence answer d would have been correct if the question were changed to ask for E1. Answers a and b are not relevant.

Question 5

Bit stuffing allows for a transmission speed of which of the following?

○ a. DS0

○ b. 64Kbps

○ c. 56Mbps

○ d. 33.6Kbps

○ e. 64Mbps

○ f. 56Kbps

Answer b is correct. Bit stuffing allows for a transmission speed of 64Kbps. In addition, with this question, you must pay attention to the detail of the answers. Some test questions are designed to test more than the knowledge of a number. Answer e, 64Mbps is the wrong magnitude for the speed and is therefore wrong. Answer a is wrong because it is simply the definition of a 64Kbps channel, not the speed at which it is being used. Answers c, d and e are wrong because they can be achieved without bit stuffing..

Question 6

Current high-speed local loop options for consumers include [Choose the two best answers]:

❏ a. Digital Local loop

❏ b. VPDN

❏ c. DSL

❏ d. X.25

❏ e. ISDN

❏ f. DSN

Answers c and e are correct. DSL and ISDN are replacing the current local-loop. ISDN provides a digital replacement to the current analog last-mile. DSL provides transmission speeds using higher frequencies than the voice box can transmit. Answer d is incorrect because X.25 is a different technology that could replace the local loop as defined. However, the question asked what consumers could choose rather than if the local-loop could be replaced. Answers a and f don't represent any technology and are, therefore, wrong. Answer b is incorrect because it does not address the speed issue. Virtual Private Dialup Networking allows the mobile user much more flexibility, but no more speed; hence answer b is wrong.

Question 7

A T3 circuit is the equivalent of how many DS0s?

○ a. 512

○ b. 24

○ c. 672

○ d. 3

Answer c is correct. Another way to phrase this question would be to ask the number of DS1s in a DS3 (28). Some questions will test the candidate's knowledge of the T carrier speeds and equivalents. There are 24 DS0s in a T1. There are 28 T1s in a T3. Therefore there are 672 DS0s in a T3. Some questions require a simple rote.

Question 8

Which two bits are bipolar violations to signify an altered string of 0s using B8ZS?

○ a. The fourth and seventh

○ b. The first and last

○ c. The fifth and eight

○ d. The fourth and fifth

Answer d is correct. B8ZS uses the fourth and fifth bit to redefine a string of 8 zeros. B8ZS changes the fourth and fifth bits to enforce one's density so that the receiving equipment does not lose clocking. Answers a, b and c do not follow the definition for B8ZS.

Question 9

The number of analog-to-digital conversions needed to communicate between PCs over a carrier network is:

- ○ a. 2
- ○ b. 4
- ○ c. 6
- ○ d. 8

Answer b is correct. It's necessary to convert from digital to analog and back
four times to cross an entire carrier network. The internal carrier network is
digital, but the last-mile to most customers is still analog. If you originate
modem connection to another user modem across a carrier network the first
digital-to-analog conversion will happen as you leave your location. Your PC
speaks digital, which is converted to analog so the carrier can take it over the
last mile to the CO, where the carrier converts it back to a digital signal. At this
point the data has undergone 2 conversions. The data is now passed on a digital backbone until it reaches the destination. The next step is to convert the
digital back to an analog signal to transmit over the last mile so the receiving
modem can convert the analog signal back to digital for the PC.

Question 10

How many samples per second are used to convert an analog signal to digital?

- ○ a. 64K
- ○ b. 8K
- ○ c. 64
- ○ d. 8

Answer b is correct. The answer is 8K or 8,000 samples per second based on
the Nyquist theory. An additional issue in this question concerns the use of the
"K". Many questions will require the candidate to be aware of the common
metric representations. The question wants more than "8" or "64"; the metric
argument as well as the speed are required. Answer a is the number of bits that
are transferred each second. By sampling 8,000 samples per second and each
sample representing 1 byte (8 bits) the transfer rate is 64Kbps.

Need To Know More?

 Cisco Press. *Cisco IOS Dial Solutions*. Macmillan Technical Publishing, Indianapolis, IN. ISBN 1-57870-055-8. This is a resource book not designed to be a good read, but it is useful as a command reference. It has many examples and reference tables in one location.

 Hardwick, Steve. *ISDN Design, A Practical Approach*. Academic Press, Inc. Harcourt Brace Jovanovich, Publishers. ISBN 0-12-324970-8. Solid treatment of the subject with many detailed descriptions of the terminology.

 Cisco Systems: Documentation CD. Any recent version of the CD has much background information on the various technologies discussed here. The search engine will allow the user to look specifically at white paper information in lieu of a command search. This gives the user a quick way to find a discussion of the search issue, not just the command to use it.

 Visit the official Cisco Web site at **www.cisco.com** for information and links to all technologies employed by Cisco.

Asynchronous
Modem Connections

Terms you'll need to understand:

√ Asynchronous signaling

√ Data Terminal Equipment (DTE)

√ Data Circuit Terminating Equipment (DCE)

√ Baud rate

√ V.90

√ Reverse Telnet

Techniques you'll need to master:

√ Configuring the physical interface of a router to communicate through a modem

√ Configuring a chat-script

√ Assigning IP addressing to a remote device

√ Configuring the physical and logical parameters for modem communication from a router

Asynchronous Signaling

Asynchronous communications represent the earliest form of internetworking. A modem (modulator/demodulator) allowed for the representation of a digital signal to traverse an analog line, as discussed in Chapter 3. The term *asynchrony* is the absence or lack of concurrence with time. *Asynchronous* signifies no timing requirements, and the transmitting device signals the start of each character.

As previously discussed, the transmitter and receiver must have a way to clock the line. *Clocking* tells the receiver when each pulse starts. For example, a long string of 1s or 0s is presented to the receiver as a steady signal without change (of course, all data transmissions are simply 1s and 0s). The clock allows the receiver to determine how many bits have been transmitted. So, if presented with five 0s in a row the receiver has to have a clock to determine if the string was five, six, or only four. Because such synchronization is needed even in our asynchronous world, we need a way to determine how many bits are 1 and how many bits are 0. With asynchronous transmission, the clocking takes place for each byte of data. A start bit and one or two stop bits are added to the end of every byte. In today's world, the most common form of asynchronous clocking is eight bits, no parity, and one stop bit (8-N-1). Thus, for every 8 bits of information you must transmit at least 10 bits, or 20 percent overhead.

Compare this process to the previous discussion on synchronous signaling, where the data itself provides the clock or start-of-bit signal. With synchronous signaling, a constant signal is sent; when eight 0s present themselves to the line, the bipolar 8 zero substitution (B8ZS) technique allows for the 1s density to remain high enough for the clocks to stay synchronized. During the initialization of an asynchronous link the modems will train upon a signal called the carrier. This carrier is a fixed sine wave format. Alterations of the carrier will signal the 1s and 0s.

Because the carrier is a fixed signal, the start bit (or 1) is needed to wake up the receiver and alert it that a byte will follow. If the sent signal is all 0s, you also need a bit to signify the end of the byte. (It could be that the initial 1 [or start bit] was a line spike that meant nothing.)

Telephone equipment is capable of recognizing 2,400 cycle changes per second. This is called the *baud rate*. In the early days of modem communication, the terms *baud* and *bits-per-second (bps)* were often interchanged. However, the terms are not the same. Today we are communicating at 2,400 baud; but the number of bits per second has increased dramatically. Such an alteration of this carrier wave is called *modulation*—the changing of amplitude, frequency, or phase of an electrical signal.

Amplitude Modulation

Amplitude modulation differentiates the 1s and 0s by changing the height of the carrier signal. When the receiver is getting an unmodulated (unchanged) carrier, it's interpreted as a 0. To signal a 1, the carrier wave amplitude is increased, as shown in Figure 4.1. An amplitude modulation modem would then be capable of sending up to 2,400bps. Again, not all of the bits represent data.

Frequency Modulation

Frequency modulation uses effectively the same principle. However, instead of heightening the signal for the sample period, the frequency itself is altered, as shown in Figure 4.2. However, the same restriction holds true for a frequency modulation modem as for an amplitude modulation modem—*only* 2,400bps can be transmitted. This speed (or lack thereof) gave rise to other methods of transmission.

Phase Modulation

The use of phase change created the divergence of the terms *baud* and *bps*. Changing the phase at the start of each signal or sample allowed the modem to send two bits per sample cycle. With four distinct phases that could be represented during a cycle or baud, the transmission was interpreted as a two-bit pattern based on the phase of the signal, as outlined in Table 4.1.

The shifting of the phases is shown in Figure 4.3. The beginning of the phase can be 0, 90, 180, or 270 degrees out of phase, signaling the bit pattern seen in Table 4.1.

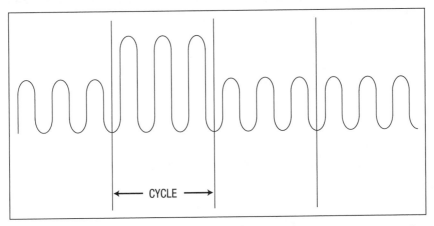

CYCLE

Figure 4.1 Amplitude modulation heightens the signal to represent a 1 bit.

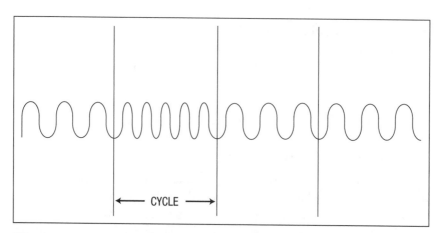

Figure 4.2 Frequency modulation changes the number of cycles per baud to represent a 1 bit.

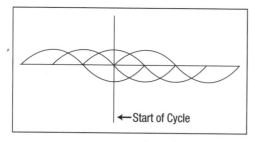

Figure 4.3 Phase shift signaling.

Table 4.1	Bit patterns for each phase shift.
Bits	**Phase**
00	0
01	90
10	180
11	270

Because four phases were possible, and only 1s and 0s were needed, the number of bits per cycle (or baud) doubled with phase modulation techniques.

With just phase modulation, the number of bits per second rose to 4,800. The next step was to combine the phase shift with one or more of the other modulation techniques—by adding these techniques, the number of bits per second could be increased even more. Even though the sample cycle remained at 2,400 baud, there were higher and higher throughputs.

Evolution Of Higher Modem Speeds

Newer techniques combine the altering of more than one physical characteristic of the carrier wave with compression techniques. The original evolution came when V.32 allowed for up to 9,600bps, then V.34 pushed the speed to 28.8Kbps, and finally the V.90 standard raised speeds to 56Kbps. 56Kps isn't usually achieved, due to line loss and interference in the telephone system and the fact that the Federal Communications Commission (FCC) limits the maximum data rate to 53Kbps.

The highest speed of 53Kbps is obtained *only* on the reverse path by avoiding the upstream analog/digital conversion, as stated in Chapter 3. Technology is pushing the limits of what can and can't be done at the current frequency and bandwidth filters, using the existing copper wires.

At this point in our discussion of modulation, there is nothing left to change. All of the physical characteristics that can be changed—the frequency, the amplitude, and the phase—have been changed. The sample rate (baud) is a fixed entity, and unless the telephone companies unite to upgrade the infrastructure, the baud will continue to be fixed.

Take heart, gentle reader. We'll talk about Digital Subscriber Loop (DSL) and Integrated Services Digital Network (ISDN) later.

Good Bits And Bad Bits

When an efficient means to get bits from one modem to another was firmly established, the next step was to find a way to tell the difference between good bits and bad bits. The earliest attempt had the modem decide whether the bit wore a black hat or a white hat, but this technique was abandoned when all the bits started sporting baseball caps of their favorite major league teams.

An alternative method was to designate one of the bits as a tattle bit, called a *parity bit*. For each seven bits that were sent, an eighth bit declared either even or odd parity. If the seven-bit pattern was 0011001 and parity was declared to be even, the eighth bit would be set to 1. This yielded a bit pattern of 00110011, or four (an even number) of 1s. The same principle holds true for odd parity. Using the same seven-bit pattern 0011001 with odd parity, the eighth bit would remain a 1; and the resulting pattern, 00110010, has three 1s (an odd number).

This method works well as long as only an odd number of bits are flipped. If a byte is interfered with or corrupted during transmission, and two bits are changed from a 1 to a 0 or vice versa, the parity would be reported correctly and the error left undetected.

The next evolution of checking for good and bad bits used a parity bit for each byte and also sent an additional byte to check for parity across a block of bytes. This method resulted in additional overhead and was reliable only up to about 80 percent.

Other forms of parity exist such as mark and space, which are only variations on the even or odd method. Using these methods, the eight-bit pattern is presented using a mark or a space for error correction. Each method is as good as the next so long as both sides of the conversation agree on which method will be used. Additionally, the parity can be set to none. In this case no line checking is done, and the responsibility is left to the higher levels of the protocol stack.

The most recent technique is the cyclic redundancy check (CRC). This technique is designed to provide 99.999 percent reliability in data transmissions. The CRC technique is a sophisticated mathematical algorithm that is based on lots of stuff. The term "lots-of-stuff" is used because the algorithm is daunting to all but a few Ph.D. mathematicians, and while it can be turned on or off, its form cannot be altered. The drawback to the CRC technique for asynchronous communications is the intensive computational need at both the transmitting and receiving ends, thus making it impractical for modem implementation.

PCs today are quite capable of quickly understanding whether the data is good or bad using a CRC technique. For asynchronous communications, the passing of the data is the most critical function. Today, the upper-level protocols and applications decide if the data is good or bad.

To summarize the last few pages in brief, set your modem to 8-N-1 and let the power of the PC and application software discover a bad bit, naturally.

Modem Signaling

The remainder of this chapter deals specifically with the facts concerning modem signaling and configuration on your Cisco router.

 Both the CMTD and BCRAN tests will examine your knowledge of the theory of communications, so understanding the technology explained in the previous sections is important. So too is memorizing many of the following facts.

The use of asynchronous data communications technology involves having a device (such as a PC) call or connect to another device (such as a server) to exchange data. The end devices are referred to as Data Terminal Equipment (DTE). These devices communicate through Data Circuit Terminating Equipment (DCE). In the original concept of a DCE device, it *was* the end of a telephone circuit. This definition is somewhat lost on us now, because the telephone company no longer owns much of the customer's equipment. Nonetheless, the terminology continues to be used.

The Electronic Industries Association/Telecommunications Industry Association (EIA/TIA) defines a standard for the interface between DCE and DTE devices called the EIA/TIA-232. This standard was previously referred to as the RS-232-C standard, where *RS* stood for *recommended standard*.

The concept of data communications is often thought of as a DTE device connecting to a DCE device; however, this is only part of the picture. My PC contacting a server over a phone line requires the use of a DTE-DCE connection (PC to modem), a DCE-DCE connection (modem to modem), and a DCE-DTE connection (modem to server).

With asynchronous communication, the eight pins are used in a 25 pin D-Shell Block (DB25) to transfer data and control the modem behavior. These pins and their definitions are shown in Table 4.2. You should pay particular attention to the direction of the signal and what type of device (DTE or DCE) recognizes the pin.

Data Transfer

The pins discussed in the previous section control the data transfer, the flow control of data, and the modem control. The pins used for data transfer are Transmit Data (TD pin 2), Receive Data (RD pin 3), and the Signal Ground (GRD pin 7). The signal ground pin allows the receiver and transmitter to reference the same ground potential to ensure that signal strength is measured against a common point. Once a call is established and the DTE device sees

Table 4.2	Standard RS-232-C definitions and codes.	
Pin Number	**Designation**	**Definition**
2	TD	Transmit Data (DTE to DCE data)
3	RD	Receive Data (DCE to DTE data)
4	RTS	Request To Send (DTE buffer available)
5	CTS	Clear To Send (DCE buffer available)
6	DSR	Data Set Ready (DCE ready)
7	GRD	Signal Ground
8	CD	Carrier Detect (DCE has carrier)
20	DTR	Data Terminal Ready (DTE ready)

the DCE post Clear To Send, the DTE device will transmit data on pin 2. Conversely, the DTE device will post Request To Send when it has buffer space available to receive from the DCE device.

TD is the signal pin for the DTE device to transmit data to the DCE device.

RD is the signal pin for the DTE device to receive data from the DCE device.

Ground provides a common signal ground for voltage measurement.

Data Flow Control

The flow of information is controlled by the Clear To Send (CTS pin 5) and the Request To Send (RTS pin 4). If you think it sounds confusing that when a device (the DTE) is ready to receive data it would raise a pin called Request To Send, you're correct. It's probably easier to think of the RTS pin as Request (or Ready) To Receive. That way all the pins can be viewed from the perspective of the DTE.

CTS means the DCE has buffer space to accept data from the DTE.

RTS means the DTE has buffer space to accept data from the DCE.

Modem Control

Modem control is handled with the Data Terminal Ready (DTR pin 20), the Data Set Ready (DSR pin 6), and the Carrier Detect (CD pin 8). DSR is raised when the modem is powered on, to let the DTE device know that the modem is ready for use. When the DTE device is ready to receive information from the DCE, the DTR pin is raised. If you've turned on your answering-machine software, the PC will raise DTR indicating to the modem that it's ready to receive incoming information. If your PC initiates a call with an AT command string, the command string will raise DTR to allow the DCE device to return information. Either way, DTR is needed for a two-way conversation between the DCE and DTE devices.

When two DCE devices establish a connection, the CD pin is held high to indicate that a carrier has been established between the DCE devices.

Because two devices constitute the DTE (PC) and DCE (modem) connection, it's necessary to allow for either to terminate the connection. If the DTE

(PC) is ready to terminate the connection because the user has finished surfing the Web, DTR is dropped. The modem must be configured to interpret the loss of DTR as the end of a conversation. Also, if the far-end modem drops the connection because the remote is lost or has disconnected, then CD is lost on the DCE. Again, the modem must be programmed to understand this scenario.

DTR is raised (or high) to tell the DCE that the DTE device will accept a call.

DSR is raised (or high) to show that the DCE device is ready for use.

CD is raised (or high) after a carrier signal is negotiated with a remote DCE.

To terminate a call:

➤ *DTE initiated termination*—Drop DTR

➤ *DCE initiated termination*—Drop CD

Modem Configuration And Reverse Telnet

In order to configure the modem, the router must be set up to talk to it. Cisco refers to this as a *reverse Telnet connection*. A host that is connected to the router can Telnet to a Cisco-reserved port address on the router and establish an 8-N-1 connection to a specific asynchronous port. The reserved port addresses are shown in Table 4.3. The router must have a valid IP address on an interface and an asynchronous port. To establish a connection to the modem connected to the asynchronous port, you can—from the router console (or a remote device with Telnet access to the router)—Telnet to the valid IP address indicating the specific port for the connection.

For example, suppose you want to set up an 8-N-1 connection to the fourth asynchronous port on a router that has the 10.44.5.6 address assigned to its E0 port. To connect in character mode using Telnet, you would issue the following command:

```
telnet 10.44.5.6 2004
```

where 10.44.5.6 is the router's E0 port, and 2004 is the Cisco-reserved port number for the fourth asynchronous port on the router. (See Table 4.3 for other port ranges.)

Table 4.3   Cisco-reserved port numbers for reverse Telnet.

Connection Service	Reserved Port Range For Individual Ports	Reserved Port Range For Rotary Groups
Telnet Protocol (Character Mode)	2000 through 2xxx	3000 through 3xxx
TCP Protocol (Line Mode)	4000 through 4xxx	5000 through 5xxx
Telnet Protocol (Binary Mode)	6000 through 6xxx	7000 through 7xxx
Xremote Protocol	9000 through 9xxx	10000 through 10xxx

 You should review and memorize port numbering and connection modes for the CMTD and BCRAN exams.

The rotary group reserved port number connects to the first available port that's in the designated rotary group. However, using rotary groups doesn't negate the ability to connect to a specific port using the individual reserved numbers.

Once a connection has been established with the modem, you can configure it (if you're using character mode) with the **AT** command set for that modem. To exit the connection, use the Ctrl+Shift+6 X sequence to **SUSPEND** the session and then issue the **DISCONNECT** command from the router prompt.

You obtain the line numbers on a router in the following manner:

1. The console port is line 0.

2. Number each asynchronous (TTY) port 1 through the number of TTY ports on the router. (Note: *TTY* refers to teletype which was the original form of asynchronous communications. The legacy of the port acronym is perpetuated.)

3. Give the Auxiliary (AUX) port the line number of the last TTY port plus one.

4. Number the Virtual Terminal (VTY) ports starting with the line number of the last TTY port plus two.

Figure 4.4 is the *show line* output for a Cisco 2522 router that has eight asynchronous ports available. Notice that the AUX port is line #10 and the VTY

```
2500router#sh line
  Tty Typ     Tx/Rx      A Modem  Roty AccO AccI  Uses  Noise  Overruns
*   0 CTY                 -   -     -    -    -     0      3      0/0
Line 1 is currently invalid
    2 TTY    9600/9600    -   -     -    -    -     0      0      0/0
    3 TTY    9600/9600    -   -     -    -    -     0      0      0/0
    4 TTY    9600/9600    -   -     -    -    -     0      0      0/0
Line 5 is currently invalid
Line 6 is currently invalid
Line 7 is currently invalid
Line 8 is currently invalid
Line 9 is currently invalid
   10 AUX    9600/9600    -   -     -    -    -     0      0      0/0
*  11 VTY                 -   -     -    -    -     1      0      0/0
   12 VTY                 -   -     -    -    -     0      0      0/0
   13 VTY                 -   -     -    -    -     0      0      0/0
   14 VTY                 -   -     -    -    -     0      0      0/0
   15 VTY                 -   -     -    -    -     0      0      0/0
```

Figure 4.4   The **show line** output from a fixed configuration 2500
series router.

ports are labeled #11 through #15. The *show line* command will produce the
output that follows:

```
BCRANrouter#sh line
```

The numbering of interfaces was expanded for the BCRAN courseware with
the introduction of the 3600 series routers. The concept of the console being
line 0 and the VTY ports being labeled after the TTYs is the same; however,
the slots gave rise to a need for a numbering system to cross slot boundaries.
Figure 4.5 shows the back plane of a 3620 and 3640 series router and the line
numbers associated with each slot.

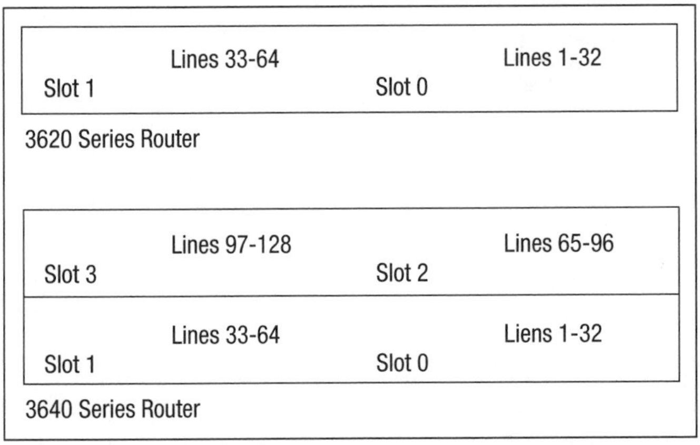

Figure 4.5   3600 line numbers.

The line number scheme is important when you're configuring a router, so take care to understand the line numbers. In the case of the 3600 and 2600 routers with the new modular interfaces, the line numbers are based upon the slot that a feature card is in. The output in Figure 4.6 is from a 3640 series router with a modem card in slot 2. You'll notice that the line numbers for the six internal modems are 65 through 70.

In order to properly configure a router, you must know the association of the line and interface numbers. The AUX port on the modular routers is the last line number *that could be* plus 1. In the case of the 3640 router used in most labs, the AUX port number is 129, and the VTY ports are 130 through 135 by default.

3600 line numbering:

➤ *Slot 0*—Lines 1 through 32

➤ *Slot 1*—Lines 33 through 64

➤ *Slot 2*—Lines 65 through 96

➤ *Slot 3*—Lines 97 through 128

Fixed configuration line numbering:

➤ *Line 0*—Console

➤ *TTYs*—1 through last TTY port

➤ *AUX*—Last TTY plus 1

➤ *VTYs*—Last TTY plus 2

```
3600router#sh line
  Tty Typ      Tx/Rx       A Modem  Roty AccO AccI  Uses   Noise  Overruns   Int
*   0 CTY                  -   -       -    -    -     0      0      0/0      -
I  65 TTY              - inout        -    -    -     0      0      0/0      -
I  66 TTY              - inout        -    -    -     0      0      0/0      -
I  67 TTY              - inout        -    -    -     0      0      0/0      -
I  68 TTY              - inout        -    -    -     0      0      0/0      -
I  69 TTY              - inout        -    -    -     0      0      0/0      -
I  70 TTY              - inout        -    -    -     0      0      0/0      -
I  97 TTY 115200/115200- inout        -    -    -     0      0      0/0      Se3/0
*129 AUX     9600/9600    -   -       -    -    -     0      0      0/0      -
  130 VTY                 -   -       -    -    -     0      0      0/0      -
  131 VTY                 -   -       -    -    -     0      0      0/0      -
  132 VTY                 -   -       -    -    -     0      0      0/0      -
  133 VTY                 -   -       -    -    -     0      0      0/0      -
  134 VTY                 -   -       -    -    -     0      0      0/0      -

Line(s) not in async mode -or- with no hardware support:
1-64, 71-96, 98-128
```

Figure 4.6   The **show line** output from a 3600 series router with a modem
card in slot 2.

The following excerpt from a configuration for a 3640 router shows the physical characteristics configured on line 97 for the asynchronous interface in slot 3/0:

```
interface Serial3/0
 physical-layer async
 ip unnumbered Ethernet0/0
 no ip directed-broadcast
 encapsulation ppp
 async mode interactive
 peer default ip address pool TESTPOOL
 no cdp enable
 ppp authentication chap
!
line 97
 password cisco
 autoselect during-login
 autoselect ppp
 login local
 modem InOut
 transport input all
 stopbits 1
 speed 115200
 flowcontrol hardware
line aux 0
line vty 0 4
 login local
!
```

Cisco has recently announced and is shipping a 3660 device that has six slots that are numbered in a like fashion to the 3620 and 3640 described here. This information is provided to give the reader updated information but has no effect on any test material.

Basic Modem Configuration

In order to configure the modem (the DCE) from the router (the DTE), you must set up the physical parameters on the line for communication to take place. The logical and physical aspects of the connection must be established. The logical aspects include the protocol addressing, the authentication method, and the encapsulation—you configure them on the asynchronous interface. The physical configuration is done on the line. The physical characteristics include the flow control, the DTE-DCE speed, and the login request.

The following configuration is an example of the commands you can use on the interface and line. Later in this chapter, we'll list each command with its arguments. Each of these commands is a prime test candidate:

```
interface Serial3/0
 physical-layer async
 ip unnumbered Ethernet0/0
 no ip directed-broadcast
 encapsulation ppp
 async mode interactive
 peer default ip address pool TESTPOOL
 no cdp enable
 ppp authentication chap
```

 Many of the Cisco exams have recently gone to a fill-in-the-blank format for some of the questions. This format requires typing the answer with the correct spelling and syntax. It's important to *not* rely on the common shortcuts. For that reason, throughout this section we present the full command syntaxes.

It should be noted here that on some of the router models (those with A/S ports), the serial ports default to synchronous, and the interface must be declared for asynchronous usage using the **physical-layer async** command. The previous sample configurations are for the second asynchronous interface on a 2522. The **physical-layer async** command is needed because this device has A/S ports.

Logical Considerations

The logical considerations are configured on the interface of the router. These include the network layer addressing, encapsulation method, authentication, and so on. The following is a sample configuration for a serial interface that will be used to receive an inbound call:

```
interface Serial2
    physical-layer async
    ip unnumbered Ethernet0
    ip tcp header-compression passive
    encapsulation ppp
    bandwidth 38
    async mode interactive
    peer default ip address pool REMOTEPOOL
    no cdp enable
    ppp authentication chap
```

The **physical-layer async** command places the serial 2 interface in asynchronous mode. Once this command is issued, the router treats the interface as an asynchronous port. This can be done *only* on those interfaces that are defined as A/S.

The **ip unnumbered Ethernet0** command declares that the interface will assume the address of the E0 interface. This command allows for the saving of IP addresses but will make the interface non-SNMP (Simple Network Management Protocol) manageable. You could replace this command with the desired IP address of the interface. For more information, see the "Asynchronous Addressing Schemes" section later in this chapter.

The **ip tcp header-compression passive** command states that if the other DCE device sends packets with header-compression, this interface will understand and will send in kind, but won't initiate the compression.

The **encapsulation ppp** command declares the encapsulation method for this interface.

The **bandwidth 38** command tells the routing protocol and the router (for statistics) the speed of the line. This command has no effect on the actual negotiated speed of the modem or the speed at which the DTE talks to the modem.

Once a connection is made, the **async mode interactive** command allows the dial-in user access to the **exec** prompt.

The **peer default ip address pool REMOTEPOOL** command specifies that the IP address assigned to the dial-in user will come from the address block defined as **REMOTEPOOL**. The syntax for the pool definition is

```
ip local pool REMOTEPOOL low-ip-pool-address high-ip-pool-address
```

defined in global configuration mode. For more information, see the "Asynchronous Addressing Schemes" section later in this chapter.

The **no cdp enable** command turns off Cisco Discovery Protocol for this interface. By default, this protocol is on; and because the interface is likely connected to a dial-in user that doesn't understand CDP, the bandwidth it would use is saved.

The **ppp authentication chap** command specifies that the Challenge Handshake Authentication Protocol (CHAP) will be used on this link. Failure of the client to honor CHAP will result in the link's not being established.

Physical Considerations

The physical characteristics are configured on the line. These include the speed, direction of call, modem setup, and so on. The following is a sample configuration used to connect to a USR Sportster modem on physical line 2:

```
line 2
    autoselect during-login
```

```
autoselect ppp
password cisco
login local
modem InOut
modem autoconfigure type usr_sportster
transport input all
stopbits 1
rxspeed 115200
txspeed 115200
flowcontrol hardware
```

The **password cisco** and **login local** commands are the same for this line as they are for the console and AUX ports. The **login local** command tells the physical line to request a password for connectivity and to look locally for a correct

```
username xxxx password xxxx
```

combination in the global configuration. (*xxxx* represents a freely chosen username and password combination).

The **autoselect during-login** and **autoselect ppp** commands automatically start the PPP protocol and issue a carriage return so the user is prompted for the login. This feature became available in the 11.0 release. Prior to the **during-login** feature, the dial-in user was required to issue an **exec** command to start the session.

The **modem InOut** command allows for both incoming and outgoing calls, as suggested by the command. The alternative to this command is the default **no modem InOut,** which yields no control over the modem.

The **modem autoconfigure type usr_sportster** command uses the **modemcap database usr_sportster** entry to initialize the modem.

 The **transport input all** command has changed with Version 12 code.

The **transport input all** command allows the processing of any protocol on the line. This command defines which protocols to use to connect to a line. The default prior to 11.1 was **all;** the default as of 12.0 is **none.**

As discussed earlier, the number of **stopbits** must be the same for both communicating DCE devices.

The **rxspeed** and **txspeed** commands are entered as a single command, as noted in the example. The command **speed** sets both transmit and receive speeds. This command is needed to lock the speed between the modem and the DTE device.

The **flowcontrol hardware** command specifies that the RTS and CTS will be honored for flow control.

This example provides a basic template for the creation of a configuration file for an asynchronous line. The next step in getting the link to establish is to ensure that the modem is properly initialized. Both the CMTD and BCRAN courseware showed a listing of Standard and Non-Standard modem commands. The Standard commands are shown in Table 4.4.

Not surprisingly, these commands were in evidence on the exams. It's important prior to taking the test to be familiar with the AT command set. It is *not* important to memorize the non-standard commands for each modem vendor. Good, huh?

The correct initialization string must be sent to the modem for proper operation. You can accomplish this by using a **chat-script** or the **modem autoconfigure** command. The common method of initialization is the **modem autoconfigure** command. Modem autoconfiguration allows for the following features:

➤ *Configure*—Configure modems without using modem commands

➤ *Autodiscover*—Autodiscover modem

➤ *Reinitialize*—Reinitialize the line each time it's reset

Table 4.4	Standard modem command strings.
Command	**Result**
AT&F	Load factory default settings.
ATS0=n	Auto answer.
AT&C1	CD reflects the line state.
AT&D3	Hang up on DTR low (actually it's AT&D2, but the courseware shows D3, and so did the CMTD exam!).
ATE0	Turn off local echo (so you don't see two characters when you type).
ATM0	Turn off the speaker. (Why?! Without the speaker how can you troubleshoot?)

The term *autoconfigure* actually relies on the modem capabilities database (**modemcap**). The modem capabilities database contains a list of modems and a generic initialization string for the modem type. The *discovery* of a modem using the autoconfigure feature uses the initialization strings from each modem in the modem capabilities database to discover the installed modem. If the modem isn't in the database, it fails, and the administrator has to add the modem to the database.

The use of the discovery feature isn't recommended because of the overhead on the router. Each time the line is reset, the modem is rediscovered. You should use the discovery feature to initially learn the modem type (if you aren't geographically near the router); then use the **type** argument to specify the entry to use in the modem capabilities database.

To discover a modem, the syntax would be

```
Modem autoconfigure discovery
```

Once the modem type is determined, the final configuration for the router interface should be

```
Modem autoconfigure type entry_name_from_modemcap
```

To see the entries in the modemcap database, use the command **show modemcap**. The listing that is produced is as follows:

```
BCRANrouter#sh modemcap

default
codex_3260
usr_courier
usr_sportster
hayes_optima
global_village
viva
telebit_t3000
microcom_hdms
microcom_server
nec_v34
nec_v110
nec_piafs
cisco_v110
mica
```

To view a particular entry in the database, add the entry name as an argument to the **show modemcap** command:

```
BCRANrouter#sh modemcap usr_sportster
2511_Router#sh modemcap codex_3260
Modemcap values for codex_3260
Factory Defaults (FD):   &F
Autoanswer (AA):   SO=1
Carrier detect (CD):   &C1
Drop with DTR (DTR):   &D2
Hardware Flowcontrol (HFL):   *FL3
Lock DTE speed (SPD):   *SC1
DTE locking speed (DTE):   [not set]
Best Error Control (BER):   *SM3
Best Compression (BCP):   *DC1
No Error Control (NER):   *SM1
No Compression (NCP):   *DC0
No Echo (NEC):   EO
No Result Codes (NRS):   Q1
Software Flowcontrol (SFL):   [not set]
Caller ID (CID):   &S1
On-hook (ONH):   HO
Off-hook (OFH):   H1
Miscellaneous (MSC):   [not set]
Template entry (TPL):   default
Modem entry is built-in.
```

The database contains most models of modems. If your entry isn't in the database, you can add it by editing the database. Creating your own entry name and specifying the attributes to use for the entry does this.

For example, if the attached modem is a Microcom xyz and it isn't listed in the database per se, the administrator would create an entry for the modem type and add those attributes that are changed from one of the other Microcom entries.

```
Modemcap edit microcom_xyz template microcom_hdms
```

This command uses the initialization string from the entry **microcom_hdms** and allows the administrator to alter the newly created **microcom_xyz**. All changes and additions to the **modemcap** database are stored in the configuration file for the router. In this fashion, Cisco can add to the **modemcap** at any release because the alterations remain with the router.

Chat Scripts

Lastly, you have the chat scripts available for asynchronous lines. These scripts allow you the ability to talk to the modem or log in to a remote system using whatever non-standard syntax is called for. Essentially, the chat script takes this form:

```
Expect-string  send-string  expect-string  send-string  . . .
```

Chat scripts can be used for the following purposes:

➤ *Initialization*—Initializing the modem

➤ *Dial string*—Providing the modem with a dial string

➤ *Logon*—Logging in to a remote system

➤ *Command execution*—Executing a set of commands on a remote system

A chat script can be manually started on a line using the **start-chap** command, or it can be configured to start for the following events:

➤ Line activation-CD trigger (incoming traffic)

➤ Connection-DTR trigger (outgoing traffic)

➤ Line reset-asynchronous line reset

➤ Startup of an active call– access server trigger

➤ Dialer startup from a dial-on-demand trigger

You should review the uses and triggers for a chat script prior to the exam for both CMTD and BCRAN.

The primary chat script to provide a modem with a number to call is as follows:

```
Router(config)#chat-script Central ABORT ERROR ABORT BUSY
    "" "ATZ" OK "ATDT \T" TIMEOUT 30 CONNECT \c
```

Take care with the case of this command. The **ABORT ERROR** and **ABORT BUSY** cause the modem to abort if it sees **ERROR** or **BUSY**. If you enter **error** and **abort** in lowercase, the modem will never see these conditions. The \T inserts the called number in the chat script from the **dial string** or **map** command. A \t causes the script to look for a table character—hence, case is important here also.

Asynchronous Addressing Schemes

A few commands were used throughout this chapter to address the dial-up interface and to assign or accept the address of the calling party. The following rules apply to the addressing for asynchronous interfaces:

➤ The interface can be assigned a unique address or be *un*numbered to another interface address on the router.

➤ The calling party can specify its own address, or the called party can dictate the calling party's address on the interface or assign it from a pool of addresses.

In the case of the called party's address, it can be assigned using the **ip address** command just like any other interface on the router. The **ip unnumbered** command can point the address assignment to another interface, which can save IP addresses. In the case of unnumbering, many asynchronous interfaces can be pointed to a single LAN or loopback interface, thus saving many IP addresses. The drawback to this practice is that the asynchronous interface can't be managed using SNMP; and, if the interface that the asynchronous line is pointed to goes down, so does the asynchronous link.

For an example of when unnumbering may be a benefit, consider a situation in which you have many dial-in links connecting to access the resource on the E0 (Ethernet 0) interface. If all the asynchronous lines are unnumbered to E0 and E0 goes down, what will the dial-in users be accessing, anyway? The main problem here will be the lack of SNMP management. The question here is, how much management information is needed for those dial links?

The receiver has the option of specifying the remote's IP address or accepting the address as given. The following commands control this process:

```
Router(config-int)#peer default ip address
    [address | pool pool-name | dhcp]
```

or

```
Router(config-int)#async dynamic address
```

In the case of the **peer default ip address** command, the called router assigns an IP address to the caller in the following fashion:

➤ **address**—Specifically assigned address for all calls to this interface.

➤ **pool** *pool-name*—Assigned address from the address pool declared by *pool-name*.

➤ **dhcp**—Address assigned by DHCP server (Dynamic Host Configuration Server).

Using the **async dynamic address** command, the calling router specifies the address that it will use for the connection. When using the **async dynamic address** command, the calling router must specify a compatible address in the range that the called router is using or no communication will take place.

A classic example of using the **ip unnumbered** feature and the **peer default** addressing would involve a large number of dial-in clients accessing resources on the Ethernet interface of the host router. If all the interfaces are unnumbered to the Ethernet interface and a pool of addresses is set aside from the Ethernet address pool, then the individual callers can be assigned an address on an as-needed basis.

Study Guide

In this chapter, we've discussed asynchronous signaling using various modulation techniques with error checking performed by parity or CRC. We described the roles of the DTE and DCE devices and covered the pin assignments for the EIA/TIA-232 cable. We also discussed the concepts of modem control, reverse Telnet, and line numbering. Finally, we outlined the concept of auto configuration and discovery using the modem capabilities database and presented *many* commands.

The following list of commands and their syntax is presented as a study aid for the CMTD and BCRAN tests. Each command *and* its arguments may be seen on the test. The reader is reminded that some questions will take the form of fill-in-the-blank, *not* multiple choice:

Global commands:

➤ **telnet** (note port for reverse telnet)

Line commands:

➤ **exec**
➤ **login**
➤ **flowcontrol**
➤ **speed**
➤ **transport input**
➤ **stopbits**
➤ **modem InOut or dialin**
➤ **autoselect**

Interface commands:

➤ **encapsulation**
➤ **async dynamic address** versus **peer default ip address**
➤ **async mode interactive** or **dedicated**
➤ **ppp authentication**
➤ **ip address**

Practice Questions

Question 1

> Given a router with an Ethernet port address of 10.1.1.1, what command will establish a reverse Telnet connection to the third asynchronous port on a router:
>
> ○ a. **telnet 10.1.1.1 3**
>
> ○ b. **telnet 2003 10.1.1.1**
>
> ○ c. **telnet 10.1.1.1 2003**
>
> ○ d. **telnet line 3**

Answer c is correct. The command Telnet 10.1.1.1 2003 will give the user access to the third asynchronous port. The static mapping of a host name to the connection is reversed using the command "ip host 2003 10.1.1.1". Static mapping commands should not be confused with the console commands. Answer b is representative of this incorrect static map command being used as a console command. Answer a is incorrect because no port number is specified, and answer d is incorrect because "line 3" is not a valid argument.

Question 2

> Chat scripts can be used for:
>
> ○ a. Initializing a modem
>
> ○ b. Executing a set of commands on a remote system
>
> ○ c. Providing the modem with a dial string
>
> ○ d. All the above

Answer d is correct. The execution of commands on a remote system can be done using the **start-chap** command. Chat scripts can be used for initializing the modem, providing the modem with a dial string, logging in to a remote system, and executing a command set.

Question 3

To assign the IP address 10.1.1.1 to a dial-in user, the command is:

○ a. **async dynamic address 10.1.1.1**

○ b. **dynamic address 10.1.1.1**

○ c. **peer default ip address 10.1.1.1 255.255.0.0**

○ d. **peer default ip address 10.1.1.1**

Answer d is correct. Note that the subnet mask isn't used in the command string. Answers a and b use the keyword dynamic, which does not exist in this context; therefore, these answers are wrong. Answer c is wrong because the assignment of a peer default address does not take the subnet mask as an argument. The peer default is assigning an address based on a range known by the router, which is assigning the number. No mask is needed.

Question 4

Which of the following best describes the TD:

○ a. Is the signal pin for the DCE device to transmit data to the DTE device

○ b. Is the signal pin for the DTE device to transmit data to the DCE device

○ c. Means the DCE has buffer available to the DTE

○ d. Means the DTE has buffer available to the DCE

Answer b is correct. The pin definitions are given from the perspective of the DTE device; in this case, the TD is the signal pin for the DTE device to transmit to the DCE device. Answers a is wrong because it is describing the function of the RD pin. Answers c and d are describing control conditions that manage the flow of data over the RD and TD pins, and, therefore, are incorrect.

Question 5

> For the DCE to terminate an existing connection it must:
>
> ○ a. Drop DTR
>
> ○ b. Drop CTS
>
> ○ c. Send ATH to the DTE
>
> ○ d. Drop CD

Answer d is correct. The DCE will signal the termination by dropping the Carrier Detect pin. Answer a would be the correct response if the DTE device were to drop the circuit. Answer b drops a control lead, and has no effect on the connection. Answer c is incorrect, although it will end the connection. A user intervening by sending ATH is asking for the modem to hang up, which will drop carrier detect, but the DCE is not the initiating action that clears the circuit. It is the user.

Question 6

> To end a reverse Telnet session on a router-attached modem, what command is used?
>
> ○ a. **clear line**
>
> ○ b. Ctrl+Shift-6+x and disconnect
>
> ○ c. **ATH** and **clear line**
>
> ○ d. **+++**

Answer b is correct. Answer a, the command **clear line,** will end the connection if the user is on the router console; however, the question asks how to end the session on the modem. Using the Ctrl-Shift-6+x will put the user back on the router and the following **disconnect** command will release the session completely. Answers c and d will both end the connection, but leave the user on the modem console. To release the reverse telnet connection, the user must use the Ctrl-shift-6 + x command.

Question 7

> Using a 3640 router, on what line would you configure the physical character-
> istics for interface serial 2/0?
>
> ○ a. Line 2/0
>
> ○ b. Line 20
>
> ○ c. Line 65
>
> ○ d. Line 64

Answer c is correct. Line 65 would be the first line in slot #2. Answer d, line
64, is part of slot #1 and answer b, line 20, is part of slot #0. Answer a, the
command 2/0, is irrelevant. The numbering of the lines on a 3640 router are
counted as 1-32 (slot 0), 33-64 (slot 1), 65-96 (slot2) and 96-128 (slot 3).

Question 8

> What command will assign an address to a caller from the IP address pool
> REMPOOL?
>
> ○ a. **peer default ip address pool REMPOOL**
>
> ○ b. **peer default pool REMPOOL**
>
> ○ c. **peer default address REMPOOL**
>
> ○ d. **peer default REMPOOL**

Answer a is correct. Syntax is key. **Peer default ip address** is the command.
The argument is *pool* and the pool name that is to be used is REMPOOL.
Answers b, c, and d are syntactically wrong.

Question 9

> The **flowcontrol hardware** command specifies that _____ will be used
> for flow control.
>
> ○ a. CD and DSR
>
> ○ b. RTS and CTS
>
> ○ c. DTR and DSR
>
> ○ d. XON and XOFF

Answer b is correct. The Request To Send and Clear To Send pins will be used for flow control. Answer a specifies Carrier-Detect and Data-Set-Ready which are used for connectivity. Answers c and d are also used for connectivity. Answer d specifies the usage of software flow control using XON and XOFF, which is incorrect.

Question 10

The **modem autoconfigure** command allows for the following features [Choose the two best answers]:

❑ a. Automatically discover the modem

❑ b. Copy the phone number from the map statement to the modem configuration register

❑ c. Configure the modem without modem commands

❑ d. Reset modem to factory defaults after each call

Answers a and c are correct. The **autoconfigure** command can be used to discover the modem and to configure the modem without modem commands. Answer b is a bit mystifying because the **modemcap** database supplies the modem commands; however, the administrator does *not* have to use the commands. Answer d is incorrect because the modem is set to the defaults specified in the modemcap database.

Question 11

The modem command to hang up on DTR low is _____.

○ a. **AT&C1**

○ b. **AT&D3**

○ c. **AT&F**

○ d. **AT&M0**

Answer b is correct. It's actually AT&D2, but both the CMTD and BCRAN material list it as AT&D3. Answer a reflects the state of the line. Answer c sets the modem to factory defaults and answer d turns off the modem speaker.

Question 12

> The signal pin CTS:
>
> ○ a. Means the DCE has buffer space to accept data from the DTE.
> ○ b. Means the DTE has buffer space to accept data from the DCE.
> ○ c. Is raised only when RTS is low.
> ○ d. Is raised only when RTS is high.

Answer a is correct. CTS means that the DCE has buffers available to take data from the DTE. The RTS pin means that the DTE has buffer space to accept data from the DCE, hence answer b is wrong. Answers c and d reflect the state of the DTE and are not linked to whether the DCE is available.

Question 13

> DTR is raised to tell the DCE that the DTE device will accept a call.
>
> ○ a. True
> ○ b. False

Answer a is correct. Data Terminal Ready indicates to the DCE device that the DTE is ready to listen on pin 3. This is what happens when the modem control software is invoked on a PC. When the "answering machine" software wants to alert the modem that it is ready to accept (or answer) a call, the DTR pin is raised.

Question 14

> The DTE device sends data on pin 2 and receives data on pin 3.
>
> ○ a. True
> ○ b. False

Answer a is correct. Transmit data is on pin 2 and receive is on pin 3. The fact that it's the DTE device is only added for confusion. The DCE and the DTE devices transmit on pin 2. The cable is reversed so that each device "listens" to pin 3.

Need To Know More?

 Cisco Press: *Cisco IOS Dial Solutions*. Macmillan Technical Publishing. ISBN 1-57870-055-8. This resource book is not designed to be a 'good read', but rather it is a useful command reference. It puts many examples and reference tables in one location.

 Motorola University Press: *The Basics Book*. Addison-Wesley Publishing Company, Inc. ISBN 0-201-56372-X. This book offers very basic information, but delivers a clear concept of data communications in an easy-to-read format.

 Cisco Systems: Documentation CD. Any recent version of the CD has much background information on the various technologies discussed here. The search engine will allow the user to look specifically at white paper information in lieu of a command search. This gives the user a quick way to find a discussion of the search issue, not just the command to use it.

 www.cisco.com Visit the official Cisco Web site for information and links to all technologies employed by Cisco.

Configuring PPP With PAP And CHAP Authentication

5

. . . .

Terms you'll need to understand:

√ Point-to-Point Protocol (PPP)

√ Dial-up

√ Callback

√ Multilink

√ Challenge Handshake Authentication Protocol (CHAP)

√ Client

√ Server

Techniques you'll need to master:

√ Understanding Compression

√ Configuring Callback

√ Understanding Negotiation

√ Configuring Authentication

Remote Access

Today's corporate environments contain more telecommuters than ever before. Because of this fact, dial-in access is a very important part of network connectivity. Although users need to have several computer components, including a Layer 3 protocol and necessary applications, this chapter will primarily cover the login process using the Point-to-Point Protocol (PPP).

PPP isn't the only dial-in type supported—Cisco routers support Serial Line Internet Protocol (SLIP) by default. The biggest problem with SLIP is that it only works with Transmission Control Protocol/Internet Protocol (TCP/IP). For users who need to send Internetwork Packet Exchange (IPX) or AppleTalk traffic, PPP is the protocol of choice.

You may configure a router to automatically accept a certain type of connection when a user dials in. Go into line configuration mods for the appropriate line and enter the command:

```
autoseclect <arap | ppp | slip | during-loin>
```

The PPP option for autoselect looks for frames that contain the hexidecimal value 7E, 01111110 in binary, in the flag field. During-login causes a username / password promt to apprear without the user needing to press any keys. The user needs to configure PPP on a Windows machin to bring up a terminal window after dialin.

Connectivity

The PPP protocol maps to a portion of the Open System Interconnection (OSI) model as shown in Table 5.1 below.

PPP consists of several types of Control Protocols (CPs) that do a variety of things:

➤ *High Level Data Link Control (HDLC)*—Not the Cisco encapsulation across serial lines. Instead, it's based on ISO standards. PPP is more than an encapsulation type and needs something to do just encapsulation.

➤ *Link Control Protocol (LCP)*—Handles the connectivity part beyond the HDLC portion. The LCP is responsible for Hello packets, authentication, and so on. This is one of the primary items to observe via debug commands if there is a problem connecting.

➤ *Network Control Protocol (NCP)*—A base form of NCP that has several extensions, much like a fork. Each tine of the fork is a protocol-specific CP that allows that protocol to transport data across a PPP connection. This is the portion that sets PPP apart from SLIP.

Table 5.1 OSI model and PPP chart.			
IP	**IPX**	**Additional Protocols**	**Layer**
IP	IPX	Other Protocols	Layer 3
IPCP	IPXCP	Other Control Protocols (CPs)	Layer 3
Network Control Protocol (directly connected to specific NCP above)			Layer 2
Link Control Protocol (LCP)			Layer 2
Standards based non-Cisco High-Level Data Link Control (HDLC)			Layer 2
Connectivity, including cables (EIA/TIA 232, v.35, and interfaces)			Layer 1

As mentioned earlier, the LCP is responsible for authentication, among other things. You have two choices for authentication: Password Authentication Protocol (PAP) and Challenge Handshake Authentication Protocol (CHAP). As with any type of authentication, a username and password are required. In addition to authentication, the PPP LCP allows for callback, compression, and multilink:

➤ *Callback*—A setting that allows the router that the user called to turn around and call the user back. If you remember the days of the BBS, some BBSs wouldn't allow a user to dial in and do whatever. Instead, the BBS software would hang up and call the user back (using the number in the user's record) to make sure that the user was who he said he was. Cisco calls this a method to provide billing consolidation, but it also increases security. Callback was first supported with IOS 11.0(3).

➤ *Compression*—Supported to allow more data to cross Wide Area Network (WAN) links than the link will natively support. Several different types of compression are supported, and they have different resource utilization levels. They will be covered in more detail later in this chapter. Compression was first supported in IOS 10.3.

➤ *Multilink*—Allows for multiple data circuits to be logically bound together to increase throughput. Frames are broken up and transmitted across the series of channels at the same time, and then recombined at the destination. Multilink was first supported in IOS 11.0(3).

Authentication

PAP and CHAP are the two types of router-based authentication supported under PPP. In addition, PPP supports sending a request to an authentication server such as TACACS+ or RADIUS.

PAP's one major problem are passwords that cross the line in clear text. The user will send a request to the router saying, "Let me in. This is my username and this is my password." The router then permits or denies the user based on that information. The connection and authentication attempt are controlled by the user.

From user to router, the authentication is one-way. The router attempts to authenticate the user, and that's it. With a router-to-router connection, each router authenticates the other. Because PAP sends passwords in clear text, there is nothing stopping someone from sniffing the wire, finding out what the password is, then playing back that password to gain access to the network.

CHAP is a bit more secure. The called router doesn't just accept whatever information is given to it—it will make sure the remote device isn't spoofing by sending a challenge to the remote device.

Next, the calling router will send its password in a hash generated with a Message Digest 5 (MD5) hashing function. The called router will compare the received hash against its copy to validate the password. This process prevents anyone sniffing the circuit from easily seeing the password.

Finally, CHAP has a third feature that makes it more desirable than PAP: the use of repeated challenges. Every two minutes, the called device will generate a challenge that the remote device must respond to. Because all of these challenges contain a random part, no one can analyze the circuit and play back the hash to gain access.

To summarize, the CHAP authentication process follows these steps:

1. The user dials into the CHAP authenticating device.

2. The called device generates a challenge. This challenge has a challenge identifier (a type 01), a sequencing ID, a random value, and the authentication name of the challenger.

3. The calling device responds to the challenge by providing its username and password, the sequencing ID, and the random value. The password, ID, and random number are hashed and put into a packet with a response ID (a type 02), the sequencing ID, and the calling device's username.

4. When the authenticating device receives the response, it looks at the sequencing ID to find the original challenge packet for the random

value. Then it places the ID, the random value, and the password the called device has for the calling device into the hashing program and generates a hash. The two hashes are compared.

5. One of two things now happens. If the authentication was successful, then a message is sent authorizing access. This message uses a type 03 CHAP message. If the comparison of hashes failed, then access will be denied with a type 04 message.

Configuring PPP For CHAP Authentication

Before we move on to options for PPP, you should know how to configure the basics. Any true geek should be champing at the bit by this point to get going. If you're not champing, then we still have a ways to go before we fully convert you.

Basic PPP Configuration Commands

The first thing you need to do is set up PPP on a serial interface using this command:

```
Router(config-if)#encapsulation <PPP | SLIP>
```

You also need to specify whether the user has a choice as to how she wishes to access the router. Use the command

```
Router(config-if)#async mode dedicated
```

if you want the user *only* to access via this method. If you want the user to be able to run PPP, SLIP, or EXEC tasks, you need to use this command:

```
Router(config-if)#async mode interactive
```

Chances are, the user will be using IP; we'll address those commands necessary for addressing. The

```
Router(config-if)# peer default ip address <IP address | pool
    pool-name | dhcp>
```

command specifies how the user will get an address generated by one of your devices. The *pool* address option also requires this command:

```
Router(config)#ip local pool pool-name starting-address
    ending-address
```

If you want the user to specify an address, use the

```
Router(config-if)#async dynamic address
```

command. This command is used when the user has a static address and the called interface *must* be in interactive mode. Finally, you can also use the command **IP unnumbered**. All these commands are explained in more detail in Table 5.2.

Table 5.2 PPP configuration commands explained.

Command	Explanation
Router(config-if)#encapsulation *ppp	slip*	Sets PPP or SLIP encapsulation on the interface. Remember, SLIP is IP only.
Router(config-if)#async mode dedicated	Places the interface into dedicated SLIP or PPP access mode with no EXEC capability.
Router(config-if)#async mode interactive	Required mode for either SLIP or PPP to access EXEC on the router.
Router(config-if)#peer default ip address *address	pool pool-name	dhcp*	Says which IP address the client will receive. You can specify an address, a pool of addresses, or that the client should use Dynamic Host Configuration Protocol (DHCP).
Router(config-if)#async dynamic address	Allows the client to specify his own IP address with a static configuration. The dial-in interface *must* be in interactive mode for this command to work.
Router(config-if)#ip unnumbered *interface-type interface-number*	Because an unnumbered interface doesn't have an IP address, it uses the address of the specified interface. Use only on point-to-point connections.
Router(config)#ip local pool *pool-name starting-address ending-address*	In order to use a pool of addresses, you actually have to configure a pool. The command **ip local pool XYZCorp 10.1.1.1 10.1.1.254** establishes a set of 254 addresses for dial-up use.
Router(config)#ip address-pool dhcp-proxy client	Tells the router to act as a proxy client for DHCP addressing. For this command to work, it's helpful to also use the command **Router(config)#ip dhcp-server** *<ip-address	name>*. Otherwise, the router won't know where to get an address.

Configuring CHAP

Once PPP and addressing are established, it takes only a couple more lines to set up CHAP authentication on two routers. Table 5.3 shows a side-by-side comparison of the commands. (We're leaving off the other configuration information to avoid confusing the issue.) Each configuration will start in Global configuration mode.

The configuration commands in the table work as follows:

➤ The first line tells the router what its name is. This is the username that is actually sent when authenticating.

➤ The second line says, "When authenticating with this device, use this password." When device One wants to call device Two, it sends its hostname and the listed password. The username is *case sensitive!*

➤ The third line tells the router we are about to configure interface serial 1.

➤ The fourth line tells the router to use PPP encapsulation on this interface.

➤ The last line tells the router to use CHAP authentication.

Additional PPP Settings

As mentioned earlier, PPP has a couple of other settings that can be useful in a corporate environment. This section will talk about PPP callback, compression, and multilink.

PPP Callback

When a user dials in, PPP still communicates and sets up the connection. The user authenticates, but then the call is disconnected. The remote device calls the user back and the connection proceeds normally.

Table 5.3   CHAP configuration comparision.

Router one	Router two
hostname one	hostname two
username two password cisco	username one password cisco
interface serial1	interface serial1
encapsulation ppp	encapsulation ppp
ppp authentication chap	ppp authentication chap

Callback is designed by Cisco to aid in bill consolidation. Instead of having numerous telecommuting employees pay long distance fees that they have to expense, the router will call them back after the person has authenticated. Although Cisco doesn't officially market callback as a security feature, many organizations use it as such.

PPP callback follows these steps:

1. The user/callback client calls the remote router/callback server. If the user is configured to request callback, callback may occur. This request is sent during the LCP negotiation phase.

2. The callback server checks its own configuration to verify that it can perform callback services.

3. Authentication takes place as normal with PPP.

4. Once the callback client has authenticated, the callback server checks its configuration to find the callback string for this specific client. The router uses the username of the client to find this information.

5. The call is disconnected.

6. The callback server uses the specified client dial string to call the client back. Only one attempt is made, so if something interferes with the callback process, the client needs to call the server again.

7. Once a connection is made when the server calls back the client, another round of authentication happens. If successful, there is now an active connection.

What can prevent the second phase of callback from completing? Anything that can interrupt a phone line. Things like someone else calling, a household member picking up the phone, or traffic on the callback server side using the last modem can all prevent the return connection from being made. Callback can be configured for both plain old telephone system (POTS) and Integrated Services Digital Network (ISDN) lines.

The commands necessary to configure callback are listed in Table 5.4.

Compressed PPP

A router interface can be configured to compress the data that passes through it. PPP supports four main types of compression:

➤ *Stacker*—Uses a Lempel-Ziv (LZ) compression algorithm to compress data. Stacker maps where data appears in a stream and sends each type

Table 5.4   Callback configuration commands explained.

Callback Command	Explanation
Router(config-if)#ppp callback request	Tells the client to request callback from the callback server it's dialing. This command is placed in the dialing interface.
Router(config-if)#dialer hold-timeout *seconds*	Tells the client to wait the specified number of seconds for callback to take place. The router will hold packets going to the destination for this period. This command is optional and can also be used on the callback server.
Router(config-if)#dialer hold-queue *packets*	How many packets the hold queue may contain. The range is 0 through 100. It's helpful if the **dialer hold-queue timeout** command has been configured, because otherwise the router will drop packets while it waits for callback.
Router(config-if)#ppp callback accept	Tells the router to accept callback requests that arrive on this interface. This is a callback server command.
Router(config-if)#ppp callback initiate	Another callback server command, as are the rest of the commands. Allows the router to start a callback session to a remote device capable of auto answering.
Router(config-line)#callback forced-wait *seconds*	Used on a line, this command tells the router to wait so many seconds before beginning callback.
Router(config-line)#script callback *script-name*	Specific AT commands the modem should use for this callback session.
Router(config)#username username <password password > <callback-dialstring phone-number> <callback-line line-number> <callback-rotary rotary-group>	Options to the usual **username name password password** configuration for CHAP authentication, including options for callback. These options are defined individually below.
callback-dialstring *phone-number*	The phone number the callback server will dial to reach this device.
callback-line *line-number*	Specifies a line to be used when calling this device.
callback-rotary *rotary-group*	Rather than specifying a particular line, specifies a group of dial-out devices by using the **callback-rotary** command.

only once. Stacker is more CPU intensive than Predictor. Use Stacker compression when you know the majority of your data isn't already compressed. Compressing already-compressed data often leads to an increase in file size.

➤ *Microsoft Point to Point Compression protocol (MPPC)*—Enables a user with a Microsoft workstation to connect to a Cisco router and compress the data that flows between them. MPPC is also an LZ algorithm. MPPC is more CPU intensive than Predictor. To easily recall what this one is used for, just remember that the *M* is for *Microsoft*. Use this type of compression when connecting Microsoft OS clients to a routed interface.

➤ *Predictor*—Examines data to see if it's already compressed. If the data isn't compressed, Predictor will compress and then forward the data. If it's compressed, Predictor won't compress the data. Predictor is more memory intensive, due to all the checking it does, than either Stacker or MPPC. Predictor uses an open source algorithm available in RFC 1978. Use Predictor compression in the opposite scenario given for Stacker: when you have quite a bit of compressed data crossing a WAN link and you don't want to use the processing cycles needed to compress already-compressed data.

➤ *TCP Header*—Doesn't do any compression on the data portion of the packet; instead, it compresses only the TCP headers. You always want to compress the largest part of a packet that you can. So if you're sending packets in which the TCP headers take up more bandwidth on average than the data portion, you use this type of compression. An example of appropriate use would be if an organization has a lot of Telnet traffic crossing a WAN link.

Table 5.5 explains the various PPP compression commands.

Multilink PPP

Multilink allows for bundling of data circuits into a larger virtual pipe. For example, ISDN has two data channels that each support up to 64Kbps. You can use each channel separately, or you can bind them together to form a virtual 128Kbps pipe. Multilink accomplishes this task by load balancing across the circuits. Multilink ensures that packets don't arrive out of order by fragmenting the packets and then shooting the fragments across the multilinked bundle.

Multilink PPP (MLP) is supported by multiple vendors under RFC 1990, which is an update to RFC 1717. This support means that you don't have to have Cisco equipment on both sides of the WAN in order to multilink. A

Table 5.5 PPP compression commands explained.	
PPP Compression Option	**Explanation**
Router(config-if)#compress stac	Use this command at the appropriate interface to enable Stacker compression.
Router(config-if)#compress predictor	This command enables Predictor compression.
Router(config-if)#compress mppc	This command enables MPPC compression.
Router(config-if)#ip tcp header-compression *passive*	This command enables TCP Header compression on an interface. The *passive* command is optional and tells the interface to compress only if it received compressed headers from the other side of the WAN.

router uses something called the Maximum Received Reconstructed Unit (MRRU) during LCP negotiation to tell the device on the far side that it's capable of forming a multilink bundle. Multilink is best used in environments where bandwidth requirements are dynamic. Cisco targets multilink usage to telecommuters and the small office/home office (SOHO) market.

 Multilink adds headers to the packet fragments so that the fragments can be reconstructed. These headers may be two, four, or eight bytes and are used for sequencing. The Cisco 700 series ISDN devices use two-byte headers, whereas Cisco IOS uses four-byte headers.

Troubleshooting PPP

You can use several commands to troubleshoot a PPP connection. These commands are explained in Table 5.6.

The following examples show actual output from a router using the **debug PPP negotiation** and **debug PPP authentication** commands.

The **debug ppp negotiation** command gives the output shown below. The output shows the authentication and LCP negotiation process. Due to page size, some lines had to be wrapped. You can tell the beginning of a new line because it has a timestamp next to it.

```
00:06:37: %LINK-3-UPDOWN: Interface Serial1/1, changed state to up
00:06:37: Se1/1 PPP: Treating connection as a dedicated line
00:06:37: Se1/1 PPP: Phase is ESTABLISHING, Active Open
00:06:37: Se1/1 LCP: O CONFREQ [Closed] id 5 len 15
```

Table 5.6 PPP Troubleshooting commands explained.	
PPP Troubleshooting Command	**Explanation**
show dialer	Gives basic information about calls, including successes and attempts for a particular phone number; current status; and, if up, what brought a link up. If the output of this command shows the name of the device your router connected to via PPP, then your PAP or CHAP authentication has completed.
show ppp multilink	Gives status information regarding multilink bundles.
debug ppp negotiation	What PPP interaction is happening during the negotiation phase. To debug this interaction successfully, it's best to turn on debugging before bringing up the link.
debug ppp authentication	The same as **debug ppp negotiation**, except this debug shows only PAP and CHAP authentication information.
debug ppp packet	Which PPP-oriented packets are being sent.
debug ppp multilink	Gives packet fragmentation information regarding a multilink bundle. Because the information is almost real time and a link often has traffic, this isn't a command to use frequently in a production environment. Consider CPU utilization before debugging multilink.
debug ppp multilink negotiation	Gives information about the status of a forming multilink bundle.

```
00:06:37: Se1/1 LCP:     AuthProto CHAP (0x0305C22305)
00:06:37: Se1/1 LCP:     MagicNumber 0x505AB72C (0x0506505AB72C)
00:06:37: Se1/1 LCP: I CONFREQ [REQsent] id 39 len 15
00:06:37: Se1/1 LCP:     AuthProto CHAP (0x0305C22305)
00:06:37: Se1/1 LCP:     MagicNumber 0x5056251B (0x05065056251B)
00:06:37: Se1/1 LCP: O CONFACK [REQsent] id 39 len 15
00:06:37: Se1/1 LCP:     AuthProto CHAP (0x0305C22305)
00:06:37: Se1/1 LCP:     MagicNumber 0x5056251B (0x05065056251B)
00:06:37: Se1/1 LCP: I CONFACK [ACKsent] id 5 len 15
00:06:37: Se1/1 LCP:     AuthProto CHAP (0x0305C22305)
00:06:37: Se1/1 LCP:     MagicNumber 0x505AB72C (0x0506505AB72C)
00:06:37: Se1/1 LCP: State is Open
00:06:37: Se1/1 PPP: Phase is AUTHENTICATING, by both
00:06:37: Se1/1 CHAP: O CHALLENGE id 2 len 25 from "p1r2"
```

```
00:06:37: Se1/1 CHAP: I CHALLENGE id 3 len 25 from "p1r3"
00:06:37: Se1/1 CHAP: O RESPONSE id 3 len 25 from "p1r2"
00:06:37: Se1/1 CHAP: I RESPONSE id 2 len 25 from "p1r3"
00:06:37: Se1/1 CHAP: O SUCCESS id 2 len 4
00:06:37: Se1/1 CHAP: I SUCCESS id 3 len 4
00:06:37: Se1/1 PPP: Phase is UP
00:06:37: Se1/1 CDPCP: O CONFREQ [Closed] id 3 len 4
00:06:37: Se1/1 IPCP: I CONFREQ [Not negotiated] id 3 len 10
00:06:37: Se1/1 IPCP:    Address 192.168.1.2 (0x0306C0A80102)
00:06:37: Se1/1 LCP: O PROTREJ [Open] id 6 len 16 protocol IPCP
  (0x80210103000A0306C0A80102)
00:06:37: Se1/1 CDPCP: I CONFREQ [REQsent] id 3 len 4
00:06:37: Se1/1 CDPCP: O CONFACK [REQsent] id 3 len 4
00:06:37: Se1/1 CDPCP: I CONFACK [ACKsent] id 3 len 4
00:06:37: Se1/1 CDPCP: State is Open
00:06:38: %LINEPROTO-5-UPDOWN: Line protocol on Interface
  Serial1/1, changed state to up
```

The **debug ppp authentication** command gives the output shown below. The output only details the authentication process. The wrapped line is the one without a timestamp.

```
00:08:19: %LINK-3-UPDOWN: Interface Serial1/1, changed state to up
00:08:19: Se1/1 PPP: Treating connection as a dedicated line
00:08:21: Se1/1 PPP: Phase is AUTHENTICATING, by both
00:08:21: Se1/1 CHAP: O CHALLENGE id 3 len 25 from "p1r2"
00:08:21: Se1/1 CHAP: I CHALLENGE id 4 len 25 from "p1r3"
00:08:21: Se1/1 CHAP: O RESPONSE id 4 len 25 from "p1r2"
00:08:21: Se1/1 CHAP: I RESPONSE id 3 len 25 from "p1r3"
00:08:21: Se1/1 CHAP: O SUCCESS id 3 len 4
00:08:21: Se1/1 CHAP: I SUCCESS id 4 len 4
00:08:22: %LINEPROTO-5-UPDOWN: Line protocol on Interface
  Serial1/1, changed state to up
```

Practice Questions

Question 1

The best compression type to use when connecting to a Microsoft client would be:

○ a. Stacker

○ b. Predictor

○ c. MPPC

○ d. TCP Header

Answer c is correct. In most cases, the best type of compression for a client using a Microsoft operating system is MPPC because most clients do not have the necessary software to activate the other types on compression. Therefore answers a, b, and d are not correct. MPPC is the only one that comes with a Windows operating system.

Question 2

The best compression type to use with primarily Telnet traffic is:

○ a. Stacker

○ b. Predictor

○ c. MPPC

○ d. TCP Header

Answer d is correct. TCP Header compression should be used when the TCP headers are larger than the data portion of the packet. Answers a and b, Stacker and Predictor, shouldn't be used because they will just slow down the router without a measurable increase in compression. Answer c, MPPC, shouldn't be used because a Microsoft client wasn't mentioned and even if it had been, MPPC would give the same result as using Stacker.

Question 3

The best compression type to use with traffic that contains a lot of compressed data would be:

○ a. Stacker

○ b. Predictor

○ c. MPPC

○ d. TCP Header

Answer b is correct. Predictor examines packets to see whether they are already compressed and, if so, won't compress them again. This process saves a small amount of bandwidth as well as CPU cycles on the receiving device. Answers a, c, and d don't examine packets to see if it will be a waste of time compressing them.

Question 4

Which dial-up encapsulations support compression?

○ a. PPP

○ b. HDLC

○ c. Frame Relay

○ d. SLIP

Answer a is correct. Answer c, Frame Relay, isn't what we would call a dial-up encapsulation type, and of the remaining choices, only answer a, PPP, natively supports compression.

Question 5

A Cisco 700 series uses what size multilink headers?

○ a. Two byte

○ b. Four byte

○ c. Eight byte

○ d. 16 byte

Answer a is correct. The 700 series isn't IOS driven and uses two-byte headers on multilink packets. *IOS* uses four-byte headers, so answer b is not correct. Answer c, eight-byte headers, is an option only for some vendors and answer d, 16 byte, is not an option.

Question 6

Which ways can CHAP send passwords? [Choose the two best answers]

- ❏ a. Encrypted using the Dijkstra algorithm
- ❏ b. Plain text
- ❏ c. MD5 encrypted hash
- ❏ d. Dijkstra encrypted hash

Answers b and c are correct. CHAP can send passwords both in plain text (not a good idea) or by using the MD5 format to create an encrypted hash. The Dijkstra algorithm is used with Link State routing protocols, not authentication. Therefore answers a and d are not correct.

Question 7

Which issues will prevent a device from calling back the device that called it when using callback?

- ❏ a. Authentication failure
- ❏ b. Another call being made or received that uses the last available interface
- ❏ c. Authentication success
- ❏ d. Interesting traffic arriving

Answers a and b are correct. Success in authenticating will continue the process but won't prevent the return call. If interesting traffic uses the last available dial-out interface, it will prevent the call, but interesting traffic itself won't stop the process. Authentication success normally continues the process, so answer c is not correct. While answer d, interesting traffic arriving, can stop the process if it uses the last available interface, the traffic arriving doesn't necessarily cause a problem.

Question 8

> The command to enable Stacker compression is:
>
> ○ a. **compression stac**
>
> ○ b. **compression stacker**
>
> ○ c. **compress stac**
>
> ○ d. **compress stacker**

Answer c is correct. The command **compress stac** is used to enable Stacker compression. Answers a, b, and d are just incorrect.

Question 9

> Which option for the command **ip tcp header-compression** tells the interface to compress TCP headers *only* if the destination device sends packets with compressed TCP headers?
>
> ○ a. **active**
>
> ○ b. **passive**
>
> ○ c. **receive**
>
> ○ d. **transmit**

Answer b is correct. The command **ip tcp header-compression passive** tells the router to compress TCP headers only if it receives a compressed header from the other device. Answers a, c, and d don't exist.

Question 10

> Cisco IOS uses which size headers on multilink packets?
>
> ○ a. Two byte
>
> ○ b. Four byte
>
> ○ c. Eight byte
>
> ○ d. 16 byte

Answer b is correct. The IOS uses four-byte headers when sending packets across multilinked lines. The 700 series ISDN devices use two-byte headers, the specification allows for eight-byte headers and 16-byte headers are not allowed. Therefore answers a, c, and d are not correct.

Need To Know More?

 Most of the PPP RFCs are in the 1900s but many of the important specifications are outside this range. You can find details about PPP Multilink in RFC 1990, LCPs in RFC 1661, Microsoft CHAP in RFC 2433, and CHAP itself in RFC 1994 at **www.faqs.org/rfcs/**.

 You can find more information on PPP and options both covered here and additional commands on the Cisco web site at: **www.cisco.com/univercd/cc/td/doc/product/software/ios113ed/ 113ed_cr/dial_c/dcprt2/dcppp.htm**.

Windows 95
Dial-Up Access

Terms you'll need to understand:

√ Briefcase

√ Modem

√ Window

√ Dial-Up Networking (DUN)

Techniques you'll need to master:

√ Deferring printing

√ Installing a modem driver

√ Setting connection properties

This chapter covers accessing a network via Windows 95 dial-up. Because this book is being written when the common operating system for new desktops is Windows 98, this chapter assumes that any configuration the reader does will be with Windows 98. So, this chapter will integrate both the 95 and 98 operating systems by using screen shots from Windows 98; and, in the text, it will explain any important differences that Cisco may test on. We have no intention of leaving out testable material—but, by the same token, we want the reader to have information regarding the most current OS.

The Basics Of Windows Dial-Up

The Windows 95/98 operating systems come with several components that make it easier for the user to work remotely. In order to accomplish remote connectivity via dial-up, the machine needs to have some type of analog or ISDN modem as well as 2 to 3MB of space available on the hard drive. You may also use Dial-Up Networking (DUN) with the Microsoft Virtual Private Networking (VPN) adapter, but many of the topics covered in this chapter won't apply to that configuration.

Remote Mail

Microsoft included an Exchange client with Windows 95 and Outlook Express with Windows 98. Both of these utilities allow the user to remotely access email by dialing in using DUN.

Briefcase

The Briefcase is one of the most underutilized tools in the Windows OS area, in our opinion. The Briefcase makes it very easy to synchronize files between two locations: Copy a file from the network to a local drive, make changes, and then synchronize, and the network file is the same as the desktop version. This process works extremely well when a file is updated often, like a corporate phone directory. The user can keep a local copy and every so often just open the Briefcase and synchronize, rather than surfing through the network drives to download a new copy. But the Briefcase has one major problem: When both files are updated at the same time, one party must download the new version and make changes again.

Deferred Printing

The ability to defer printing is useful for traveling users who print often. It allows them to work in an airport, set up a job to print, and then go to the next task. Once they plug into a printer, the jobs spool automatically.

Windows 95/98 automatically decides by default that you must be dialing to a Point-to-Point Protocol (PPP) enabled device. In many cases this is true, but not always. PPP has the most flexibility of the connection types supported, but you may have to make changes if you aren't dialing to a PPP device. Table 6.1 shows the protocol options for each connection type. A walk-through of setting up dial-up connectivity will appear in the next section of the chapter, along with a figure showing this particular window.

> When configuring DUN, Windows will default to PPP connectivity with all protocols configured for networking enabled for PPP. As a result, if the network card in the machine has IPX bound to it, IPX will also be enabled in PPP. This can occasionally create some weird errors on the client.

Installing Dial-Up Networking

Configuring a dial-up client is usually a fairly brainless task if you're familiar with the Windows wizards. Normally, any problems occur within the modem installation phase; so once it's working, any future phone number additions generally work.

Installing A Modem

There are many small steps to installing a modem and getting a connection going. Here are many of those steps explained.

1. Click on the Start button and choose Settings and then Control Panel. You should see a window displaying Control Panel icons, as shown in Figure 6.1.

Table 6.1 Dial-Up Networking protocols.	
DUN Connection	**Protocols Allowed**
NetWare Connect	IPX/SPX
PPP for Internet, NT Server, and Windows 98 connectivity	TCP/IP (Transmission Control Protocol/Internet Protocol), IPX/SPX (Internetwork Packet Exchange/Sequenced Packet Exchange), NetBEUI
RAS (Remote Access Server) for NT 3.1 or Windows for Workgroups 3.11	NetBEUI
SLIP (Serial Line Internet Protocol) and CSLIP (Cisco SLIP)	TCP/IP

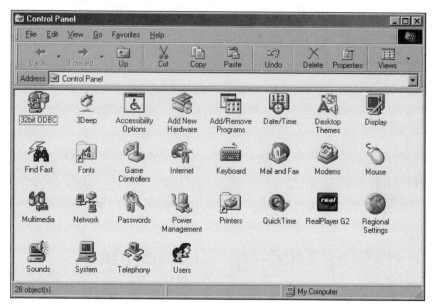

Figure 6.1 Control Panel.

2. Double-click on the Modems icon. The Install New Modem Wizard window should appear, as shown in Figure 6.2. Either click on Next to make Windows search for a plug-and-play modem, or check the Don't Detect My Modem box and select your modem from a list.

3. Windows will search for your modem as shown in Figure 6.3. If it doesn't detect a modem, you'll have to install the modem yourself as

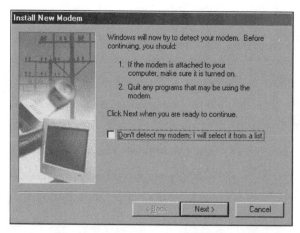

Figure 6.2 New Modem Installation Wizard.

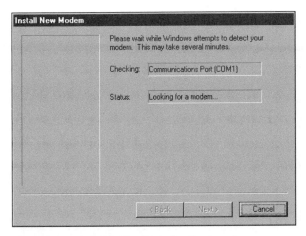

Figure 6.3 Wizard looking for the modem.

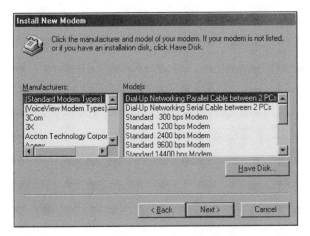

Figure 6.4 Installing the modem yourself.

shown in Figure 6.4. This process may involve using the drivers that came with the modem.

4. Click on Next to make Windows install the modem driver. Once installation is complete, click on Finish to open the call connection properties window.

5. Enter your area code, country, and dialing method as shown in Figure 6.5. Click on OK twice to end the modem installation step.

Installing Dial-Up Networking

This section shows how to add Dial-Up Networking to a computer if it doesn't already exist.

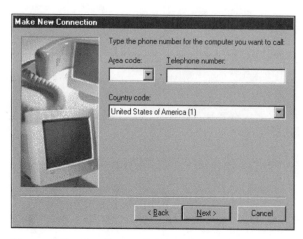

Figure 6.5 Configure dial properties.

1. From Control Panel, double-click on the Add/Remove Programs icon. Then, select the Windows Setup tab at the top of the window to display optional applications, as shown in Figure 6.6.

2. Double-click on Communications and check the Dial-Up Networking box, as shown in Figure 6.7. Click on OK on each of the two screens to

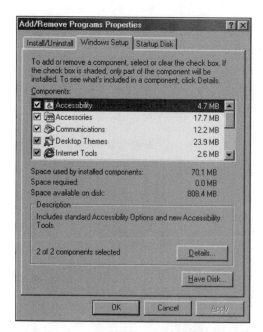

Figure 6.6 Add/Remove Programs.

Figure 6.7   Adding DUN from the Communications options.

exit the Add/Remove Programs window and begin copying information from the CD.

3. When told, restart the client machine.

Configuring Dial-Up Networking

This section explains how to start the process of creating a new configuration for a connection.

1. From the Start menu, select Programs|Accessories|Dial-Up Networking. You can also double-click on My Computer and then double-click on Dial-Up Networking. Doing so will start the Make New Connection Wizard, shown in Figure 6.8.

2. Enter the area code and phone number of the number you wish to have the client dial.

3. Click on Next to create a connection configuration. Clicking on Finish will save the configuration.

Configuring Dial-Up Networking Properties

Setting up DUN is easy if the client machines don't go anywhere; but if the users travel around, they need to be familiar with some additional options. Open Dial-Up Networking as described previously and right-click on the icon

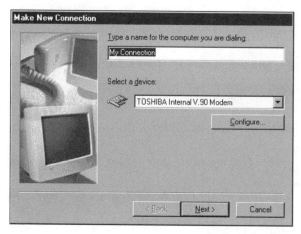

Figure 6.8 Making a new DUN configuration.

that represents the location you wish to call. Doing so opens a pop-up menu from which you need to select Properties. On the first screen, shown in Figure 6.9, you can reconfigure the phone number or go to a different property area.

Clicking on the Server Types tab at the top of the window takes you to the screen shown in Figure 6.10. Here, you can select the type of connection you wish, as shown in Figure 6.11; Windows 95 and 98 default to PPP. You may also select/deselect the protocols you wish to use, as well as move into TCP/IP

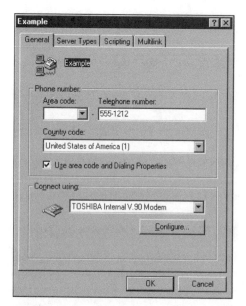

Figure 6.9 Dial-Up Networking property window.

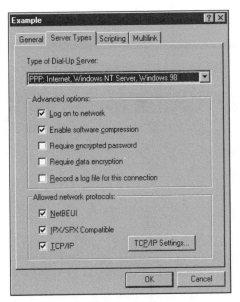

Figure 6.10   Choose the type of connection you want and the protocols.

settings or choose to record the details of your connection via the Record A Log File For This Connection check box.

The default TCP/IP settings, shown in Figure 6.12, are fine when connecting to most ISPs. In most cases, the ISP wants to assign an IP address via Dynamic

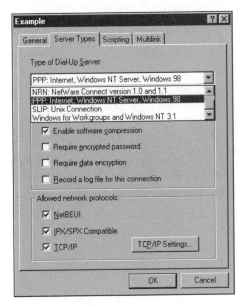

Figure 6.11   Connection Types.

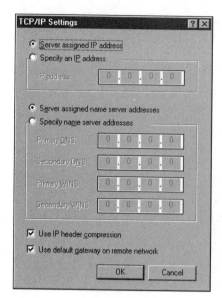

Figure 6.12 TCP/IP settings.

Host Configuration Protocol (DHCP), and this address will include items like the Domain Name System (DNS) address. You may configure static IP addressing, though, if your connection allows.

You may also need to adjust your dialing properties. This is accomplished by double-clicking on the Modems icon in Control Panel. Select the modem you want and click on Dialing Properties to open the window shown in Figure 6.13.

In this dialog box, you'll configure any special information regarding access: whether you need to dial 9 to reach an outside line, long-distance access codes, calling card billing, and so on. The window also includes an Area Code Rules button, which is a nice option to have given how often area codes currently change. Clicking this button opens the dialog box shown in Figure 6.14.

The most important part is the 10-digit dialing check box. You can also specify that when dialing certain outside area codes, the modem should not dial 1. This option is useful in many cities.

Trying to access a remote network address when DUN is not active will cause Windows to start DUN by default. If you wish to turn this feature off, go to the Dial-Up Networking window and click on Connections|Settings, then click the Don't Prompt To Use Dial-Up Networking radio button.

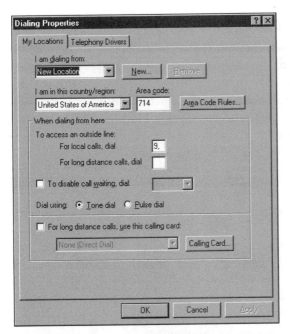

Figure 6.13   Location-specific dial properties.

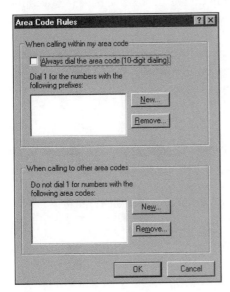

Figure 6.14   Area Code configuration.

Troubleshooting DUN

Troubleshooting a dial-up connection can be an exercise in frustration, because you don't have firm data regarding what is happening on the other side of the connection or what is happening in between. This section highlights two logs that can help you figure out what is going wrong. Most of the items that look confusing are covered in other sections of this book. The examples below illustrate the information available at the Windows client—they don't provide an in-depth explanation, repeating material in other chapters.

PPPLOG.TXT

The PPPLOG.TXT file can give you extremely low-down, basic information about forming a connection with your dial-in device. The PPPLOG.TXT log doesn't run automatically; you must enable it. In order to enable the PPPLOG, you need to right-click on the specific DUN icon for the location you want to call. Click on Properties, then click the Server Types tab at the top of the window. In the middle of the open window you will see a box next to Record A Log File For This Connection; click that box until a checkmark appears. Refer back to Figure 6.10 for a screen shot of this window.

Listing 6.1 is an example log taken from calling an ISP. We have removed the majority of the "Transmitting 32 bytes, Receiving 6 bytes" messages because a couple of pages of nearly identical code would just waste space. The data portions regarding the login process have also been removed. This data would appear in the <Data snipped> sections, but it's usually several-to-many lines. Due to page width, some lines have been broken apart. You can recognize the beginning of a line by the fact that it has a time stamp.

Listing 6.1   PPPLOG.TXT display.

```
10-04-1999 23:18:06.44 - Microsoft Dial Up Adapter log opened.
10-04-1999 23:18:06.44 - Server type is  PPP (Point to Point
    Protocol).
10-04-1999 23:18:06.44 - FSA : Adding Control Protocol 80fd
    (CCP) to control protocol chain.
10-04-1999 23:18:06.44 - FSA : Adding Control Protocol 803f
    (NBFCP) to control protocol chain.
10-04-1999 23:18:06.44 - FSA : Adding Control Protocol 8021
    (IPCP) to control protocol chain.
10-04-1999 23:18:06.44 - FSA : Adding Control Protocol 802b
    (IPXCP) to control protocol chain.
10-04-1999 23:18:06.44 - FSA : Adding Control Protocol c029
    (CallbackCP) to control protocol chain.
10-04-1999 23:18:06.44 - FSA : Adding Control Protocol c027
    (no description) to control protocol chain.
```

```
10-04-1999 23:18:06.44 - FSA : Adding Control Protocol c023
    (PAP) to control protocol chain.
10-04-1999 23:18:06.44 - FSA : Adding Control Protocol c223
    (CHAP) to control protocol chain.
10-04-1999 23:18:06.44 - FSA : Adding Control Protocol c021
    (LCP) to control protocol chain.
10-04-1999 23:18:06.44 - LCP : Callback negotiation enabled.
10-04-1999 23:18:06.44 - LCP : Layer started.
10-04-1999 23:18:06.44 - PPP : Transmitting Control Packet of
    length: 25
<Data snipped>
10-04-1999 23:18:09.45 - PPP : Transmitting Control Packet of
    length: 25
<Data snipped>
10-04-1999 23:18:09.54 - PPP : Received Control Packet of
    length: 9
<Data snipped>
10-04-1999 23:18:09.54 - LCP : Received configure reject for
    callback control protocol option.
10-04-1999 23:18:09.54 - PPP : Transmitting Control Packet of
    length: 22
<Data snipped>
10-04-1999 23:18:09.63 - PPP : Received Control Packet of
    length: 22
<Data snipped>
10-04-1999 23:18:11.34 - PPP : Received Control Packet of
    length: 26
<Data snipped>
10-04-1999 23:18:11.34 - LCP : Received and accepted ACCM of 0.
10-04-1999 23:18:11.34 - LCP : Received and accepted magic number
    412dbb83.
10-04-1999 23:18:11.34 - LCP : Received and accepted protocol
    field compression option.
10-04-1999 23:18:11.34 - LCP : Received and accepted
    address+control field compression option.
10-04-1999 23:18:11.34 - LCP : Received and accepted
    authentication protocol c023 (PAP).
10-04-1999 23:18:11.34 - PPP : Transmitting Control Packet of
    length: 26
<Data snipped>
10-04-1999 23:18:11.34 - LCP : Layer up.
10-04-1999 23:18:11.34 - PAP : Layer started.
10-04-1999 23:18:11.34 - PPP : Transmitting Control Packet of
    length: 20
<Data snipped>
10-04-1999 23:18:11.79 - PPP : Received Control Packet of
    length: 22
```

```
<Data snipped>
10-04-1999 23:18:11.79 - PAP : Login was successful.
10-04-1999 23:18:11.79 - PAP : Layer up.
10-04-1999 23:18:11.79 - IPXCP : Layer started.
10-04-1999 23:18:11.79 - IPCP : Layer started.
10-04-1999 23:18:11.79 - IPCP : IP address is 0.
10-04-1999 23:18:11.79 - NBFCP : Layer started.
10-04-1999 23:18:11.79 - CCP : Layer started.
10-04-1999 23:18:11.79 - PPP : Transmitting Control Packet of
    length: 32
<Data snipped>
10-04-1999 23:18:11.79 - PPP : Transmitting Control Packet of
    length: 42
<Data snipped>
10-04-1999 23:18:11.79 - PPP : Transmitting Control Packet of
    length: 110
<Data snipped>
10-04-1999 23:18:14.80 - PPP : Transmitting Control Packet of
    length: 32
<Data snipped>
10-04-1999 23:18:14.89 - PPP : Received Control Packet of
    length: 6
<Data snipped>
10-04-1999 23:18:41.80 - IPXCP : Layer finished.
10-04-1999 23:18:41.80 - FSA : Last control protocol failed.
10-04-1999 23:18:53.03 - Remote access driver is shutting down.
10-04-1999 23:18:53.03 - CRC Errors            1
10-04-1999 23:18:53.03 - Timeout Errors        0
10-04-1999 23:18:53.03 - Alignment Errors      0
10-04-1999 23:18:53.03 - Overrun Errors        0
10-04-1999 23:18:53.03 - Framing Errors        0
10-04-1999 23:18:53.03 - Buffer Overrun Errors 0
10-04-1999 23:18:53.03 - Incomplete Packets    0
10-04-1999 23:18:53.03 - Bytes Received        989
10-04-1999 23:18:53.03 - Bytes Transmittted    3255
10-04-1999 23:18:53.03 - Frames Received       20
10-04-1999 23:18:53.03 - Frames Transmitted    45
10-04-1999 23:18:53.03 - LCP : Layer down.
10-04-1999 23:18:53.03 - PAP : Layer down.
10-04-1999 23:18:53.03 - IPXCP : Layer started.
10-04-1999 23:18:53.03 - IPCP : Layer down.
10-04-1999 23:18:53.03 - NBFCP : Layer started.
10-04-1999 23:18:53.03 - CCP : Layer started.
10-04-1999 23:18:53.03 - PPP : Transmitting Control Packet of
    length: 6
<Data snipped>
10-04-1999 23:18:53.11 - PPP : Received Control Packet of
    length: 6
```

```
<Data snipped>
10-04-1999 23:18:53.11 - LCP : Received terminate acknowledgement.
10-04-1999 23:18:53.11 - LCP : Layer finished.
10-04-1999 23:18:53.11 - Microsoft Dial Up Adapter log closed.
```

As you can see, the ISP in question is using Password Authentication Protocol (PAP) authentication and rejected doing callback. Neither of these is a problem with the current configuration. At the end, you can see that 45 frames were transmitted, 3255 bytes were sent, and 989 bytes were received. All of this data is just for negotiation and authentication.

MODEMLOG.TXT

The MODEMLOG.TXT file runs automatically in Windows 98. You can view the contents by going to the dial-up connection properties, selecting Configure, clicking on the Connection tab, and then clicking on the Advanced button. (Imagine if Microsoft wanted to make this option hard to find!) Once you're in the Advanced Connection Settings window, click on the View Log button. Again, some lines have been broken because of length and the beginning of lines are still referenced with a time stamp. An example of the log can be found in Listing 6.2.

Listing 6.2 MODEMLOG.TXT.

```
10-04-1999 23:17:30.56 - TOSHIBA Internal V.90 Modem in use.
10-04-1999 23:17:30.57 - Modem type: TOSHIBA Internal V.90 Modem
10-04-1999 23:17:30.57 - Modem inf path: LTMODEM4.INF
10-04-1999 23:17:30.57 - Modem inf section: Modem_PNP_DSVD
10-04-1999 23:17:30.87 - 115200,N,8,1
10-04-1999 23:17:30.87 - 115200,N,8,1
10-04-1999 23:17:30.87 - Initializing modem.
10-04-1999 23:17:30.87 - Send: AT<cr>
10-04-1999 23:17:30.88 - Recv: AT<cr>
10-04-1999 23:17:30.88 - Recv: <cr><lf>OK<cr><lf>
10-04-1999 23:17:30.88 - Interpreted response: Ok
10-04-1999 23:17:30.88 - Send: AT &F E0 &C1 &D2 V1 S0=0\V1<cr>
10-04-1999 23:17:31.01 - Recv: AT &F E0 &C1 &D2 V1 S0=0\V1<cr>
10-04-1999 23:17:31.01 - Recv: <cr><lf>OK<cr><lf>
10-04-1999 23:17:31.01 - Interpreted response: Ok
10-04-1999 23:17:31.01 - Send:
    ATS7=60S30=0L0M1\N3%C1&K3B0B15B2N1\J1X4<cr>
10-04-1999 23:17:31.01 - Recv: <cr><lf>OK<cr><lf>
10-04-1999 23:17:31.01 - Interpreted response: Ok
10-04-1999 23:17:31.01 - Dialing.
10-04-1999 23:17:31.01 - Send: ATDT;<cr>
10-04-1999 23:17:34.00 - Recv: <cr><lf>OK<cr><lf>
10-04-1999 23:17:34.00 - Interpreted response: Ok
```

```
10-04-1999 23:17:34.00 - Dialing.
10-04-1999 23:17:34.00 - Send: ATDT#########<cr>
10-04-1999 23:18:06.31 - Recv: <cr><lf>CONNECT 50666
    V42bis<cr><lf>
10-04-1999 23:18:06.31 - Interpreted response: Connect
10-04-1999 23:18:06.31 - Connection established at 50666bps.
10-04-1999 23:18:06.31 - Error-control on.
10-04-1999 23:18:06.31 - Data compression on.
10-04-1999 23:18:53.15 - Hanging up the modem.
10-04-1999 23:18:53.15 - Hardware hangup by lowering DTR.
10-04-1999 23:18:54.36 - WARNING: The modem did not respond to
    lowering DTR.  Trying software hangup...
10-04-1999 23:18:54.36 - Send: +++
10-04-1999 23:18:55.41 - Recv: <cr><lf>OK<cr><lf>
10-04-1999 23:18:55.41 - Interpreted response: Ok
10-04-1999 23:18:55.41 - Send: ATH E1<cr>
10-04-1999 23:18:55.54 - Recv: <cr><lf>OK<cr><lf>
10-04-1999 23:18:55.54 - Interpreted response: Ok
10-04-1999 23:18:55.54 - 115200,N,8,1
10-04-1999 23:18:56.78 - Session Statistics:
10-04-1999 23:18:56.78 -                 Reads : 1097 bytes
10-04-1999 23:18:56.78 -                 Writes: 3374 bytes
10-04-1999 23:18:56.78 - TOSHIBA Internal V.90 Modem closed.
```

This log file shows a lot of communication from the OS to the modem. Once the modem starts dialing, it took 32 seconds before getting a **Connect**. At this point, the savvy reader will note that the PPP log file begins. In this log file, the connection was closed manually. The connection didn't drop—instead, we ended the connection from the systray icon.

Practice Questions

Question 1

How much space does the installation of Windows DUN require?

○ a. 1MB

○ b. 3MB

○ c. 5MB

○ d. 7MB

Answer b is correct. DUN requires 2 to 3MB of available storage for installation. Therefore, answers a, c, and d are not correct.

Question 2

Which protocols does SLIP support?

○ a. AppleTalk

○ b. Decnet

○ c. IPX

○ d. NetBEUI

○ e. TCP/IP

Answer e is correct. TCP/IP is the only protocol supported by SLIP. On a Cisco exam, just because you can select multiple answers doesn't mean that more than one is correct, unless it tells you to choose a certain number of answers. If you want to use AppleTalk, NetBEUI, or IPX you need to use PPP. Therefore, answers a, c, and d are not correct. NetBEUI also needs bridging instead of routing. Decnet need a third-party utility for dial-up, so answer b is incorrect.

Question 3

What line protocol is the only one that will allow for multiple network protocols?

○ a. CSLIP

○ b. PPP

○ c. RAS

○ d. SLIP

Answer b is correct. PPP is the only line protocol that will support multiple network protocols like TCP/IP and IPX. Answer a, CSLIP, is a Cisco version of answer d, SLIP. Answer c, RAS, stands for Remote Access Server, a device that connects across long distance via a dial-up connection.

Question 4

A user is on a trip and wishes to update a file on his laptop. The file from which he wants to update is on a network server. When he attempts this update, he discovers the file has been orphaned. What could be the cause?

○ a. The user is using PPP to connect, and Briefcase requires NetBEUI support.

○ b. The file's name has been changed.

○ c. The server file has been marked as read-only.

○ d. Someone is currently modifying the file.

Answer b is correct. Answer d means that the user won't get the latest version until the person is done, and b describes the problem that will lead to a file no longer being linked. Answer a isn't right because PPP supports NetBEUI and answer c is incorrect because as long as the user can read the file, he can update his copy of the Briefcase

Question 5

Which log files exist for troubleshooting? [Choose the two best answers]

❑ a. PPPTXT.LOG

❑ b. MODEMLOG.TXT

❑ c. PPPLOG.TXT

❑ d. MODEMTXT.LOG

Answers b and c are correct. PPPLOG.TXT and MODEMLOG.TXT are the two log files that exist to show what is happening with a connection. Answers a and d don't exist.

Question 6

Windows 95/98 include support to dial into which types of devices? [Choose the three best answers]

❑ a. A NetWare server

❑ b. A Unix server

❑ c. An NT Server

❑ d. An AppleTalk server

Answers a, b, and c are correct. Native AppleTalk dial-in, answer d, is not supported by Windows 95/98.

Question 7

In order to dial in to a device, Dial-Up Networking must be installed on the workstation. If it isn't, where is it installed from?

○ a. The Windows CD: Pop it in and select the components.

○ b. The Windows CD, but you have to use Explorer to get to the directory.

○ c. Directly off the Microsoft Web site.

○ d. From Add/Remove Programs in Control Panel.

Answer d is correct. Go into Control Panel and double-click on Communications to add Dial-Up Networking to the machine. Answers a and b are partially correct because you will most likely need the CD to install the components. If you answered c, how did you propose to access the web site?

Question 8

> Which email clients come with Windows 95/98? [Choose the two best answers]
>
> ❑ a. Eudora
> ❑ b. Exchange
> ❑ c. Groupwise
> ❑ d. Outlook Express
> ❑ e. Lotus Notes

Answers b and d are correct. Windows 95 comes with the Exchange client, whereas Windows 98 comes with Outlook Express. If you selected answers a, c, or e, you'll want to review Microsoft's product line because those choices are products of competitors.

Question 9

> Deferred printing refers to what?
>
> ○ a. Not having to pay for the printer until a later date
> ○ b. Configuring a printer as a backup for when the primary isn't available
> ○ c. Holding print jobs when a printer isn't available

Answer c is correct. With deferred printing, the client machine holds onto the print job because the selected printer isn't available for spooling. Answers a, and b are not correct.

Question 10

The protocols that DUN automatically configures for a connection are:

○ a. TCP/IP

○ b. IPX/SPX

○ c. NetBEUI

○ d. None of the above; you have to configure each on the connection

○ e. All of the above

○ f. Some of the above, depending on which protocols are enabled in
       Network Neighborhood Properties

Answer f is correct. DUN will automatically allow all protocols that are configured within Network Neighborhood Properties at the time the dial-up configuration is made. So, if only IPX is established within Network Neighborhood, only IPX is configured for the DUN connection.

Need To Know More?

 Jang, Michael H. *MCSE Windows 98 Exam Prep*. The Coriolis Group. ISBN 1-57610-290-4. Because Dial Up Networking is tested in detail in the Microsoft MCSE exams, the Coriolis Windows 98 *Cram* and *Prep* books are good sources for extensive information regarding Dial-Up Networking.

 Stewart, James Michael and Ed Tittel. *MCSE Windows 98 Exam Cram*. The Coriolis Group. ISBN 1-57610-289-0.

 The Microsoft web site at **www.microsoft.com** has an extensive amount of information on Dial-Up Networking but it can be difficult to wade through. This URL focuses in on some common issues: **http://support.Microsoft.com/support/ServiceWare/Windows/Win98/76J77EM3K.ASP**.

ISDN And DSL

Terms you'll need to understand:

√ Integrated Services Digital Network (ISDN)

√ Digital Subscriber Loop (DSL)

√ Q921

√ Q931

√ Bandwidth on demand

√ Multilink Point-to-Point Protocol (PPP)

√ Leaf network

√ Bearer channel

√ Reference points

Techniques you'll need to master:

√ Configuring an ISDN interface for Dial-on-Demand Routing (DDR)

√ Troubleshooting an ISDN connection

√ Aggregating multiple channels with Bandwidth on Demand (BOD)

√ Describing an ISDN call setup

√ Describing an ISDN call tear down

Introduction To ISDN And DSL

Integrated Services Digital Network (ISDN) allows for the extension of digital services to the end user. The target audience for ISDN varies depending on whom you talk to. Many people see ISDN as an enabler for telecommuters and high-speed Web access from the home. Others see ISDN as a passing technology that never reached its full potential and will be replaced by Digital Subscriber Line (DSL). Regardless of which camp you're in, ISDN is fielded widely in many carrier markets. ISDN is an end-to-end digital solution, removing the digital-analog conversion that created the bottleneck for dial-up users.

The use of ISDN and DSL now provide the home user a digital last mile. These technologies are replacing the existing modems for those who require a higher-speed remote connection. The target markets here are the telecommuters and the small office/home office (SO/HO) users.

This chapter discusses both the ISDN world and the DSL world. The DSL discussion is included for those who will be taking the original CMTD exam. The DSL section and related information were dropped when the course was revamped to become BCRAN. It's thought that the DSL information will be included in a future Cisco course, but for those who are taking the current CMTD exam, a basic understanding of DSL is required.

Integrated Services Digital Network (ISDN)

The physical characteristics of ISDN provide two circuits for use: the Basic Rate Interface (BRI) and the Primary Rate interface (PRI). The BRI is comprised of two B channels (referred to as *bearer* channels) and 1 D channel (referred to as the *delta* channel). Each B channel is 64Kbps, and the D channel is 16Kbps. The PRI is 23 B channels and 1 D channel (23B+D). (The European E1 is 30B+D, which is based on E1 signaling.) Each B channel is 64Kbps, and the D channel is also 64Kbps for the PRI.

As was discussed in Chapter 3, the T-carrier system was developed here in the United States. The E-carrier system was used in Europe, hence the nomenclature.

The B channel is a carrier channel that provides clear-channel capability. As discussed in Chapter 3, the use of clear channel in North America requires the lines to be bi-polar 8 zero substitution (B8ZS) to ensure 1s density. In some areas, alternate mark inversion (AMI) (or *robbed bit signaling*) still is deployed; hence, some calls will be limited to 56Kbps.

The D channel is used for call setup and signaling. The D channel is out-of-band signaling, sometimes called *common-channel* signaling. The D channel for the BRI is a shared channel used for low-level packet switching and signaling. The Cisco routers currently *do not* use the packet-switching provision. The BRI D channel uses a specific bit in the multiplexed 2B+D signal. The PRI D channel is used for signaling only; it uses a specific "byte" in the multiplexed signal. The signaling is used for D channel messaging, such as "alerting", "connect", "setup acknowledge", and so on, to establish and tear down calls.

In short, a PRI is a T1 with 23 B channels and 1 D channel. The B channels are DS0s which are 64Kbps. The D channel uses one of the 24 DS0s making up the T1 span and carries the signaling information that sets up the call and manages the link for all of the B channels. Much ado is given to the various speeds used by each piece in both the CMTD and BCRAN courseware, although the BCRAN text is more comprehensive. The following information should be understood before taking the exam.

The ISDN BRI specifies:

➤ Two 64Kbps bearer channels and one 16Kbps delta channel

➤ Framing and synchronization of 48Kbps

➤ Total speed is (2 x 64) + 16 + 48 = 192Kbps

The North American ISDN PRI specifies:

➤ Twenty-three 64Kbps bearer channels and one 64Kbps delta channel

➤ Framing and synchronization of 8Kbps

➤ Total speed is (23 x 64) + 64 + 8 = 1.544Mbps

The European ISDN PRI specifies:

➤ Thirty 64Kbps bearer channels and one 64Kbps delta channel

➤ Framing and synchronization of 64Kbps

➤ Total speed is (30 x 64) + 64 + 64 = 2.048Mbps

During the exam it's critical to be aware of what question is being asked about the speed of an ISDN line. The total speed of a BRI is in fact 192Kbps; however, the user data transfer rate is 128Kbps.

The physical layout for ISDN can be viewed in Figure 7.1. The International Telegraph and Telephone Consultative Committee Communications Standards Organization (CCITT) created a reference model that described the functional groupings of the components used in ISDN. Each grouping represented

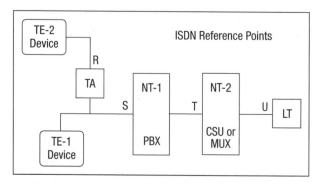

Figure 7.1 The CCITT reference model.

a function rather than a specific piece of equipment. In Figure 7.1, for example, the TE-2 device is simply a device that doesn't speak digital and has to be converted to digital signaling by a TA device. Using this thought process, a refrigerator would be considered a TE-2 type device. It doesn't send out a digital signal, does it? More in keeping with data communications, an analog phone would require a TA to convert the analog signal to a digital signal to be presented to a Network Termination Point 1 or 2 (NT-1 or NT-2) device.

The following list describes general meaning for each reference point or interface detailed by the CCITT:

➤ The TE-2 is connected to the TA that is connected to the leg bone, which is connected to the thighbone or something like that. (OK, not really.)

➤ The TE-2 is a device that is non-ISDN equipment (like my car).

➤ The TA is a device that converts non-ISDN signaling to ISDN digital signaling.

➤ The TE-1 is a device that is ISDN subscriber equipment or speaks ISDN.

➤ The NT-1 is a device that converts the two-wire (telephone company [telco] circuit) to the four-wire (subscriber circuit). This is commonly a Private Branch eXchange (PBX) device.

➤ The NT-2 is a device that converts the two-wire (telco circuit) to the four-wire (subscriber circuit). This is commonly a channel service unit (CSU) or MultipleXing Unit (MUX).

➤ LT is the Loop Termination (or Line Termination) point, which is commonly called the demarcation point (DEMARC), or the end of the telco's responsibility).

➤ ET is the Exchange Termination point or the terminus of the last mile at the central office equipment.

The lettered reference points describe the connection between each of the functional groupings. This glue between the devices allows for the development of products without regard to the entire puzzle. As an example, I could develop a TA that would successfully convert output from a soda machine to proper ISDN signaling to be presented to an NT-2 (or PBX), which would phone in an order for a refill of Joe-Bob's Dew Drop tea. This ability is a leap from the simple signaling of an analog circuit. Emergency services, alarm companies, and banks are seeing and using the D channel for its fast dedicated link. Alarm service companies use the D channel to signal a break-in or alert. Banks are taking advantage of the D channel signal for their ATM machines. A connection isn't required—just the delivery of a small amount of signaling information. The reference points are defined by Cisco as follows:

➤ *R (Rate Reference Point)*—The interface between non-ISDN equipment and the TA.

➤ *S (System Reference Point)*—The interface between the NT-1 or NT-2 and the subscriber equipment TA device.

➤ *T (Terminal Reference Point)*—The interface between the NT-1 and the NT-2 equipment.

➤ *U (User Reference Point)*—The interface between the LT and the NT1 or NT2. This reference point is unique to North America, because the NT devices in Europe are considered carrier equipment.

➤ *V*—The interface between the ET and LT. This reference point was not declared by Cisco, hence, it is simply a letter designated reference point as all the reference points were initially.

The reference points are on the exams. Knowing that the S reference point stands for *system* is important, and so on.

Both the S and T reference points represent the conversion point from the two-wire to four-wire. Whether it's a PBX (NT-2) or a CSU (NT-1) device isn't relevant to the router. Some of the routers present an S/T interface, and some come with a built-in NT-1 and present a U interface. It's important to remember though that a serial interface is capable of using ISDN. However, it must be connected to an external TA, which is then connected to an NT-1 device, which is connected to the LT, which is connected to the ET, which then, of course, is connected to the leg bone. Can a serial port be used to connect to ISDN? Yes.

The protocols involved are standards that allow the creation of equipment that provides the functionality between these device groupings. Table 7.1 shows the protocols that are used at the Datalink and Network layers of the Open Systems Interconnect (OSI) model for the B and D channels.

At the Physical layer (layer 1) of the model, the S/T interface is controlled by the ITU-T I.430 standard and the U interface is governed by the ITU-T I.431 standard. Simply speaking, the I.430 standard controls the BRI, and the I.431 standard controls the PRI. The PRI is connected to the Channel Service Unit/ Data Service Unit (CSU/DSU) and multiplexes the 23 channels (plus the D channel signaling) at the U (or User Reference Point). The I.430 standard must allow for multiple signals (and collisions) at the S/T interface.

Troubleshooting The ISDN Installation

When troubleshooting an ISDN installation, the following debug commands are most useful. It may not be appropriate to turn them all on at once, because the output may become daunting; however, by stepping through the process, you'll generally find it's quite clear where (if at all) a breakdown occurs. However, before you start any debug, we recommend using the **show isdn status** command:

```
    BCRANrouter#sh isdn status

Global ISDN Switchtype = primary-5ess
ISDN Serial1/0:23 interface
dsl 0, interface ISDN Switchtype = primary-5ess

Layer 1 Status:
ACTIVE

Layer 2 Status:
TEI = 0, Ces = 1, SAPI = 0, State = MULTIPLE_FRAME_ESTABLISHED

Layer 3 Status:

0 Active Layer 3 Call(s)
Activated dsl 0 CCBs = 0

Total Allocated ISDN CCBs = 0
```

Table 7.1 D and B channel protocols.		
OSI Layer	**D Channel**	**B Channel**
Datalink (layer 2)	Q.921(LAPD)	LAPB/PPP/HDLC/FR
Network (layer 3)	Q.931 IP/IPX	

The layer 1 status should be **ACTIVE**—if it isn't, then no amount of debugging will provide a solution, because the physical layer is down. If it's plugged in, it's time to call the carrier.

Once you have an active layer 1, the following debug commands can provide any other needed troubleshooting information:

➤ **DEBUG DIALER**—Shows the Dial-on-Demand Routing (DDR) trigger and what phone number is being used. Not surprisingly, if the phone number is wrong, a connection will not be made. Refer to Chapter 8 for additional information.

➤ **DEBUG ISDN Q921**—Shows the Datalink layer conversation between the router and the switch. This is a very chatty debug command, but it shows that a discussion is ongoing.

➤ **DEBUG ISDN Q931**—Displays the network layer conversation over the D channel as the call is set up or torn down.

You should understand both the setup and tear down of a call for the exam. Remember that the conversation displayed is strictly between the router and the central office (CO) switch to which the router is connected. See the details in the next section.

➤ *DEBUG PPP Negotiation*—Gives the details for the negotiated parameters during the PPP setup. The three negotiated parameters during this step will be multilink, authentication, and compression. Both sides must declare multilink or it is not optioned. Both sides must declare compression or it is not optioned. But if either case isn't optioned, that fact doesn't affect the establishment of the link.

Of the authentication methods declared on both sides of the link—Password Authentication Protocol (PAP), Challenge Handshake Authentication Protocol (CHAP), MicroSoft Challenge Handshake Authentication Protocol (MS-CHAP), or None), one authentication method *must* be common for each side or the link will fail to be established. Refer to Chapter 5 for more information.

➤ *DEBUG PPP AUTHENTICATION*—Shows the result of the authentication. It will clearly show if the username and password pair is found, and whether it is verified or not verified.

Call Setup And Teardown

Because the conversation is between the router and the CO switch, all the steps necessary to set up or tear down a call are seen with the Q931 debug information. The following summary is provided as a study aid, and it is important to memorize the "flow" on the D channel for the exam. The arrows in the following summary indicate the direction of the packet (← toward the router, or   toward the switch).

Calling Party Setup

➤ *SETUP*   —Calling party requests a connection to a remote number

➤ *SETUP ACK* ←—Switch acknowledges the Setup message

➤ *CALL PROCEEDING* ←—Switch progress message (generally associated with voice calls)

➤ *ALERTING* ←—Switch progress message

➤ *CONNECT* ←—Connection is established to the CO

➤ *CONNECT ACK*   —Router acknowledges the connection

The **CALL PROCEEDING** and **ALERTING** messages may or may not be seen. You may also see other progress messages prior to the **CONNECT**. The number and sequence of messages can vary from carrier to carrier depending on the implementation. Again, remember that the D channel signaling can be used for a variety of applications.

Called Party Setup

➤ *SETUP* ←—Incoming call setup string asks for connection

➤ *CALL PROCEEDING*   —Acknowledgement of the setup request

➤ *ALERTING*   —Switch progress message

➤ *CONNECT*   —Connection is established to the CO

➤ *CONNECT ACK* ←—Switch acknowledges the connection

Again, the **CALL PROCEEDING** and **ALERTING** messages may or may not be seen.

 The sequence for calling and called party setup is a test item. It's important to remember that the router talks *only* to the local switch. So, the perspective (calling or called) of the router is key.

The disconnection or *tear-down* of a circuit can be initiated by either the calling or called party. The release procedure is based on a three-step approach after a **DISCONNECT** message.

Disconnection Initiation

➤ *DISCONNECT*   —Releasing part issues to the local switch

➤ *RELEASE*   —Signal to terminate the circuit

➤ *RELEASED* ◄—Local switch acknowledges release

➤ *RELEASE COMPLETE*   —Circuit is down

The device that initiates the release of the call sends out an initial **DISCONNECT** to its local switch. The local switch forwards that on to the far side; however, the initiating device doesn't receive confirmation that the far end has indeed seen the message. The initiator follows with a **RELEASE** message to the switch, expecting the switch to respond by closing the circuit and sending the **RELEASE COMPLETE** message. The **RELEASE COMPLETE** is effectively the acknowledgement to the switch prior to closing the circuit from the initiating device.

Disconnection Reception

➤ *DISCONNECT* ◄—Switch signals disconnect

➤ *RELEASED*   —Signal to terminate the circuit

➤ *RELEASE COMPLETE* ◄—Circuit is down

The receiver of the disconnect acknowledges to the local switch that it understands it must end the call and sends the switch the **RELEASED** command, and the switch acknowledges by **RELEASE COMPLETE**.

Global Configuration Parameters

The remainder of this section deals with the configuration parameters for ISDN. The configuration of ISDN on a router requires the global configuration of the switch type, the specification of the interface parameters and call triggering (DDR), and includes a group of optional parameters.

The one global configuration parameter that must be set is the switch type. You set the switch type in global configuration mode using the following command:

```
Router(config)#isdn switch-type switch-model
```

The *switch-model* is specified as a *basic-switch-model* or a *primary-switch-model*. For example, you'd set the switch type for a North American AT&T 5ess model used on a router with a BRI interface as follows:

```
Router(config)#isdn switch-type basic-5ess
```

The same switch type configured for a router with a primary rate interface (PRI) would look like this:

```
Router(config)#isdn switch-type pri-5ess
```

Until version 11.3 (with a patch) or version 12.0, you couldn't specify the switch type on a per-interface basis. Although this wouldn't seem to be a major problem, the Internetwork Operating System (IOS) was altered to allow for the switch type to be overridden on a per interface basis.

If it's a PRI interface, you must configure the controller for the line coding, framing, and timeslots to be used. The controller must be configured for the North American or European facilities using the following command:

```
Router(config)#controller [t1 | e1] {slot/port | unit-number}
```

The *slot/port* specifies the physical location of the controller or interface card. The *unit-number* specification is for the 4000 series routers that didn't use slot numbering. On the controller, you then define the coding, framing, and timeslots using the following commands:

```
Router(config-controller)#framing [sf | esf | crc4]
Router(config-controller)#linecode [ami | b8zs | hdb3]
Router(config-controller)#clock source
    [line primary or secondary | internal]
```

Super Frame (SF) is used for some older T1 carrier configurations. Extended Super Frame (ESF) is used for T1 PRI configurations. Cyclic Redundancy Check 4 (CRC-4) is used for E1 PRI configurations. The line coding is Alternate Mark Inversion (AMI) for T1, B8ZS for T1 PRI, high-density bi-polar 3 (HDB3) for E1 PRI configurations.

You can set the clocking of the line to line or internal. Typically, it will be set to line because it's uncommon for the carrier to accept clocking from a customer. If there are multiple controllers in a specific router, each other controller will be declared as a secondary. If there are three controllers in a 7000 series router, one will be primary (typically line) and two will be secondaries.

In addition to the clocking and coding of the line, you must configure the number of time slot (64Kbps) channels as follows:

```
Router(config-controller)#pri-group timeslots range
```

The *range* of time slots is counted from 1 through 24; the range declares the number of channels being used for this controller. Because this is a PRI declaration, the D channel slot must be specified. You do this with the **interface** command, because all configuration is done on the D channel. The curious catch is that the channels for D channel selection are counted from 0 through 23. You configure the D channel as follows:

```
Router(config)#interface serial [slot/port | unit] [23 | 15]
```

The last (twenty-third) channel is used for D channel signaling on a T1 PRI; the center (fifteenth) channel is used for E1 PRI.

An optional configuration command that you can use for **interface** is **isdn incoming-voice modem**. This command allows analog calls coming in over the PRI to be terminated locally on internal modems. This feature turns on the software that examines the D channel information to determine if the call is a true ISDN call or an analog signal that has been converted to digital signaling. If it's an analog call, it must be converted back to digital data by the modem.

There is little, if any, flexibility in the configuration of the controller, because it's based on provider settings. The common configuration for a North American T1 PRI provided by an AT&T 5ess with the capability to receive both analog and digital calls is shown here:

```
Central(config)#isdn switch-type pri-5ess
Central(config)#controller t1 3/0
Central(config-controller)#framing esf
Central(config-controller)#linecode b8zs
Central(config-controller)#clock source line primary
Central(config-controller)#pri-group timeslots 1-24

Central(config)#interface serial 3/0:23
Central(config-int)#ip address 100.1.1.1 255.255.0.0
Central(config-int)#isdn incoming-voice modem
```

This configuration is for a 3600 series router with a T1 card located in the 3 slot, using an internal modem card for analog terminations.

No other global settings related to ISDN are required for the configuration. However, because these links will generally be used as dial-up links, you'll need to create static or default routes so the router will have knowledge of the remote networks. This process is also a global configuration function. The creation of static and default routes is discussed in the next section as it relates to the Dial-on-Demand Routing (DDR) functionality.

Dial-On-Demand Routing

Dial-on-Demand Routing (DDR) was presented in both the CMTD and BCRAN courseware. With the remake of the class to the BCRAN format, DDR over ISDN became a subchapter in the ISDN section; the asynchronous DDR commands were put into a separate chapter. The following discussion will touch on some of the needed asynchronous commands where appropriate, even though they may seem out of context in a discussion of ISDN. For a fuller discussion of all DDR properties, please see Chapter 8. The focus in this chapter is on DDR usage within the ISDN arena, although some definitions may be replicated in both chapters.

The implementation of DDR is used for low-volume periodic traffic, typically from a small branch office or remote site where a dedicated link wouldn't prove cost effective. The packets delivered to the interface are deemed interesting or not based on the router administrator's selection. The declaration of whether the packets are interesting is made using either a dialer-list or an access-list (discussed in the next section). In either case, *permitting* a packet means to make the call and *denying* a packet means not to make the call.

The steps for DDR are as follows:

1. Packet arrives at the router and is processed for routing.

2. Packet is routed to a DDR interface (generally due to a static or default route).

3. Packet is determined to be interesting or not based on the dialer-list.

4. If interesting, the call is made to the appropriate phone number for the receiving router.

5. After a configured idle time, the call is hung up, and no additional charges are incurred.

With DDR, the receiving site isn't constantly connected—hence, you can't use classic routing protocols to exchange route information. Typically, a static or default route will be used to maintain route information. When configuring a leaf node or stub network, use a default route to point all non-local traffic to a central router or network.

> *Note: A leaf node or stub network is a network with one connection back to the main or core network and no additional routes behind it. Because there is one and only one way to reach any other network (through the central router), the leaf need only know that one path.*

Routing In A DDR Environment

Static or default routes eliminate the need for a router to maintain an expensive leased line facility or continually trigger a DDR call. Whenever DDR is configured, it's imperative to monitor the link for a period of time to ensure that it's being called only for interesting traffic. Any error of omission or syntax in the statement of interesting traffic within the dialer-list could result in a large phone bill at the end of the month.

To create a static route, use the following syntax:

```
Ip route remote-network network-mask next-hop-address
    [administrative-distance]
```

For example,

```
Ip route 144.5.6.0 255.255.255.0 122.4.5.6 130
```

To reach the 144.5.6.0 network, the next hop is 122.4.5.6. The subnet mask is needed to let the router know what part of the address is the network portion. The next hop address lets the router know where the packets are to be delivered, and the administrative distance is the believability of this particular route.

Figure 7.2 shows an example network that uses this route.

The stub router has knowledge of the 144.5.6.0 network and also knows that to reach that network, the next hop is 122.4.5.6. Because the leaf node dialer interface is 122.4.5.5 (on the same network as the next hop), the packet is given to that interface for delivery. The interface is labeled a *dialer interface* in Figure 7.2 because it could be either BRI or asynchronous. It's a given that the users on the stub must have some reason to try to reach the remote 144.5.6.0 network. This could be accomplished from a DNS lookup or simply by user knowledge. In this case, the administrative distance isn't relevant because there is only one route to the destination.

Each remote site that the stub must dial requires a static route. If the network is truly stubby and only one connection is required, setting a default route

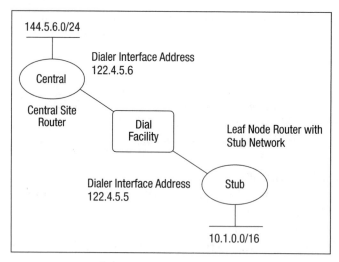

Figure 7.2 Leaf node or stub network.

could accomplish the same task. You would configure the central router for a static route to the remote network and configure the remote as follows:

```
IP route 0.0.0.0 0.0.0.0 122.4.5.6
```

This is the preferred method for establishing a default route for the stub side. Figure 7.3 shows this configuration.

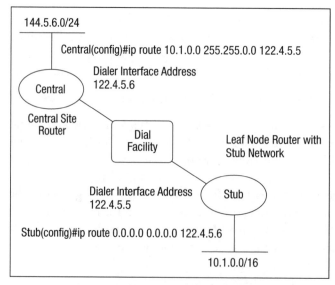

Figure 7.3 Leaf or stub network with a default route.

In this fashion, the central router has knowledge of the stubbed network on the remote router and the stub router knows that anything non-local should be sent to the central router for processing. Take care to control DDR, to avoid a large phone bill. Each protocol or packet declared interesting destined for *anywhere* will cause the link to activate.

To extend the idea of a central network in which multiple routes are available to the stub, it's clear to see the importance of the default route. Configuration of every route in the central core could become tedious, at best, for the stub. We need two additional concepts to further control the workload for the central and stub routers: *route redistribution* and *passive interfaces*.

In order for the other routers in the central network to have knowledge of the remote 10.1.0.0 network, the static route must be redistributed into the route table being propagated by the routing protocol being used in the central network. If the central network is using Internet Group Routing Protocol (IGRP) (a fine choice), the following commands are required for the static route to be transmitted throughout the central network of routers:

```
Central(config)#router igrp 100
Central(config-router)#network 122.0.0.0
Central(config-router)#network 144.5.0.0
Central(config-router)#redistribute static
Central(config)ip route 10.1.0.0 255.255.0.0 122.4.5.5
```

The result will be that routers beyond the central router in the core network will have knowledge of the remote 10.1.0.0 network.

Lastly, to control or eliminate the updates from IGRP on the dialer interfaces, you set those interfaces to be **passive** for the protocol. Because a static route exists on the central router and a default route exists on the stub, there is no reason to propagate route information on the dialer interfaces. To stop these updates, use the following commands under the protocol definition on each router:

```
Central(config)#router igrp 100
Central(config-router)#passive-interface bri0
```

This example assumes that the dialer interface is the first BRI port on both the central and stub routers. Now that the router has the ability to reach a remote network, the interesting packets must be declared to trigger the link.

Declaration Of Interesting Traffic

As mentioned earlier, the router administrator must define what traffic is interesting. This determination is a critical piece in the effective establishment of

DDR. For example, suppose a remote office periodically must synchronize its local database with that of the central office. The trigger could be all FTP traffic or just FTP traffic destined for a particular remote destination. Again, take care when defining interesting traffic to ensure that the link is established *only* when required.

You must create a dialer-list to control DDR. The list syntax is as follows:

```
Dialer-list dialer-group-number protocol protocol-name
               {permit|deny|list access-list}
```

The **Dialer-list** command creates the list and takes as its argument a freely chosen number (from 1 through 10) for the *dialer-group-number*. The **protocol** keyword then declares which protocols are to be checked. The arguments to the **protocol** keyword are *ip, ipx, appletalk, vines,* and so on.

You can also have the dialer-list point to an access-list. In short, you can create the dialing conditions a number of ways. Some examples are:

➤ All IP traffic triggers a call (maybe not a good idea):

```
Dialer-list 1 protocol ip permit
```

➤ All FTP traffic triggers a call:

```
Dialer-list 1 protocol ip list 101
Access-list 101 permit tcp any any eq ftp
```

The first example uses only the **Dialer-list** command. However, all IP traffic will trigger the call on an interface where it's activated. This setup may not be a good idea because it provides little, if any, control over what establishes a link. The second example uses an access-list to declare what brings up the link. In this case, any FTP traffic will create the link. Again, it may be more prudent to exactly specify the destination, to ensure that the link is established only for its designed purpose.

Using the example in Figure 7.4 as a basis, you can use the following configuration information to control the periodic resynchronization of the stub network database server with the central server:

```
Stub(config)#dialer-list 1 protocol ip list 101
Stub(config)#access-list 101 permit tcp
    host 10.1.0.5 host 144.5.6.12 eq ftp
Stub(config)#interface bri0
Stub(config-int)#dialer-group 1
```

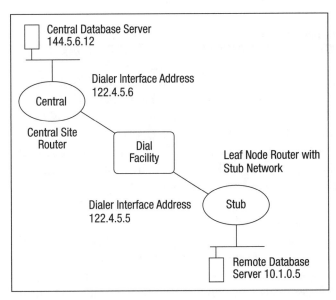

Figure 7.4 Only FTP traffic from the remote system triggers a call to the central router.

The BRI0 interface is used for the example, although any dialer interface could be substituted.

To turn on the dialer-list, use the command **dialer-group** on the interface. Doing so is similar to using the **access-list/access-group** command pair for packet control. This is *not* to say that once the link is established, the dialer-group will prevent other traffic from crossing the link. If you're talking on the phone and the kids are making noise in the background, the person you're talking to will hear the background noise. If you don't want the background noise to carry across the link, you *must* also use the **access-list/access-group** pair.

The **dialer-group** interface command is used *only* to determine whether to make a call. Once the call is established, the dialer-group command doesn't control the flow of data. If the same traffic that is interesting for making the call is the only traffic to be sent on the link, then you should also use the **access-group** interface command.

When you're describing interesting traffic, it's preferable to determine what traffic *should* trigger the call, rather than what traffic should *not* trigger it. The implicit deny at the end of an access-list will keep uninteresting traffic from triggering a call. Another point to keep in mind is the interplay within protocol suites. The following example configuration shows this:

```
Central(config)#access-list 101 deny
    protocol tcp any any eq telnet
Central(config)#access-list 101 permit protocol tcp any any
```

The point of the access-list is to ensure that Telnet traffic would not bring up the link. After the denial of the Telnet traffic, it appears that all other traffic will be permitted; however, only other Transmission Control Protocol (TCP) traffic will be permitted. Unfortunately, no User Datagram Protocol (UDP) traffic will cause a connection, because it's implicitly denied at the end of the list. Notice that any UDP traffic will not match either of the criteria, and hence, will match the last implicit deny statement.

Dialer Maps And Interface Dialers

Now that the router has a route and interesting traffic has been declared, the router must make a phone call to the remote location. This can be done in a number of ways. The simplest way is to associate a phone number with an interface using the **dialer string** command, so that all calls made from the interface go to the same location. Doing so doesn't scale well, however, because you'd need a physical interface for each location to be dialed. Because DDR is generally used for periodic traffic, it would seem logical that a single interface could be used to call multiple destinations. For this purpose, you can use the **dialer map** command.

The **dialer map** statement allows you to configure the physical interface to call multiple different remote locations based on the destination IP address. A single physical channel, however, can call only one location at a time. We use the term *channel* because in the case of a BRI, it's possible to have each channel connected to a different remote location.

The next step in allowing for a more flexible dial plan is to implement *dialer interfaces*. A dialer interface is a logical interface created in the same fashion as a loopback interface. The logical interface has all the configuration needed to connect to a remote site, but isn't tied to a specific physical interface. You can then put the physical interfaces into a pool that the logical interfaces can use when a call is to be made.

Associating a number with a physical interface using the **dialer string** command is akin to Batman or Robin picking up the handset of the Bat phone and the phone automatically ringing at Commissioner Gordon's office. This configuration is simple and would be very useful when the remote site calls only one central location. The addition of **dialer map** statements can allow a single channel the option of calling multiple locations; however, if you have four children and only one phone, the competition may be more than desirable. By allowing for the creation of logical interfaces (dialer interfaces), the router func-tions as a bank of phones—the caller just picks a line that isn't currently busy and makes the call. Any phone will do. This last scenario would be very useful in a central site where many remotes are called on an as-needed basis; in such a case, 4 or 5 channels could satisfy 10 or more remote locations.

Let's look at three configurations that detail each of the methods discussed. Figure 7.5 shows a configuration for a one-to-one connection.

In the one-to-one case, only Telnet is allowed between the stub network (10.1.0.0) and the central network (144.5.6.0). The static route points to the next hop address of 122.4.5.6, which is associated with the BRI interface on the stub router. The access-list 101 is associated with dialer-list 1 and the **dialer-group** interface command activates it on the interface. This stub net-work only needs to reach the central site.

To allow for a location to call multiple sites, the following example extends the capacity of the router. To call multiple locations, use the **dialer map** command. The syntax is as follows:

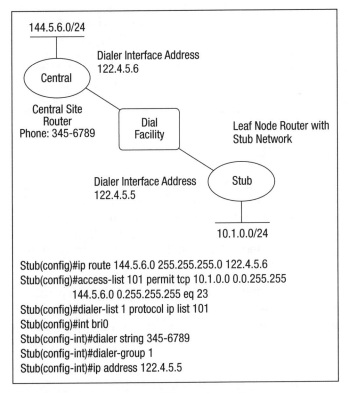

Figure 7.5   One-to-one DDR configuration.

```
Central(config-if)#dialer map protocol next-hop-address

                              [name hostname]

                              [modem-script script-name]

                              [system-script script-name]

                              [broadcast]

                              dial-string
```

The following are the definitions for each of the arguments associated with this command.

➤ **dialer map**—Specifies the map statement

➤ *protocol next-hop-address*—Declares the protocol and the associated next-hop-address

➤ **name** *hostnam*—Defines the remote system name

➤ **modem-script**—Optionally declares a script file for making the connection

➤ **system-script**—Optionally declares a script file for login to the remote system

➤ *broadcast*—Specifies whether broadcast packets for the protocol should be sent

➤ *dial-string*—Remote location phone number

 The syntax for the **dialer map** statement can be very cumbersome. In the classroom labs, the script files aren't used; however, you should review *all* arguments to the **map** statement for the test. The optional commands are shown in brackets in the statement syntax. In some documentation, the dial-string is also listed as optional, but this is not true.

Figure 7.6 shows the configuration for a central site router that can place calls to multiple remote sites. The commands differ little from the one-to-one configuration, other than the multiple **route** statements and the **map** statements themselves.

The configuration for a one-to-many scenario is suited for a central site that must make occasional calls to a number of remote locations. In this example, the authentication method has been declared as PPP CHAP. Take care that

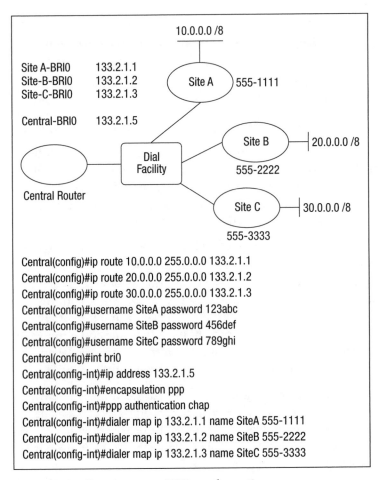

Figure 7.6   One-to-many DDR configuration.

the name in the **map** statement and the username/password pair are *exactly* the same. Even though it isn't a requirement for the administrator to be case con- science in a CHAP environment, the router will fail to find the route if it isn't the same case. For more information, refer to Chapter 5.

The most flexible of the dial configurations uses *dialer profiles*. The use of di- aler profiles lets the administrator associate the physical interface to the profile for the duration of the call on a per-call basis. A virtual interface called a *dialer interface* is created to use for the *dialer profile*. The *dialer profile* is a concept that is defined using a *dialer interface*. The dialer profiles provide many new features to the DDR command set and add the following benefits:

➤ Free the BRI B channels to act independently. Prior to dialer profiles, both B channels operated based on the BRI physical configuration.

➤ Can be used as the source for dial backup to a physical interface. Prior to dialer profiles, when another physical interface was put into backup status it could not be used except for the explicit backup of the primary.

➤ Eliminate the need for complex **dialer map** statements in a multi-protocol environment.

The elements used by a dialer profile and associated with a *dialer interface* are:

➤ *Dialer interface*—The logical configuration for the connection. All the associated interface characteristics are configured in this logical profile, such as protocol addressing, phone number, authentication, encapsulation, and so on. Note that the **dialer map** command is a valid entry in a dialer interface, although its particular benefit is minimal.

➤ *Dialer pool*—The grouping of physical interfaces that the dialer interface can use. Each physical interface can belong to more than one pool, and the physical interfaces in the pool can be prioritized for their usage. A good example would be a case in which the pool consists of both BRI and asynchronous ports. It may be more expedient to use the BRI B channels, due to the faster setup time, or it may be more cost effective to use the asynchronous ports. Either way, the physical ports can be offered for servicing the dialer profiles in a prioritized manner.

➤ *Optional map class*—Can be associated with a particular dialer interface or a group of dialer interfaces. The **map** class operates like an **include** statement to the dialer profile. You associate the **map** class with a particular phone number being called by adding the class argument to the **dialer string** or **dialer map** command.

 From a test perspective, it's hard to distinguish that the dialer pool and the physical interfaces are components of the dialer interface. However, both the CMTD and BCRAN courseware declare that the four components of a dialer interface are:

➤ Dialer interface

➤ Dialer pool

➤ Map class (optional)

➤ Physical interfaces that make up the pool

The configuration for a dialer profile is very similar to the configuration for a one-to-one connection. However, the configuration is put into the logical dialer interface. Figure 7.7 provides an example of a configuration for a dialer interface.

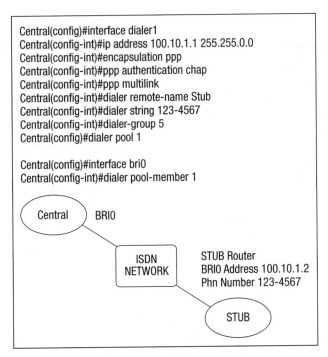

Figure 7.7   Dialer interface configuration.

In this example the dialer interface is using pool 1, which has as a member only the BRI0 interface. The physical interface, however, has been disassociated from the logical or Network layer address. The **dialer-group** statement is associated with the dialer-list for the interface (not shown in the diagram).

To further the functionality of the dialer interface, you can add the **map-class** command to the **dialer string** command. The **map-class** command can specify the same values to be used for many calls. The commands that can be placed in the **map-class** command are:

➤ **dialer isdn speed 56**—Used only when the ISDN line speed is 56Kbps (using robbed-bit signaling).

➤ **dialer idle-timeout**—The idle timeout specified in seconds to hang up the line when no interesting traffic is seen.

➤ **dialer fast-idle**—The idle timeout period when a call is pending and no lines are available (more on this later).

➤ **dialer wait-for-carrier-time**—The period of time the router will wait for a synchronized carrier signal before declaring the call has failed.

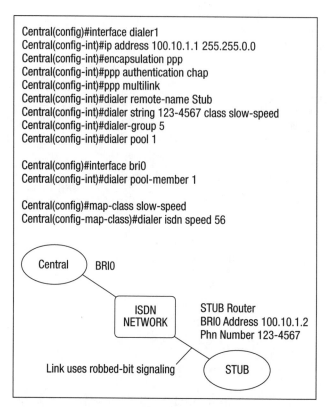

```
Central(config)#interface dialer1
Central(config-int)#ip address 100.10.1.1 255.255.0.0
Central(config-int)#encapsulation ppp
Central(config-int)#ppp authentication chap
Central(config-int)#ppp multilink
Central(config-int)#dialer remote-name Stub
Central(config-int)#dialer string 123-4567 class slow-speed
Central(config-int)#dialer-group 5
Central(config-int)#dialer pool 1

Central(config)#interface bri0
Central(config-int)#dialer pool-member 1

Central(config)#map-class slow-speed
Central(config-map-class)#dialer isdn speed 56
```

Central   BRI0

ISDN
NETWORK   STUB Router
                 BRI0 Address 100.10.1.2
                 Phn Number 123-4567

Link uses robbed-bit signaling   STUB

Figure 7.8 Optional **map-class** command added.

The use of the **map-class** command can save you keystrokes if all the calls follow the same rules for timeouts and speeds. The example shown in Figure 7.8 adds the **map-class** command to the previous configuration.

 Both the CMTD and BCRAN texts clearly point out that the **dialer isdn speed** command does *not* take 64Kbps as an argument.

The placement of physical interfaces in the pools can be prioritized and overlapped, as seen in the following configuration script:

```
Central(config)#interface bri0
Central(config-int)#encapsulation ppp
Central(config-int)#ppp authentication chap
Central(config-int)#dialer pool-member 1 priority 10

Central(config)#interface bri1
Central(config-int)#encapsulation ppp
```

```
Central(config-int)#ppp authentication chap
Central(config-int)#dialer pool-member 2 priority 10

Central(config)#interface async 1
Central(config-int)#encapsulation ppp
Central(config-int)#ppp authentication chap
Central(config-int)#dialer pool-member 1 priority 1
Central(config-int)#dialer pool-member 2 priority 1
```

Notice that the asynchronous interface was placed into both pools, but with a lower priority. In this fashion the asynchronous interface will be used as a secondary resource after the BRI interfaces.

Optional Configuration Tasks

You can use a number of optional commands to enhance or adjust the dial facilities that you've set up. It's important to understand that these additional tasks aren't necessary, but they can be very helpful in creating a cost-effective dial plan for small or remote offices. Each command essentially stands on its own. The commands are detailed in the remainder of this section.

Multilink PPP And Bandwidth On Demand

Multilink PPP is an open standards method for the aggregation of multiple individual links to create the appearance of a larger point-to-point circuit. The term Bandwidth on Demand (BOD) is the generic name given to the philosophy of aggregating the links. The IOS supports BOD and can implement BOD using either Multilink PPP or a proprietary algorithm for link aggregation.

Using BOD gives the administrator the option to establish additional links if the first link becomes too busy. The definition of *busy* is up to you. To establish what is considered busy, you use the command

```
Router(config-int)#dialer load-threshold
    load [inbound | outbound | either]
```

The *load* is declared as a value from 1 to 255 that is related to the bandwidth used on the link. A load of 128 would declare the link busy when it reached 50 percent saturation. If the busy condition exists, a second link will be established until the load is reduced on the aggregated link to below the threshold. The arguments **inbound, outbound,** and **either** declare the direction of the load to be monitored. By default the direction is outbound. The outbound direction may not be the most suitable selection in many remote environments if the remote generates requests for download. Because the request is only a small part of the conversation, it may never enable a second link even though the download is massive.

Once a threshold has been established, the router must be told what method to use for the aggregation. If no declaration is made, the Cisco router will try to use the proprietary method. This, of course, won't work if the receiver isn't another Cisco router. To select Multilink PPP as the aggregation method, use the command

```
Router(config-int)#ppp multilink
```

Multilink PPP (MPPP) can be configured on:

➤ *Individual BRI interfaces*—Both B channels by default are a two-link rotary group.

➤ *Multiple BRI interfaces in a rotary group*—MPPP is configured on the rotary interface, not on the BRI interface. This is an outbound call, which takes its configuration information from the **int dialer**.

➤ *Multiple BRI interfaces in dialer profiles*—MPPP is configured on the dialer interface for outgoing calls. (The configuration parameters come from the dialer profile.) MPPP is configured on the BRI for incoming calls, because the physical interface answers the call. If MPPP is required for both incoming and outgoing calls, it must be specified in both places.

➤ *PRI B channels in a rotary group*—MPP is specified on the serial interface associated with the PRI.

➤ *Asynchronous serial interfaces*—MPPP is configured in the **int dialer**, which will use the asynchronous interface as part of the dial rotary.

➤ *Synchronous serial interfaces*—MPPP is configured on the serial interface itself.

 Multilink PPP can be used on BRI, BRIs in rotary groups, BRIs in dialer pools, PRI rotary groups, asynchronous interfaces, and synchronous serial interfaces. Most often it's associated incorrectly with only BRI interfaces.

Caller Identification

Caller identification (Caller ID) is available for ISDN lines that are supported by providers that supply the called number value as part of the setup request for the link. Most providers now offer that feature. Caller ID allows for the verification of the caller number prior to establishing the call, thereby eliminating any unwanted charges. To enable caller ID, use the command

```
Router(config-int)#isdn caller number
```

The *number* is the calling party number passed by the provider during the setup of the link. Exercise caution when you create the list of caller numbers that will be accepted, because Caller ID records the number exactly as sent by the provider. Depending on the provider implementation, the number may be sent with or without an area code prefix. If no **isdn caller** command is present, then all calls will be accepted and processed. If only one caller is specified with a single **isdn caller** command, then *only* that caller will be accepted.

You can configure the **isdn caller** command to accept calls from specific numbers up to 25 characters in length. Use the *X* character to specify wildcard spaces in the caller number. For example,

```
Router(config-int)#isdn caller 212-123-XXXX
```

would accept all calls from area code 212, within exchange 123.

Rate Adaptation

In some cases where the provider doesn't use the default DS0 configuration for 64Kbps, it's necessary to specify the alternative of 56Kbps. You do so on an outgoing call-by-call basis specified in the **dialer map** statement using the **speed** argument, as follows:

```
Router(config-int)#dialer map ip 10.2.2.2 name Central
    speed 56 123-4567
```

As stated earlier, the omission of the **speed** argument declares the default 64Kbps, and 64Kbps is *not* a valid argument to the **speed** argument.

The **dialer idle-timeout** Command

The **dialer idle-timeout** value specifies how long to wait in seconds before disconnecting a call when no interesting traffic has been seen. The default is 120 seconds (2 minutes). The administrator should be aware of how much time the initial call yields. For most long-distance calls, once the connection is made the first minute is paid for; and for some overseas calls, the first three minutes are owned once the connection is put through. If the interesting traffic is very short in nature (such as Simple Mail Transfer Protocol (SMTP)), you should set the timer so that the maximum connect time is achieved without incurring additional minute charges.

The configuration of the idle timeout is placed on the interface as follows:

```
Router(config-int)#dialer idle-timeout seconds
```

The **dialer fast-Idle** Command

The **dialer fast-idle** command is used when all resources (physical dial interfaces) are busy and another call is pending. This condition places all the dial interfaces into a fast idle condition using the number of seconds specified in the command. The default fast idle timer is 20 seconds. When a call is pending with no resource, the physical lines will use the fast idle timer for disconnect. The configuration for the fast idle is also placed on the interface as follows:

```
Router(config-int)#dialer fast-idle seconds
```

Using the fast idle can be different for each interface so that when a call is pending, certain interfaces can become candidates for disconnect earlier than others. The fast idle doesn't ensure that a line will come available—only that the period of non-interesting traffic is shorter. If all the lines are streaming interesting traffic, the idle time won't be reached, and the pending call will fail when it reaches the **dialer wait-for-carrier-time** discussed next.

The **dialer wait-for-carrier-time** Command

The **dialer wait-for-carrier-time** command specifies how long to wait before declaring that the destination isn't there (for whatever reason). A continuous ring with no answer, no carrier detected, no dial tone received, and so on, are reasons that a call may not go through. The **dialer wait-for-carrier-time** command sets an upper limit to the call failure. An example would be if the number called didn't answer. The router, being a mechanical device, won't say to itself after 10 rings, "Gee, maybe they aren't there." As the hunk of metal it is, it will happily sit in the rack and listen to the ring ad infinitum. The default wait period is 30 seconds. This may or may not be long enough for some asynchronous lines, which have to dial 9 to get an outside line and then wait for the modems to train and the carrier to be established. In some cases it may be necessary to declare a longer time. Here are the carrier wait time syntax and an example in which the time has been increased to 60 seconds from the 30-second default:

```
Router(config-int)#dialer wait-for-carrier-time seconds
```

For example,

```
Router(config-int)#dialer wait-for-carrier-time 60
```

The **dialer in-band** Command

The **dialer in-band** command is used for asynchronous dial interfaces only. ISDN uses the D channel for call setup, or out-of-band signaling. This command is placed on the asynchronous interfaces in order for dialing to take place. The syntax is as follows:

```
Router(config-int)#dialer in-band
```

It takes no arguments.

The **dialer hold-queue** Command

The hold queue is exactly what it seems. The **dialer hold-queue** command establishes a queue in which interesting packets are held during the establishment of a call. The queue can be configured for 1 to 100 packets. The use of the hold queue has little impact for asynchronous links that can take 30 to 40 seconds to establish the call. In this case, if the application sending the packet is waiting for an acknowledgement, it will probably have timed the packet out. However, a hold queue could be useful in the ISDN world, where setup times are generally less than two seconds. The syntax to create the queue is

```
Router(config-int)#Dialer hold-queue packets
```

The **dialer rotarygroup** Command

Dialer rotary groups allow a logical set of commands to be associated with a group of interfaces. This arrangement is similar to the use of dialer interfaces, only in a reverse fashion. By placing an interface into a rotary group, the interface will use the command structure associated with the interface dialer. In this fashion, multiple physical interfaces can point to a single interface dialer for configuration information.

The use of the interface dialer takes on a dual role here. When using the interface dialer for outbound calling, the dialer interface points to a pool of physical interfaces to use for dial-out. In this case the physical interfaces accept their configuration details from the dialer interface.

In the case of the rotary group, the dialer interface is configured to supply the command structure for a group of interfaces, and the interfaces point to the dialer interface using the **dialer rotary-group** *group-number* command.

Troubleshooting And Verification

The **show** and **debug** commands to verify connectivity were listed earlier in the chapter and include:

➤ **DEBUG ISDN Q921**—Shows the Datalink layer conversation between the router and the switch. This is a very chatty debug, but it shows that a discussion is ongoing.

➤ **DEBUG ISDN Q931**—Displays the network layer conversation over the D channel as the call is set up or torn down. Remember that the conversation displayed is strictly between the router and the CO switch to which the router is connected.

➤ **SHOW INTERFACE BRI 0**—Displays the D channel information associated with the BRI. The following is an example output from this command:

```
BRI0 is up, line protocol is up (spoofing)
  Hardware is BRI
  Internet address is 10.140.0.1/24
  MTU 1500 bytes, BW 64 Kbit, DLY 20000 usec, rely 255/255,
    load 1/255
  Encapsulation PPP, loopback not set
  Last input 00:00:00, output 00:00:00, output hang never
  Last clearing of "show interface" counters never
  Input queue: 0/75/0 (size/max/drops); Total output drops: 0
  Queueing strategy: weighted fair
  Output queue: 0/64/0 (size/threshold/drops)
    Conversations  0/1 (active/max active)
    Reserved Conversations 0/0 (allocated/max allocated)
  5 minute input rate 0 bits/sec, 0 packets/sec
  5 minute output rate 0 bits/sec, 0 packets/sec
    1763 packets input, 8983 bytes, 0 no buffer
    Received 0 broadcasts, 0 runts, 0 giants
    0 input errors, 0 CRC, 0 frame, 0 overrun, 0 ignored, 0 abort
    1761 packets output, 8967 bytes, 0 underruns
    0 output errors, 0 collisions, 5 interface resets
    0 output buffer failures, 0 output buffers swapped out
    3 carrier transitions
```

➤ **SHOW INTERFACE BRI 0 1 2**—Displays the B channel information associated with the BRI. In the following example, both B channels (1 and 2) are displayed for physical interface BRI0. The example output for this command is shown here:

```
BCRANrouter#sh int bri0 1
BRI0:1 is down, line protocol is down
  Hardware is BRI
  MTU 1500 bytes, BW 64 Kbit, DLY 20000 usec, rely 255/255,
    load 1/255
  Encapsulation PPP, loopback not set, keepalive set (10 sec)
  LCP Closed
  Closed: IPCP, CDP
```

```
Last input never, output never, output hang never
Last clearing of "show interface" counters never
Input queue: 0/75/0 (size/max/drops); Total output drops: 0
Queueing strategy: weighted fair
Output queue: 0/64/0 (size/threshold/drops)
   Conversations  0/0 (active/max active)
   Reserved Conversations 0/0 (allocated/max allocated)
5 minute input rate 0 bits/sec, 0 packets/sec
5 minute output rate 0 bits/sec, 0 packets/sec
   0 packets input, 0 bytes, 0 no buffer
   Received 0 broadcasts, 0 runts, 0 giants
   0 input errors, 0 CRC, 0 frame, 0 overrun, 0 ignored, 0 abort
   0 packets output, 0 bytes, 0 underruns
   0 output errors, 0 collisions, 5 interface resets
   0 output buffer failures, 0 output buffers swapped out
   0 carrier transitions
```

The key issue here is that when the command **show interface BRI0** is used, output shows the D channel as line protocol is up (spoofing). This condition is necessary because the protocol must be up for the router to maintain the route information associated with this interface. To see if a call is actually in progress, you need the B channel information.

 You obtain D channel information using the **show interface BRI0** command without any arguments. To obtain B channel information, add the B channel of interest as an argument to the **show** command.

Digital Subscriber Link (DSL)

This section is provided for the specific use of those candidates who will be taking the CMTD exam. The section on DSL was removed from the BCRAN course and, according to Cisco, will be added to another course in the future. The treatment of DSL was only cursory in the CMTD class and will likely be expanded in a future course. Cisco has a broad range of DSL products at this point, but only its 90i was presented in the courseware. It is assumed that in a later release of courseware that the DSL product line will be given more exposure. Because the treatment of DSL was superficial, the understanding of the technology and concepts were the focus points on the exam.

In a nutshell, DSL is nothing more than a new modem technology. The modulation technique drives high data rates over the telephone companies' unused frequencies. It's similar to a doggie whistle—Rover can hear it, but you can't. DSL uses high frequency (greater than 4400 Hz, up to 1 MHz) to signal over the existing copper pair that supplies voice communication. Because it's unde-tectable to the human ear, the signaling can take place without disrupting the regular telephone service. The generic DSL implementation is shown in Figure 7.9.

From the home user, the existing copper line to the Central Office is used to carry the high frequency DSL signal. The splitter at the CO redirects the higher frequencies to a data network. The normal voice frequencies are sent to the voice switch. The following characteristics of DSL are presented in the CMTD courseware:

➤ Delivers high data rates

➤ Copper condition, distance, and crosstalk affect DSL performance

➤ Diverts data traffic off the telephone company switch

These three characteristics are somewhat disjointed. True, DSL will deliver higher data rates due to the frequency used. The copper condition is a limiting factor, however, because some of the existing copper can't reliably support the higher frequencies. Some estimates say that only 20 percent of the existing copper last mile can handle DSL. But that statistic is somewhat insignificant

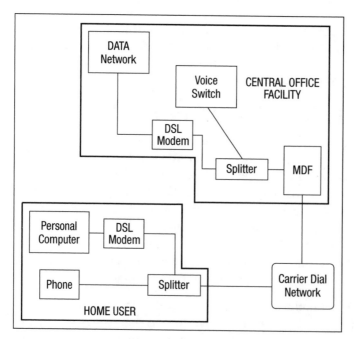

Figure 7.9 DSL implementation.

from the user's point of view. The fact that DSL will offload the telephone company switch is significant only to the telco. I pay for my telephone connection on a monthly basis, and I expect service. The fact that my connection to the Internet is now diverted to a data network prior to crossing the telephone CO switch is irrelevant to me. However, this is a large bonus to the provider.

The fact that my Internet connection terminates at the CO allows the telco to control my selection of providers for Internet access. It also lessens my impact on the CO switch for Internet service provider (ISP) access. DSL allows the telco to exact charges twice for the use of the same copper pair running into its facility. Lily Tomlin would be proud: We are the phone company.

The fact that DSL can provide high bandwidth capacity for the last mile is significant when compared to ISDN. Many people believe that DSL will be the demise of ISDN, but this is yet to be proven. No current standard exists for DSL equipment, and the service areas are spotty at best. High bandwidth DSL is generally available in high-density areas where the copper infrastructure is relatively new. However there are many flavors of DSL technology. Therefore, saying that DSL is available doesn't specifically say what flavor is being offered.

The flavors of DSL are as follows:

➤ *IDSL*—ISDN DSL. Distance limitation is 18,000 ft from the CO. Speeds are 56, 64, and 128Kbps.

➤ *SDSL*—Single Line DSL. Distance limitation is 9,000 ft from the CO. Speeds up to 768Kbps, symmetrical.

➤ *HDSL*—High Data Rate DSL. Distance limitation is 12,000 ft from the CO. Speeds from 384Kbps to 2,000Kbps, symmetrical.

➤ *ADSL*—Asymmetric DSL. Distance limitation is 18,000 ft from the CO. Speeds up to 8,000Kbps downstream and 640Kbps upstream.

➤ *RADSL*—Rate Adaptive DSL. Distance limitation is 18,000 ft from the CO. Speed adapts to line condition.

➤ *VDSL*—Very High Data Rate DSL. Distance is 4,500 ft from the CO. Speeds up to 52,000Kbps downstream, and 2,000Kbps upstream.

The speeds and distance limitations for each of the DSL technologies are considered fair game on the CMTD exam. Take care to remember the speeds and distances for each variation.

IDSL

IDSL is a leased-line variation of ISDN. There is no dial and no D channel signaling: It's a point-to-point connection to the CO, where the termination of the link is on a dedicated device. The CMTD courseware presented the 90i as an add-in card for a channel bank that could terminate up to four connections. The advantage is that it uses in-place ISDN equipment so it would be less expensive to deploy. The main disadvantage is the limited speed that would be available.

SDSL

SDSL is an extension of HDSL over a single wire pair. However, it is of limited use because of the distance limitation to the CO facility. The higher data rates that can be achieved are attractive and may become a solution for small business use where moderate speed DSL is a fit.

HDSL

The main drawback to HDSL is that it requires two pair. This may not be a dramatic limitation as HDSL continues to become a viable alternative to a T1 leased line. The driving issues will be the cost and availability. The reduction of the overhead to the CO switch facility should be attractive enough for the telcos to position this competitively.

ADSL

The critical issue with ADSL is the new and as-yet-unproven equipment. ADSL has been touted as the emerging DSL standard, and rightly so. The asymmetry of the line would be attractive to an end user whose main interest is in the download speed, because most uploads are merely requests for data. One of the critical pieces to the ADSL equipment puzzle is the Digital Subscriber Link to Asynchronous Transfer Mode (DSL-ATM) multiplexer (DSLAM). The DSLAM concentrates the remote ADSL connections for delivery to what the Cisco courseware calls the *back-haul* network.

RADSL

It has been predicted by some that Rate Adaptive DSL will likely be the next generation of ADSL. The fact that the data rate will adapt to the line conditions is an advantage to the circuit provider. The end user who is paying for the circuit could perceive this as a disadvantage: "What price do I pay for an unknown bandwidth?" If RADSL is to be the replacement to ADSL, the change will likely be driven as much by technology as by marketplace perception.

VDSL

Very high data rates can be achieved with the emerging VDSL technology. The major drawback to this technology is the distance limitation to the CO facility. This technology could become very attractive to corporate clients in a high-density area.

The Future Of DSL

As DSL gains a larger foothold in today's changing market, the providers will necessarily have to provide a higher-speed network. The limiting factor for the end user today is the analog facility for the last mile and the load on the CO switch. As more and more users move to a higher-speed connection on the CO data network, the backbone will need to be enhanced to meet the demand.

The pricing for ISDN and leased-line facilities may be affected by DSL as we move forward toward a deregulated data network. The public is now more aware than ever of the technologies that are available and is demanding faster methods to surf the Web. A recent advertisement on the side of a bus read, "Tired of ISDN, too slow? Try DSL." That advertisement showed me that the American public is ready for new technology. Cisco states in its CMTD courseware that it will "support whichever technologies customers ask for." For this reason, I believe that DSL will be added into the courseware when the public has spoken.

Practice Questions

Question 1

A Basic Rate Interface is comprised of _____.

○ a. 2B + D

○ b. 2D + B

○ c. 23B + D

○ d. 23D + B

Answer a is correct. It's 2B + D, or 2 bearer channels and 1 Delta channel; therefore, answers b, c, and d are incorrect.

Question 2

An NT device can be _____. [Choose the three best answers]

❑ a. CSU

❑ b. MUX

❑ c. Repeater

❑ d. PBX

❑ e. DSU

❑ f. Router

Answers a, b, and d are correct. An NT-1 is commonly a PBX, whereas an NT-2 is a CSU or MUX. Answer c, a repeater, is a physical layer device and not germane to ISDN. Answer f, a router, can have an NT device built into it but by definition is not an NT device per se. Answer e is not correct.

Question 3

The D channel signaling during a call setup seen by the calling part would include which of the following?

○ a. **SETUP**, **NUMBER TRANSFER**, **CONNECT**, and **CONNECT ACK**

○ b. **SETUP ACK**, **CALL PROCEEDING**, **ALERTING**, and **CONNECT**

○ c. **ALERTING**, **SETUP**, **CALL PROCEEDING**, and **Q921**

○ d. **ALERTING**, **SETUP**, **CALL FORWARDING**, and **CONNECT ACK**

Answer b is correct. The terms **NUMBER TRANSFER, CALL FOR-WARDING**, and **Q921** are not D channel messages, which eliminates answers a, c, and d.

Question 4

Choose the true statement(s) given the following sample script:

```
Dialer-list 1 protocol ip list 101
Access-list 101 permit tcp any any eq ftp
!
Interface BRIO
Dialer-group 1
```

[Choose the three best answers]:

❑ a. All FTP traffic will trigger a call.

❑ b. The **dialer-group** statement will deny all packets that are not FTP.

❑ c. All packets will be sent over the link once it's established.

❑ d. The access-list will prevent Telnet traffic from triggering the call.

❑ e. Only FTP packets will be sent over this link.

Answers a, c, and d are correct. All the FTP traffic will trigger the call and once the link is up, all traffic will be allowed to flow because the dialer-group is only interested in creating the link. The access-list, because it's associated with the dialer-list, will prevent Telnet traffic to initiate the call. Answers b and e are not correct.

Question 5

> The following arguments can be used on the **dialer map** command: [Choose the two best answers]
>
> ❑ a. **name**
>
> ❑ b. **AS number**
>
> ❑ c. **system-script**
>
> ❑ d. **dialer-group**

Answers a and c are correct. The **name** and **system-script** are arguments to the dialer map command. Answers b and d are not correct.

Question 6

> The **broadcast** keyword in the **dialer map** statement allows:
>
> ○ a. All traffic destined for MAC address FFFF.FFFF.FFFF to be sent over the interface if it's up.
>
> ○ b. All traffic destined for the network address 255.255.255.255 to be sent over the interface if it's up.
>
> ○ c. All traffic for the Network layer broadcast address of the specified protocol to be sent.
>
> ○ d. All traffic to be sent if the link is up.

Answer c is correct. The **broadcast** keyword specifies that all broadcast traffic for the specified protocol in the dialer map statement will be sent. If the dialer map is for IPX, then no IP traffic will be sent, etc. Answer a is close, but only for the protocol specified in the map. If the map statement were for IPX and the FFFF.FFFF.FFFF packet was originated by an IP client, the packet would *not* be forwarded. Answers b and d are not correct.

Question 7

> Given the following interface command:
>
> Isdn caller 212-123-XXXX
>
> Which statement is true?
>
> ○ a. No calls will be accepted.
>
> ○ b. All calls for the area code 212 and exchange 123 will be accepted.
>
> ○ c. All Calls originating in the 212 area destined for the 123 exchange will be accepted.
>
> ○ d. This feature depends on the provider's configuration.

Answer d is correct. This feature is dependent upon the provider configuration. The caller number is the number as sent by the provider. Answer b, all calls for 212-123-xxxx might be correct if the telephone service provider *always* passes the area code with the number. This may seem like a picky question, but the courseware painstakingly points out the problem with this assumption in a production environment. Answers a and c are not correct.

Question 8

> The bandwidth of a BRI including the signaling channel is _____.
>
> ○ a. 64
>
> ○ b. 128
>
> ○ c. 144
>
> ○ d. 192

Answer d is correct. The candidate should note that the question asks for the bandwidth of the BRI *including* the signaling channel. This includes both B channels at 64Kbps each, plus the D channel at 16Kbps *and* the signal information which is an additional 48Kbps. (2x64) + 16 + 48 = 192. Answers a, b, and c are not correct.

Question 9

Which of the following is a true statement?

○ a. Dialer profiles eliminate the need for complex dialer map statements.

○ b. Dialer profiles can't be used for dial backup.

○ c. Dialer profiles treat BRI interfaces as a single interface.

○ d. Dialer profiles can't use dialer map statements.

Answer a is correct. Dialer profiles eliminate the need for complex dialer map statements. It isn't common for a dialer profile to use **dialer map** statements; however, it is possible. Answers b, c, and d are not correct.

Question 10

Which of the following statements describes DSL? [Choose the two best answers]

❑ a. It is another digital option for the last mile.

❑ b. It can be affected by crosstalk.

❑ c. It reduces the load on the CO switch.

❑ d. It uses out-of-band signaling for call setup.

❑ e. It requires a DSLAM at the provider site.

Answer b is correct. DSL can be affected by crosstalk because it uses the higher frequencies and may be bundled at the collection facility for the provider. It will also reduce the load on the CO switch because it is split off prior to reaching the voice network. Answers a, c, d, and e are not correct.

Question 11

A leaf node is a network that:

○ a. Is connected to a branch router that is connected to a core

○ b. Is connected in series to a branch router

○ c. Is connected to a core network with no other routes available

○ d. Is connected using DDR

Answer c is correct. This nomenclature is used by Cisco to refer to a stub network. Both "stub" and "leaf node" carry the same meaning. Answers a, b, and d are not correct.

Question 12

The default direction for the **dialer load-threshold** command is:

○ a. Inbound

○ b. Outbound

○ c. Either

○ d. None

Answer b is correct. While answer a, inbound, is not correct, answer c would be a good choice if the traffic pattern were not known and PPP was wanted. It is especially important to be aware that when connected to an ISP the default is outbound, since inbound traffic is likely to be what the user will want PPP to trigger on.

Question 13

When the following information is displayed from the **show interface** command:

```
BRI0 is up, line protocol is up (spoofing)
```

Which statement is true?

○ a. The BRI0 interface is spoofing IPX.

○ b. The route table maintains the interface address.

○ c. The BRI0 interface is not connected.

○ d. All processing on the interface is suspended.

Answer b is correct. The BRI0 interface may or may not be connected. The **BRI0 is up, line protocol is up (spoofing)** is a D channel message. Answers a, c, and d are not correct.

Question 14

> The distance limitation for IDSL is _____ feet and the maximum speed
> is _____Kbps.
>
> ○ a. 18,000; 64
> ○ b. 18,000;128
> ○ c. 24,000; 64
> ○ d. 24,000; 128

Answer b is correct. IDSL is ISDN DSL, which allows for two B channels at 64Kbps each for a maximum of 128Kbps transmission speed. Therefore, answers a and c are not correct. 18,000 feet is, by definition, the distance from the Central Office facility the user can be. Therefore, answer d is not correct.

Question 15

> The 90i can terminate up to _____ IDSL connections at the CO.
>
> ○ a. 12
> ○ b. 24
> ○ c. 8
> ○ d. 4

Answer d is correct . Multiple 90i can be put into a D4 channel bank, but each card can terminate only 4 ISDN DSL connections, so answers a, b, and c are not correct.

Question 16

Datalink B channel signaling can be_____. [Choose the three best answers]

❏ a. PPP

❏ b. LAPD

❏ c. LAPB

❏ d. X.25

❏ e. HDLC

❏ f. CSMA/CD

❏ g. SDLC

Answers a, c, and e are correct. PPP, LAPB, and HDLC can be used over the B channel. FR encapsulation can also be used, but it isn't listed here. Answers b, d, f, and g are not correct.

Question 17

To determine the physical layer status of an ISDN link, the command _____ is used.

The answer is **show isdn status**.

Question 18

Debug Q931 shows:

◯ a. The B channel conversation between the router and the local switch

◯ b. The D channel conversation between the router and the local switch

◯ c. The D channel conversation between the local switch and the remote switch to set up the call

◯ d. The B channel conversation between the remote and local switches

Answer b is correct. Q931 is the D channel conversation for the router to connect to a local telephone switch and request a call to be set up, so answers a and d are not correct. It is important to remember that the router can speak only to the local switch, and not to the remote end over a D channel. Therefore, answer c is not correct.

Question 19

> The options for line coding on a T1 are _____. [Choose the three best answers]
>
> ❑ a. SF
>
> ❑ b. AMI
>
> ❑ c. CRC4
>
> ❑ d. B8ZS
>
> ❑ e. HDB3
>
> ❑ f. ESF

Answers b, d, and e are correct. Answers a, c, and f are framing options.

Question 20

> Which of the following correctly defines a static route from router B's BRI0 port to the 124.5.6.0/24 network on router A's Ethernet interface, if router A's dial number is 555-1212?
>
> ○ a. **Ip route 124.5.6.0 255.255.0.0 bri0 120**
>
> ○ b. **Ip route 124.5.6.0 255.255.255.0 bri0 130**
>
> ○ c. **Ip route 124.5.6.0 0.0.0.255 bri0**
>
> ○ d. **Ip route 124.5.6.0 255.255.255.0 555-1212**

Answer b is correct. Admittedly, the phone number and the administrative distance aren't relevant to this answer; however, this is the only correct solution available because answers a, c, and d are incorrect based on the information given.

Question 21

To associate interesting traffic with an interface for dial purposes, the command is _____.

- ○ a. **dialer-list**
- ○ b. **dialer-group**
- ○ c. **dialer-interface**
- ○ d. **dialer-map**

Answer b is correct. Answer a is incorrect because the **dialer-list** command *defines* what is interesting. The **dialer-group** command *activates* the list on the interface. Answers c and d are not correct.

Question 22

Choose the **dialer map** statement that is most correct:

- ○ a. **dialer map ip 133.2.3.0 255.255.255.0 name SiteA 5551000**
- ○ b. **dialer map protocol ip 133.2.3.4 name SiteA 5551000**
- ○ c. **dialer-map protocol ip 133.2.3.4 name SiteA broadcast 5551000**
- ○ d. **dialer map ip 133.2.3.4 name SiteA 5551000**

Answer d is correct. This question could be tricky if you aren't comfortable with the **dialer map** command. The **map** command isn't hyphenated, there is no **protocol** keyword, and the IP address is the next-hop address without a mask. Answers a, b, and c are not correct.

Question 23

In order for statically defined routes using a next hop address as the destination to be included in the update table for RIP or IGRP, which routing protocol configuration command is used?

- ○ a. Propagate static
- ○ b. Redistribute static
- ○ c. Static update
- ○ d. No command is required

Answer b is correct. Routing Information Protocol (RIP) and Internet Gateway Routing Protocol (IGRP) must be told under the router configuration mode to include (or *redistribute*) the static routes defined. Answers a, c, and d are not correct.

Question 24

The **system-script** command is for:

- ○ a. Creating the connection to a remote system
- ○ b. Logging into a remote system
- ○ c. Setting the modem parameters
- ○ d. Declaring the dial string to be used for a connection

Answer b is correct. This is specific to the term *system-script*. The creation, setting of the modem, and declaration of the dial string would take place in a *dialer-script*, so answers a, c, and d are not correct.

Question 25

A DSLAM device does which of the following? [Choose the two best answers]

- ❑ a. Connects to an ATM network
- ❑ b. Multiplexes ADSL signaling
- ❑ c. Converts amplitude signal changes to DSL signaling
- ❑ d. Is used for IDSL
- ❑ e. Is a 90i, for example
- ❑ f. Is a high-priority D channel for multiple PRIs

Answer b is correct. A DSLAM concentrates or multiplexes remote ADSL connections for delivery to an ATM network. Answers a, c, d, e, and f are not correct.

Need To Know More?

 Cisco Press. *Cisco IOS Dial Solutions*. Cisco Press. ISBN 1-57870-055-8. This is a resource book not designed as a "good read", but as a useful command reference. It has many examples and reference tables in one location.

 Cisco Systems. Documentation CD. Any recent version of the CD has much background information on the various technologies discussed here. The search engine will allow the user to look specifically at white paper information in lieu of a command search. This gives the user a quick way to find a discussion of the search issue, not just the command to use it.

 Visit the official Cisco Web site at **www.cisco.com** for information and links to all technologies employed by Cisco.

Dial-On-Demand Interfaces

8

Terms you'll need to understand:

√ Profile

√ Map class

√ Buffering

√ Rotary group

Techniques you'll need to master:

√ Configuring Dial-on-Demand Routing (DDR)

√ Configuring Dialer profiles

√ Configuring Dialer interfaces

This chapter introduces the concept of dial up configuration; how you can configure a router for efficient dial-up and dial-out communication and several options you have.

Dialer Profiles

A dialer profile separates configuration components from each other. Some items (such as physical interface characteristics) reside in one type of configuration, whereas others (such as a phone number) reside in another configuration. This arrangement allows for mixing and matching of configuration components depending on the need.

Dialer profiles allow fairly complex dial-up networks to have more flexibility in what they support. Gone are the days of mapping a single IP address or phone number to a serial port and using that interface to call only that one location. In order for this flexibility to take place, though, you need to define some new configurations.

When using a dialer profile to make calls, your options for encapsulation become more limited. You have the option of using Point-to-Point Protocol (PPP) or Cisco High Level Data Link Control (HDLC). Dialer profiles do allow more flexibility when it comes to Integrated Services Digital Network (ISDN), though. You can set different call properties to different ISDN B channels, use different encapsulation types per B channel, put two B channels into separate dialer pools, and even configure B channels with separate network addresses. Entering the command **interface dialer #** creates a dialer rotary group on the router.

Dialer Interface

A *dialer interface* is a logical interface that contains configuration information for a specific dial-up location. The dialer interface can be configured for most settings that would normally go on a serial port. This interface is where you configure an IP or other Layer 3 address, encapsulation type, compression, dialer maps, dialer string, remote device name, PPP authentication format, dialer list number, dialer, group number, dialer pool number, dialer idle timeout settings, and—on asynchronous serial devices—a dialer in-band.

You can use all of the commands listed in Table 8.1 in **interface dialer** *number* configuration mode unless otherwise specified.

```
Here is an example dialer interface configuration for dialer
interface 1:   ip address 192.168.4.9 255.255.255.252
    encapsulation ppp
    dialer remote-name corporate
    ppp authentication chap
    dialer-group 5
```

```
dialer pool 3
dialer string 5551212
dialer hold-queue 20
```

Table 8.1   Dialer interface commands.

Command	Explanation
ip address *address subnet-mask*	Puts the specified IP address on the dialer interface.
dialer remote-name *name*	States the remote device name that the router is calling. This command is used to determine authentication.
dialer string *string* **class** *map-class*	Specifies the phone number of the remote location. The **class** part of the command is optional and refers to a map class (covered later in this chapter).
dialer load-threshold *load-value* **<inbound I outbound I either>**	In brief, the **dialer load-threshold** command specifies the load level at which an additional line should be brought up in multilink. The *load-value* is in a range from 1 to 255, with 255 being 100 percent link utilization.
dialer hold-queue *number*	When dialing, there is a delay until connection, but no delay in arriving data. This command sets up a set of buffers to hold packets. The *number* value is in a range from 0 through 100 packets.
dialer pool *number*	The dialer pool is a group of physical interfaces that the dialer interface should use when making a call. Although a physical interface can be a member of multiple pools, you want a dialer interface pointing to one pool.
dialer-group *number*	Specifies which **dialer-list** command will be used to determine interesting traffic.
dialer map *protocol next-hop-address* **<name** *remote-device-name>* **<speed** *56 I 64>* **<broadcast>** **<modem-script** *script-name>* **<system-script** *script-name>* *<phone-number-of-remote-device(ISDN-subaddress)>*	A fairly complex animal, but allows for a lot of flexibility when using dialer interfaces. The original **dialer string** command allowed for only one location to be called, whereas the **dialer map** command allows for multiple calling locations per interface. The **protocol** configuration wants a Layer 3 protocol like Internet Protocol (IP) or Internetwork Packet Exchange (IPX) followed by the address of the device you're connecting to. Every other command is optional. You use the **name**

(continued)

Table 8.1	Dialer interface commands (continued).
Command	**Explanation**
	option when using PPP authentication. Use speed when selecting between 56Kbps and 64Kbps ISDN channels. The broadcast option is needed to send broadcast packets, such as Routing Information Protocol (RIP) routing updates, across the wire. The modem-script and system-script commands allow for custom scripts to be used per connection. If you want to dial out, you also need to put in the remote device's phone number. The ISDN subaddress is also optional; this command must be last in the dialer map statement.
ppp multilink	Establishes this interface as a member of a multilink relationship with other circuits.
**ppp authentication <pap	chap>**	States that when calling this location, the specified authentication type will be used.

Dialer Pools

A *dialer pool* is a group of physical interfaces. You need to configure each physical interface you want to be a member of the pool with a pool ID and priority information. Once an interface is a member of a pool, a dialer interface that uses the pool will use the physical interface that has the highest priority for an outgoing call. Use the command

```
dialer pool-member number priority priority
```

to configure a dialer pool in Interface configuration mode.

An interface may belong to multiple pools. If a pool contains multiple interfaces, you need to configure a priority level for the physical interface. The highest-level available interface will be used on the next call. If you do not assign a priority, then interfaces will be used in the order that they appear in the configuration.

The following example shows two Basic Rate Interface (BRI) interfaces that have each been configured to be members of two dialer pools:

```
Router(config)#interface BRI 0
Router(config-if)#dialer pool-member 1 priority 200
```

```
Router(config-if)#dialer pool-member 2 priority 150
Router(config)#interface BRI 1
Router(config-if)#dialer pool-member 1 priority 150
Router(config-if)#dialer pool-member 2 priority 200
```

Map Classes

A map class is a very useful part of a dialer profile. Although map classes are optional components, they can be used to specify different Layer 1 characteristics for a call on a per-destination basis. These commands, shown in Table 8.2, tend to revolve around connection characteristics.

Table 8.2   Map class commands.

Command	Explanation
map-class dialer *class-name*	Creates a map class with the specified unique name and puts you in map class configuration mode.
dialer idle-timeout *seconds*	Tells the router when to kill the link when a call is in progress but no interesting traffic is crossing the line. By default, the router will drop the line 120 seconds after the last piece of interesting traffic crosses.
dialer fast-idle *seconds*	Kicks in if no interesting traffic is crossing a link and packets are waiting to use the interface to call a different destination. Rather than waiting two minutes for the idle timeout timer to expire, the fast idle timer activates only when there is contention for an interface. It also expires much more quickly; the default value of the timer is 20 seconds.
dialer wait-for-carrier-time *seconds*	Useful on analog lines, because it tells the router how long to wait for a carrier signal. When used in conjunction with an asynchronous interface, the timer includes the time needed for the chat script to run. The default is 30 seconds, but Cisco recommends 60 seconds on asynchronous interfaces.
dialer isdn speed *speed*	Gives you a choice between 56Kbps and 64Kbps when making a connection via ISDN. Check with your service provider to make sure it supports 64Kbps ISDN channels.

Incoming Calls With Rotary Groups

When you have multiple lines and only one phone number for incoming calls, you need to use a *rollover* or *hunt group*. In the Cisco world we call them *rotary groups*. This is the same concept that many companies use for customer service: Call one number, and the next available person will pick up the phone. We use the same concept here, except for data calls. You can use this technique if you have lots of people calling from outside your organization—for example, if you're with an Internet Service Provider (ISP). Give your customers one number that can reach a large number of modems, and the next available one will answer.

Rotary groups can also be used for outgoing calls, but they have largely been replaced with dialer profiles to provide greater flexibility. With incoming calls, though, you have a little more predictability—most low-speed traffic is done across analog lines, and you can often dictate settings to people calling in. You don't have to worry much about different switch types and speeds for ISDN, because this technique is most often used for analog dial-up.

Configuring Rotary Groups

When configuring a rotary group, you need to specify a dialer interface as well as tell the router which physical interfaces will participate in the hunt group. You do this with the **interface dialer** *number* command and the **dialer rotary-group** *number* command, as explained in Table 8.3.

When configuring a rotary group for outgoing calls, you'll need to configure dialer strings on the dialer interface. Don't forget to put the **dialer inband** command on interfaces with modem to turn on DDR.

Table 8.3 Rotary group commands.	
Command	**Explanation**
Router(config-if)#dialer rotary-group *number*	Tells a physical interface that it's going to participate in the hunt group defined by the dialer interface with the specified number.
Router(config)#interface dialer *number*	From Global configuration mode, sets up a dialer interface of the specified number. The number of the rotary group and the dialer interface need to be the same. The number range is from 0 through 255.

Configuration Example And Explanation

Figure 8.1 illustrates a WAN design to connect from one router out four BRI lines to six locations.

Use the following Global configuration mode commands:

```
dialer-list 1 protocol ip permit
ip route 20.1.1.0 255.255.255.0 10.1.2.1
ip route 20 1.2.0 255.255.255.0 10.1.3.1
ip route 21.1.2.0 255.255.255.0 11.1.2.1
ip route 21.1.3.0 255.255.255.0 11.1.3.1
ip route 22.1.2.0 255.255.255.0 12.1.2.1
ip route 22.1.3.0 255.255.255.0 12.1.3.1
username router1 password cisco
username router2 password cisco
username router3 password cisco
username router4 password cisco
username router5 password cisco
username router6 password cisco
```

The **dialer list** command tells the router what traffic is considered interesting. In this case, all IP traffic is interesting and will bring up a link pointing to

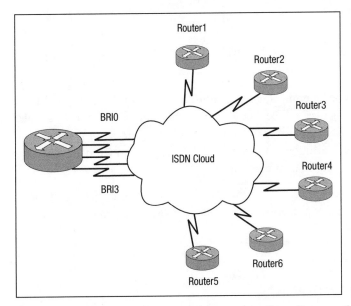

Figure 8.1   BRI WAN design with more locations than available interfaces.

dialer list 1. You may also specify an access list to get more granular. You need to make sure this command exists or your interface will not activate.

The **ip route** statements tell the router that in order to get to the specified network, you need to send packets to the specified IP address. This is a remote address.

The **username** and **password** statement state that when the router calls a remote device with a hostname equal to the username in the example code, it needs to use the associated password.

Next we add routing to the router and include the static routes in our routing updates:

```
router rip
network 10.0.0.0
network 11.0.0.0
network 12.0.0.0
redistribute static
```

This code allows other devices to know where to send packets, to us, if they need to get packets to the remote networks. The **redistribute static** will put the static routes in our routing tables that are distributed to other routers.

We configure the physical interfaces using the following lines:

```
interface bri 0
encapsulation ppp
dialer-pool member 1 priority 200
ppp multilink
```

Encapsulation, pool membership, and multilink need to be configured here, whereas everything else will be configured on the dialer interfaces. The **dialer pool** statement tells the router that this interface is a member of dialer pool 1; and because it has a higher priority than the other interface in pool 1, this interface will be used first for dial out.

The following code does the same thing as the previous code on this interface, except this interface is a member of two pools:

```
interface bri 1
encapsulation ppp
dialer-pool member 1 priority 150
dialer-pool member 2 priority 200
ppp multilink
```

The interface has a high priority on one pool and a medium priority on the other. The way we're configuring the pools means that this interface is the primary for pool 2 and the secondary for pool 1.

The next two interface configurations are very similar to the previous one:

```
interface bri 2
encapsulation ppp
dialer-pool member 2 priority 200
dialer-pool member 3 priority 150
ppp multilink

interface bri 3
encapsulation ppp
dialer-pool member 3 priority 200
ppp multilink
```

The dialer interfaces get most of the configuration information:

```
interface dialer 1
ip address 10.1.1.1 255.255.0.0
ppp authentication chap
dialer map ip 10.1.2.1 name router1 dial-string 5551212
dialer map ip 10.1.3.1 name router2 dial-string 5551313
dialer-group 1
dialer pool 1
```

We need to configure IP addressing on this interface; we can either configure the interface so that the network overlaps with both destinations, or we can configure two IP addresses and specify one as a secondary address.

The code sets up Challenge Handshake Authentication Protocol (CHAP) authentication, specifies that this interface will use physical interfaces that are a member of dialer pool 1 to make our calls, and specifies dialer group 1 to determine interesting traffic (see dialer list 1, earlier).

The **dialer map** statements allow us to call multiple sites from one interface by specifying a remote IP address, the remote router name used for authentication, and the phone number we need to call to get there.

The final two dialer interface configurations are similar to the first:

```
interface dialer 2
ip address 11.1.1.1 255.255.0.0
ppp authentication chap
dialer map ip 11.1.2.1 name router3 dial-string 5551414
```

```
dialer map ip 11.1.3.1 name router4 dial-string 5551515
dialer-group 1
dialer pool 2

interface dialer 3
ip address 12.1.1.1 255.255.0.0
ppp authentication chap
dialer map ip 12.1.2.1 name router5 dial-string 5551616
dialer map ip 12.1.3.1 name router6 dial-string 5551717
dialer-group 1
dialer pool 3
```

Practice Questions

Question 1

> When configuring a rotary group, you need to specify an interface and inter-
> face number that other interfaces will be members of. What type of interface
> collects the multiple interfaces?
>
> ○ a. Serial
> ○ b. Dialer
> ○ c. Rotary
> ○ d. BRI

Answer b is correct. A dialer interface is responsible for collecting all physical
interfaces that the rotary group will use. Serial and BRI interfaces are physical
interfaces that the rotary group can use. There is no such animal as a rotary
interface. Therefore, answers a, c, and d are incorrect.

Question 2

> The maximum value for a dialer group number is:
>
> ○ a. 2
> ○ b. 16
> ○ c. 64
> ○ d. 255

Answer d is correct. The range goes up to 255. Answers a, b, and c are incorrect.

Question 3

> What command enables DDR on a serial interface?
>
> ○ a. **dialer inband**
> ○ b. **dialer async**
> ○ c. **dialer outband**
> ○ d. **dialer inout**

Answer a is correct. The **dialer inband** statement needs to be placed on synchronous and asynchronous serial interfaces to tell the interface that it needs to interact with an external device. The **dialer inout** command is used to enable both incoming and outgoing calls on an interface while the other two aren't commands. Therefore, answers b, c, and d are incorrect.

Question 4

When an interface is in use and a packet stream needs to make a call, it waits until an interface times out. What command speeds up the timeout value when there is contention for an interface?

- O a. **dialer wait-for-carrier**
- O b. **dialer fast-idle**
- O c. **dialer idle-timeout**
- O d. None of the above

Answer b is correct. The **dialer fast-idle** command tells the router to use a different timeout value when there is contention for an interface. The **dialer idle-timeout** command specified the default timeout value of an interface, not the sped up value. The **dialer wait-for-carrier** command is actually an abbreviation of the **dialer wait-for-carrier-time** command, which states how long the router should wait for a dial tone. Therefore, answers a, c, and d are incorrect.

Question 5

Dialer profiles consist of what three major elements? [Choose the three best answers]

- ❏ a. Map class
- ❏ b. Dialer interface
- ❏ c. Dialer pool
- ❏ d. Dialer string

Answers a, b, and c are correct. The dialer string is a part of the dialer interface and specifies the phone number to be dialed. The other three options are elements of a dialer profile. Therefore, answer d is incorrect.

Question 6

Dialer profiles accept which types of encapsulation? [Choose the two best answers]

❑ a. SDLC

❑ b. PPP

❑ c. X25

❑ d. Frame Relay

❑ e. HDLC

Answers b and e are correct. Cisco HDLC and PPP are supported encapsulation types for dialer profiles. The others are not supported by dialer profiles. Therefore, answers a, c, and d are incorrect.

Question 7

What command is used to make an interface participate in a dialer pool?

○ a. **dialer pool-member** (at the interface)

○ b. **dialer pool** (at the interface)

○ c. **dialer interface** (at the pool)

○ d. **dialer priority** (at the pool)

Answer a is correct. The **dialer pool-member** command is configured at the interface and tells the interface to participate in a pool. The **dialer pool** command tells the dialer interface what pool to use when selecting an interface. The dialer pool does not contain configurable options, so answers b, c, and d are incorrect.

Question 8

While a conversation is waiting for an interface, the packets need to be buffered. What command sets up the holding area for the packets?

○ a. **dialer buffer**

○ b. **dialer queue**

○ c. **dialer fast-idle queue**

○ d. **dialer hold-queue**

Answer d is correct. The **dialer hold-queue** command tells the router how much buffer space to set aside for waiting packets. The other commands don't exist; therefore, answers a, b, and c are incorrect.

Question 9

The maximum number of packets that may be queued is:

○ a. 25
○ b. 50
○ c. 64
○ d. 100
○ e. 128
○ f. 255

Answer d is correct. You may store up to 100 waiting packets if the router is so configured. Therefore, answers a, b, c, e, and f are incorrect.

Question 10

The default value for the fast-idle timer is:

○ a. 10 seconds
○ b. 20 seconds
○ c. 30 seconds
○ d. 60 seconds

Answer b is correct. The default is 20 seconds. Therefore, answers a, c, and d are incorrect.

Need To Know More?

 Cisco IOS Dial Solutions by Cisco Systems is a book that contains the same info found on the Web site but many people find it easier to digest. Beware, it's over 1,500 pages and retails for $70.

 The Cisco Web site contains additional information regarding configuring dial-on-demand interfaces. Check out **www.cisco.com/univercd/cc/td/doc/product/software/ios113ed/113ed_cr/dial_c/dcprt4/index.htm**.

Configuration
And Features Of
The 700 Series Router

Terms you'll need to understand:

√ Profile

√ Small office/home office (SOHO)

√ Remote office (RO)

√ Dynamic Host Configuration Protocol (DHCP)

√ Port address translation (PAT)

Techniques you'll need to master:

√ Configuring the 700 for connection to an Internet
Service Provider (ISP)

√ Configuring the 700 for routing in an IP and IPX
environment

√ Configuring the 700 as a DHCP server or helper

The 700 series router was originally a product offering from a company that Cisco purchased in the last three years. The purchase gave Cisco two ISDN products targeted for the telecommuter and small office/home office (SOHO) markets: the 700 series router (a Basic Rate Interface [BRI] product) and the 900 series (a Primary Rate Interface [PRI] product). The PRI product line was discontinued, and the 700 product line has been marketed in the SOHO arena. The primary reason for the discontinuation of the 900 product was that it competed internally with other models of the Cisco product line and offered no clear advantage to other proven models. The 700 series provides BRI connectivity, which also targets the telecommuter market. The 700 product is compatible with the full Cisco router product line; however, it doesn't use the same command line structure for configuration.

The command-line interface for the 700 router has been likened to the Cisco switch product line command interface by some, but they aren't the same. They both use **set** as the main command verb; however, the similarity ends there.

The 700 offers a fixed configuration product that has a BRI port and an Ethernet port, thus allowing the user to take advantage of the higher-speed Integrated Services Digital Network (ISDN) for Wide Area Networking (WAN) connectivity and providing the Local Area Networking (LAN) interface for connectivity. A more detailed discussion of the port-level benefits and features is presented later in this chapter.

For those who are familiar with the Internetwork Operating System (IOS) command set, the 700 command language can be less than intuitive. The good news is that little command syntax associated with the 700 is on the CMTD and BCRAN tests. The major thrust is to understand the concept of configuration.

The BCRAN and CMTD classes are the only ones that use the 700s in the labs. To its credit, Cisco didn't put detailed questions on the exam concerning the syntax and configuration of the 700 series. Instead, the focus of the exam questions is on the positioning of the device in the market, the features available, and the use of profiles to control the connections. Remember, the SOHO and telecommuter communities are the target markets for the 700 series router.

700 Features

The 700 series router can be described by looking at its three feature sets: networking; routing and WAN; and ISDN and telephony features.

Networking

The 700 offers full Point-to-Point Protocol (PPP) support, which includes Password Authentication Protocol (PAP), Challenge Handshake Authentication Protocol (CHAP), and Multilink PPP. You can add data compression by purchasing an upgraded software feature set. The 700 can also function as a Dynamic Host Configuration Protocol (DHCP) server or relay agent, and will perform port address translation (PAT).

Routing And WAN

Internet Protocol (IP) and Internet Packet eXchange Protocol for Novell (IPX) are the only protocols supported on the device; however, the 700 can function as a bridge for any other protocol. Routing Information Protocol (RIP) v1 and RIPv2 are supported for IP, and RIP for IPX is also supported. Cisco's snapshot routing features are supported. Dial-on-Demand Routing (DDR) and Bandwidth-on-Demand (BOD) features are also available on the platform.

ISDN And Telephony

The 700 series supplies tone for the telephone service on plain old telephone support (POTS) interfaces. The models that end in an *even* number provide the built-in Network Termination 1 interface (NT1). The models that end in an *odd* number provide an S/T interface, and the customer must supply the NT1 device. In the United States, this built-in NT1 provides a complete solution. The NT1 in the international community, however, is a telephone company device—hence the need for the different models. The S and T have no meaning other than as a reference point, as was discussed in Chapter 7.

The four model types that are currently shipping are the 765/766 and the 775/776. All the models provide POTS support in the form of two RJ-11 jacks. The difference between the 760s and the 770s is the number of Ethernet ports: The 770 series provides four Ethernet hub ports for additional direct connection to the device.

 The CMTD courseware places more emphasis on the software available for the device, specifically concerning the SOHO and remote office (RO) versions of the software. The SOHO version supports 4 users, and the RO version supports 1,500 users. Note that an Internet Ready Pack version now supports 20 users.

Configuration And Profiles

The key to the configuration of a 700 is the arrangement of the profiles on the device. Each profile is akin to a subdirectory in a DOS or UNIX environment. The commands for each connection are declared in a profile or subdirectory. The following sections detail the profile and the configuration.

Profiles

The 700 utilizes profiles to store the configuration parameters associated with a remote location. This approach is not unlike the IOS command-line syntax that most engineers associate with a Cisco router. In a 2500 series router, the phone number, authentication, and addressing could be associated with a dialer interface. Using the same concept, the 700 calls the stored information for a connection a profile.

The 700 can store a maximum of 20 profiles: 16 user profiles (or 16 definitions for remote connections), 3 permanent profiles (LAN, standard, and internal), and the system profile. The system profile is also referred to as the *global profile* in some Cisco documentation.

 The total number of profiles is 20. There are 3 permanent profiles: LAN, standard, and internal. The system profile doesn't count as a permanent profile. There can be a maximum of 16 user profiles defined. Do not study the number 20; study the number and names of the profiles. If the exam question is truly, "What is the maximum number of profiles?" then answer 20—but look for the word "user" or "permanent" to make sure you're answering the right question.

The LAN profile is used to define the connection to the Ethernet port. It's used for routing. The parameters set here are similar to the configuration on the E0 using the familiar IOS command strings. The parameters are similar—the syntax isn't.

The *standard* profile is used for inbound ISDN calls that don't have an associated profile. This profile won't support routing. As an aside, if the caller is unknown, then why are they calling your router?

The *internal* profile is used when routing is enabled; it provides the configuration parameters to pass data between the bridge engine and the route engine.

Much ado is made about routing in the profiles. Simply stated, an unknown call won't be handled with the route engine: The *standard* profile doesn't support routing. A known call, or one with an associated profile, will be passed to the *internal* profile if IP or IPX routing has been declared for the profile and then sent to the route engine for processing to the LAN.

Cisco offers the following guidelines for profile use:

➤ *Functions*—LAN and internal profiles provide the same basic function.

➤ *LAN routing*—Any protocol routed in the LAN must be routed in the user profile. If a user profile doesn't declare routing, the LAN profile won't route it.

➤ *Bridging*—Any protocol routed in the internal profile may be routed or bridged in the user profile.

➤ *Pinging*—If IP routing is on for the internal profile, the router can be pinged.

The system, LAN, and a user profile must be configured to establish a call. The system level is similar to the IOS global configuration mode; you enter the switch type, the Service Profile Identifier for each channel (SPIDs) if it is needed, and the local directory numbers at this level. In the LAN profile, you establish the IP address and mask for the Ethernet interface and the routing protocol. Again, this is similar to the configuration of interface E0 using the IOS command set. The user profile declares the phone number, frame type, encapsulation, static routing, and authentication for this connection.

Once you've created the profiles, they must be activated. An active profile is ready to accept a demand call. To activate a profile once it's created, use the command **set active** *profile-name*.

> *Note: Some commands issued on the 700 don't become active until the system is rebooted. All currently created profiles will become active on a reboot of the system. You need the **set active** profile-name command if a new profile is created and the 700 isn't rebooted. It would be difficult to memorize the commands that require a reboot and those that don't; hence, we recommend that a reboot follow a configuration change to the router.*

Profile Configuration

The following example encompasses all of the basic commands to establish an IP session with a central site router. The configuration is based on the schematic shown in Figure 9.1 and the script file follows:

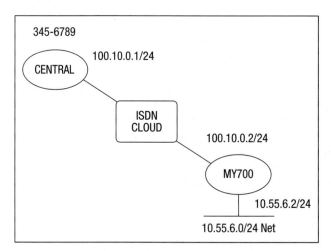

Figure 9.1 A remote 700 router named MY700 is connecting to a central site router with a hostname of CENTRAL.

```
————————————System Section————————————
>set system my700
my700>set switch 5ess
my700>set encapsulation ppp
my700>set ppp authentication incoming chap
my700>set ppp authentication outgoing chap
my700>set ppp secret
prompt for password
prompt for password
my700>cd lan
————————————LAN Section————————————
lan>set bridging off
lan>set ip  10.55.6.2
lan>set ip netmask 255.255.255.0
lan>set ip routing on
lan>cd
my700>set user central
————————————USER Section————————————
my700:central>set bridging off
my700:central>set ip 100.10.0.2
my700:central>set ip netmask 255.255.255.0
my700:central>set ip routing on
my700:central>set number 345-6789
my700:central>set ip route destination 0.0.0.0/0 gateway 100.10.0.1
my700:central>cd
my700>set active central
```

The **system** commands establish the hostname of the 700, the switch type, the encapsulation, and the authentication type and password. The command **cd lan** changes to the LAN profile. In the LAN section, the IP address and mask are assigned and routing is enabled. In the last section shown, the user central is created with the command **set user central**. Note that once the user central is created, you can access it with **cd central** like any other profile.

In the user section, an IP address for the WAN is set and routing is turned on so it will participate with the LAN profile. The phone number is set, and the default gateway is established. In effect, the static route says, "If it isn't for me, send it to 100.10.0.1 (the other side of the WAN link)." It's important to note that a static route is required on the central router to gain access to the Ethernet or LAN of the 700, because RIP updates have not been turned on.

The key issue isn't to memorize each command, but to understand the profile location of the commands, the interoperability with the IOS commands, and the features available on the router.

The user interface uses DOS-like commands to move from profile to profile. The System profile is the root, and all other profiles are *subdirectories* from the root. The router prompt indicates which profile you're currently in and is followed by a >. All the parameters are preceded by the **set** keyword, and to undo or erase a command from Nonvolatile random access memory (NVRAM), you use the keyword **reset**. This command is analogous to the usage of **no** in the IOS syntax.

To perform a **write erase/reload** on the 700, the command is **set default**. Take care using this command, because it both erases and then reloads the system without prompting. The **upload** command is analogous to the **show running** command using the IOS. There is no concept of stored and running configurations. Most commands are effective immediately and written to NVRAM. Some commands require a reload to take place before they are active, as stated previously.

DHCP And PAT

The 700 can provide a small office with a great deal of flexibility because it can perform the functions of a DHCP server and PAT. DHCP automates the IP addressing of the devices on the network. The client PC can request an IP address that is leased from the pool on the DHCP server. You can configure the 700 to act as the DHCP host or as a relay agent for another DHCP host. The following syntax is required to set up the 700 for DHCP hosting:

```
Set DHCP server
Set DHCP address 155.20.1.1 200
Set DHCP Netmask 255.255.255.0
Set DHCP Gateway Primary  188.0.0.1
Set DHCP DNS Primary 188.0.0.2
Set DHCP WINS Primary 188.0.0.3
Set DHCP Domain BigCorp
```

The settings for the gateway, Domain Name Server (DNS), WINS, and domain are self-explanatory. The address range bears discussion. The address range specified here runs from 155.20.1.1 through 155.20.1.200. The second number used in the **Set DHCP address** command specifies the number of addresses to use starting with the address shown, 155.20.1.1. The second number indicates "how many" addresses should be used, not the ending address assignment. There is some confusion in the CMTD documentation, but it has been corrected in the BCRAN notes.

When the 700 is acting in the role of a relay agent, it functions the same way as an IOS router when it sees a DHCP request on an interface with an **IP HELPER ADDRESS** configured: It sends the request to the address designated in the command. Syntactically, to specify the 700 as a proxy/relay/helper for DHCP, the command is:

```
SET DHCP RELAY dhcp-ip-address
```

The use of PAT isn't covered in this chapter, but we'll present it in Chapter 14. In the CMTD courseware, the PAT discussion is part of the 700 section, but it's moved to the Network Address Translation (NAT) chapter in the BCRAN course. The information and slides haven't changed, but the flow of the material is enhanced. It's sufficient at this point to be aware that the 700 can support PAT as a feature.

Optional Interface Configuration Features

The 700 supports Caller ID, callback, and Multilink PPP. Caller ID screening is done in the same fashion as the IOS; however, the syntax of the commands is somewhat different. The implementation of callback on the 700 is unique because it can be set with *or* without authorization.

To use Caller ID, the IOS command set declares

```
Isdn caller phone-number
```

The corresponding command on the 700 is

```
Set callidreceive phone-number
```

In addition to setting the numbers that will be answered by the 700, the command **set caller id on** enables Caller ID for the device.

The CMTD courseware emphasizes the use of Caller ID with no authorization and with authorization. BCRAN only touches upon the use of caller ID. Those taking the CMTD exam should be aware that the options exist; to ensure that the correct caller is being called back, the additional command is **caller id on**.

Multilink PPP is declared in a similar fashion on the 700 and within the customary IOS. To enable Multilink on the 700, the command is **set ppp multilink on**; within the IOS it's simply **ppp multilink**.

700 Series Router Command Summary

The features of the 700, which define the 700's position in the market, are significant to the exam. It was designed for a SO/HO environment and can perform the functions of a larger router, but it has limited throughput and address tables. Again, it isn't necessary to study the entire command reference guide; however, you should become familiar with the management commands prior to taking the exam. A summary of commands for the router follows:

Pay particular attention to the creation of a user (**set user xxx**), the router reset (**set default**), the movement to and from the profiles (**cd**), and the static route definition.

➤ Profile commands

  ➤ System
```
set switch
set encapsulation
set ppp authentication incoming
set ppp authentication outgoing
set ppp secret
set active
```

  ➤ LAN
```
set bridging off
set ip
```

```
set ip netmask
set ip routing on
```

➤ User

```
set user central
set bridging off
set ip 100.10.0.2
set ip netmask 255.255.255.0
set ip routing on
set number 345-6789
set ip route destination 0.0.0.0/0 gateway
```

➤ Management commands

```
Set user
Upload
Set default
Reset
```

➤ DHCP commands

```
Set DHCP server
Set DHCP address
Set DHCP Netmask
Set DHCP Gateway Primary
Set DHCP DNS Primary
Set DHCP WINS Primary
Set DHCP Domain
```

Practice Questions

Question 1

> The three permanent profiles are [Choose the three best answers]:
>
> ❑ a. Standard
>
> ❑ b. System
>
> ❑ c. LAN
>
> ❑ d. Internal

Answers a, c, and d are correct. Answer b is not correct because the system profile is *not* considered to be a permanent profile.

Question 2

> LAN and Internal profiles provide the same basic function.
>
> ○ a. True
>
> ○ b. False

Answer a is correct. The LAN profile describes to the router what route functionality should be used on the ethernet interface. The internal profile provides the same function for those packets that are crossing the router. It is important to remember that a protocol *must* be routed in *both* the LAN and internal profiles for routing to take place.

Question 3

> Any protocol routed in the Internal profile must be routed in the user profile.
>
> ○ a. True
>
> ○ b. False

Answer b is correct. Just because a protocol is declared for routing in the Internal profile *does not* mean it must be routed in a user profile.

Question 4

Once a profile is created, in order for it to establish a virtual connection with a remote device the profile must be _____.

- ○ a. Linked
- ○ b. Given a phone number
- ○ c. Set active
- ○ d. Called

Answer c is correct. It's true that the 700 may be powered off and back on to accomplish the same thing, but the command **set active** allows the profile to become usable without a system reset.

Question 5

To reset the 700 for factory defaults, what command is used?

- ○ a. **erase** and **reload**
- ○ b. **reset** and **reload**
- ○ c. **set default**
- ○ d. **eset default**

Answer c is correct. **Set default** is analogous to the write/erase sequence used in the customary IOS.

Question 6

The 770 provides _____ but the 760 series does not.

- ○ a. Telephony support
- ○ b. A data call button
- ○ c. A built-in NT1
- ○ d. AUI connectors

Answer b is correct. This button allows for a manual-connect or disconnect of a data call.

Question 7

> The 700 series supports routing of the following protocols [Choose the two best answers]:
>
> ❑ a. IP
>
> ❑ b. PPP
>
> ❑ c. IPX
>
> ❑ d. AppleTalk

Answers a and c are correct. *Only* IP and IPX routing are supported on the 700 series.

Question 8

> Which of the following IOS features are compatible with the 700 series router? [Choose the three best answers]
>
> ❑ a. Combinet proprietary protocol (CPP)
>
> ❑ b. IP Routing Information Protocol (RIP) v2
>
> ❑ c. Demand RIP
>
> ❑ d. IP Internet Group Routing Protocol (IGRP)
>
> ❑ e. Snapshot routing
>
> ❑ f. Internet Protocol Control Protocol (IPCP) framing

Answers b, e, and f are correct. The key is to recognize that the question is asking about the features of the IOS. Answers a and c, CPP and Demand RIP, are functions of the 700 router, and answer d, IGRP, is *not* supported on the 700. If nothing else, the process of elimination gives the answer. Snapshot routing is supported on the 700 using the **set ip rip snapshot** command on the 700. IPCP and RIP version 2 are both open standards that are supported within each platform.

Question 9

Which command will create a user profile to connect to a central router, hostname VPNServe2?

○ a. **md VPNServ2**

○ b. **set VPNServ2**

○ c. **set default VPNServ2**

○ d. **set user VPNServ2**

Answer d is correct. Remember the **user** keyword for the **set** command.

Question 10

To specify that *only* calls originating from 234-5678 will be accepted, what command is needed on the 700 series router?

○ a. **isdn caller 2345678**

○ b. **set caller id on**

○ c. **set callidreceive 2345678**

○ d. **set isdn caller 2345678**

Answer c is correct. **Set caller id on** enables Caller ID on the interface, but it doesn't specify which number to respond to.

Need To Know More?

 Cisco Systems. *Cisco 700 Series Router Software Configuration Guide.* This book is the standard documentation set that comes with the 700 series and is the most informative source for explanations.

 Cisco Systems. Documentation CD. Any recent version of the CD has much background information on the various technologies discussed here. The search engine will allow the user to look specifically at white paper information in lieu of a command search. This gives the user a quick way to find a discussion of the search issue, not just the command to use it.

 Visit the official Cisco Web site at **www.cisco.com** for information and links to all technologies employed by Cisco. Specifically for the 700 series documentation and information you can access **www.cisco.com/univercd/cc/td/doc/product/access/acs_fix/ 750/index.htm**

X.25

Terms you'll need to understand:

✓ Packet Assembler Disassembler (PAD)

✓ X.25

✓ X.121

✓ Circuit

✓ **modulo**

✓ Window

✓ Tunneling

Techniques you'll need to master:

✓ Windowing

✓ Understanding Circuit organization

✓ Using Data country codes

✓ Tunneling

X.25 is an extremely widespread form of communication. Developed during the early 1970s, X.25 is the technology that is most used for data connectivity worldwide. Originally developed for use over analog phone lines, it has found acceptance in the less developed areas of the world as a very reliable method of transport. In the U.S., Japan, Western Europe, and other more developed areas of the world, X.25 has led to the use of Integrated Services Digital Network (ISDN) and Frame Relay. Although X.25 isn't used in the U.S. as much as it was in the past, many organizations still continue to use this method of data communication.

The X.25 protocol stack maps neatly to the first three layers of the OSI model. At Layer 1, X.25 has a Physical layer; at Layer 2, it has a Link Access Procedure, Balanced (LAPB) layer; and at Layer 3 it has an X.25 layer. Because X.25 uses Layer 3, in order to transport network layer protocols across it, you must use some form of logical mapping or tunneling.

As we've discussed in previous chapters, X.25 uses the concept of Data Circuit-Terminating Equipment (DCE) and Data Terminal Equipment (DTE). The DTE is the subscriber's router or Packet Assembler Disassembler (PAD). The DCE is the switch that leads to the Public Data Network (PDN). A PAD is a device that takes packets it receives and converts them into conversations that terminal devices attached to the X.25 network can understand. The communication methods are defined by the International Telecommunication Union Telecommunications Standardization Sector (ITU-T).

X.25 uses an unusual addressing mode called X.121. X.121 addresses use decimal format and are assigned by the service provider. When you think of network addressing, you usually think of a stream of characters with dots interspersed throughout. This format isn't the case with X.25. It uses a fairly long address for each device with no dots separating address portions to make the address easier for administrators to read. The first four decimal characters identify the Data Network Identification Code (DNIC). The first three decimal characters identify the particular country, as listed in Table 10.1; and the fourth character tells who the service provider is. These values are assigned by the ITU-T.

Once you've determined the country code and service provider ID for your X.25 network, a third portion of the address is unique on your network. This *host* portion will be an additional 8 to 11 digits long.

The maximum length for an X.25 address is 15 decimal characters, and the minimum length is 1. If you're creating a private X.25 network for your organization's use, you may use whatever values you're comfortable with.

Table 10.1 X. country code list.	
Country	Value Or Range
Europe	200 through 299
France	208 through 209
U.K.	234 through 237
Germany	262 through 265
North America	300 through 399
Canada	302 through 303
U.S.	310 through 316
Asia	400 through 499
Japan	440 through 443
Australia and South Pacific	500 through 599
Australia	505
New Zealand	530
Africa	600 through 699
South Africa	655
South America	700 through 799
Brazil	724

Tunneling Layer 3 Traffic Across X.25

In order to move Layer 3 traffic across an X.25 network, the router must be told of the association. You need to provide **x25 map** statements in order for the router to understand that to reach the IP network to which it wants to send packets, it must send those packets across an X.25 link. Functionally, this **x25 map** command is the equivalent to the IP Address Resolution Protocol (ARP). Unlike Frame Relay, which is covered in Chapter 11, X.25 doesn't have a dynamic way of forming the association between an IP address and an X.25 address. An administrator must configure these commands manually on the router.

The **x25 map** command needs to be configured as follows while in interface configuration mode:

```
X25 map <protocol> <remote layer 3 address for that protocol>
<reomote X.121 address> <options>
```

A popular option is Broadcast, which tells the router to forward broadcast packets to the given Layer 3 address. An example of this configuration on a router where the X25 address of the remote device is 310093456789 and the remote device's IP address is 192.168.10.4 would be:

```
X25 map ip 192.168.10.4 310093456789 broadcast
```

Encapsulation

Encapsulation is the process of adding and removing a Layer 3 packet inside a frame that is specific to the type of network that needs to be crossed; see the left-hand side of Figure 10.1 for an example. An IP packet crosses an Ethernet segment inside an Ethernet frame and then enters the router. Once the packet is inside, the router throws away the Ethernet-specific frame in order to get to the Layer 3 information. After the router determines which network interface to send the packet out of, it places the packet inside a new frame specific to the new topology.

Tunneling follows the same format, except it places a Layer 3 packet (such as an IP packet) inside another Layer 3 packet (such as an X.25 packet). See the bottom of Figure 10.1 for an example. To the X.25 network, the IP packet with all of the associated IP headers is just the data portion of the X.25 packet. Yes, X.25 is a Layer 3 protocol. LAPB is the Layer 2 component and, as mentioned earlier, X.25 uses network and device addressing. X.25 even has routing ability, although we won't discuss that here.

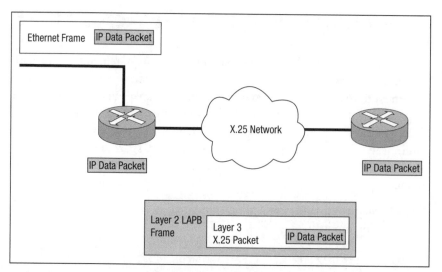

Figure 10.1   Encapsulation and Tunneling.

In order to start X.25 on an interface, you must issue the **encapsulation x25** command at the interface, unless the router is a DCE device. In that case, you need to issue the **encapsulation x25 dce** command.

Circuits

X.25 uses the term Virtual Circuit (VC). A VC is the connection from one X.25 device to another. VCs may be either Permanent (PVC) or Switched (SVC). A PVC is an always-up connection, whereas an SVC requires call setup and isn't always up. Because less configuration hassle is required, PVCs are the circuit of choice.

Both PVCs and SVCs may be used to provide for greater throughput. Up to eight circuits may support a single protocol from router to router, allowing for greater data transfer and a larger window size on the application than X.25 natively supports.

A single X.25 circuit may also carry traffic from multiple protocols, beginning with IOS v10.2. A single circuit may have up to nine protocols mapped to it, and these protocols may be mapped with a single statement. Of course, each protocol comes with associated overhead, so be sure not to over-utilize the circuit.

Data Transmission

X.25 uses packet sizes and windowing just like the other Layer 3 protocols. It comes with some defaults that will work, but they usually aren't very desirable on clean lines. Because X.25 was developed for slow, noisy lines, the defaults for the X.25 standard are for it to send a couple of small packets and wait for a reply. On lines that are very reliable, the limits can be raised.

Virtual Circuit Ranges

X.25 uses specific circuit ranges for data transmission. If the circuit is an SVC, the circuit range depends on whether the circuit is incoming only, two way, or outgoing only. Keep in mind that the addressing of circuits may only go up to 4095, as outlined in Table 10.2.

When you're using a switched VC, you must decide whether to let the router make the decisions on circuit numbering or do it yourself. If you do it yourself, you need to use the same circuit ID on both ends of the wire, from router to X.25 switch. Note that this doesn't mean all the way across the X.25 cloud—this ID applies only on the local connection.

Circuit addressing uses some default values, and those defaults mean that only two-way circuits are allowed without additional configuration. If you require unidirectional circuits or a mix of PVCs and SVCs, then you need to configure according to Table 10.3.

The first thing to remember is that *all* PVC circuit IDs must come before *any* SVC circuit IDs. Next, remember that SVCs have a specific order, as well. Incoming-only circuit IDs must come before two-way IDs, which must come before outgoing-only IDs. Once you've figured out which type of circuits you need to define, you need to start configuring using the odd abbreviations.

An example configuration might look like the following, focusing in on the circuits:

```
Interface Serial 1
     X25 encapsulation
     X25 lic 5
     X25 hic 20
     X25 ltc 21
     X25 htc 1024
     X25 loc 1025
```

Table 10.2 Virtual circuit ranges and commands.

VC Type	Max Range	Default	Command
All PVCs	1 through 4095	None	**x25 pvc** *circuit*
SVC, incoming Only	1 through 4095	0	**x25 lic** *circuit*
	1 through 4095	0	**x25 hic** *circuit*
SVC, two-way circuit	1 through 4095	1	**x25 ltc** *circuit*
	1 through 4095	1024	**x25 htc** *circuit*
SVC, outgoing only	1 through 4095	0	**x25 loc** *circuit*
	1 through 4095	0	**x25 hoc** *circuit*

Table 10.3 Virtual circuit commands explained.

Command	Definition
lic	Low incoming circuit (LIC)
hic	High incoming circuit (HIC)
ltc	Low two-way circuit (LTC)
htc	High two-way circuit (HTC)
loc	Low outgoing circuit (LOC)
hoc	High outgoing circuit (HOC)

Once encapsulation has been established, this configuration does the following, beginning on the third line:

➤ Reserves the PVC circuits. This task is accomplished by leaving room for them at the bottom of the range. By establishing the LIC on circuit 5, you leave circuits 1 through 4 for PVCs.

➤ Establishes the HIC as circuit 20, giving a total of 16 circuits for incoming-only traffic.

➤ Sets up the LTC as circuit 21.

➤ Establishes the HTC as circuit 1024, giving you more than 1,000 circuits to use for two-way traffic.

➤ Establishes the LOC as circuit 1025. You don't need an HOC ID, because everything above the LOC will be allocated to outgoing circuits. You could set a high end to the range if you wanted to limit available circuits.

You need to remember that any type of SVC that has a value of 0 will not be used. In Table 10.3, note that by default, both incoming-only and outgoing-only circuits have 0 as the default value. As a result, you need to configure them in order for the router to support these types of circuits.

PVCs require a different method of reating a map than SVCs do. The method of creating an X25 map was illustrated earlier with the command:

```
X25 map <protocol> <remote layer 3 address for that protocol>
<remote x.121 address>
```

PVCs, where the circuit is always up, must reference the circuit number in the map statement. When you sepcify the existence of the circuit, the router automatically maps the PVC, so the way you create an X25 map for a PVC is similar but a bit different from the way we create a map for an SVC:

```
X25 pvc <circuit number> <remote layer 3 address> <remote X25
address> <option>
```

As you can see, the major difference between creating a map for an SVC and a PVC is that for a PVC you replace the word "map", with "pvc" and add the circuit number right aftter the word "pvc".

Packet Size

The default X.25 packet size is 128 bytes. Acceptable values are 16, 32, 64, 128, 256, 512, 1,024, 2,048, and 4,096. If you don't wish to use the default packet size, you may change it either coming into the router, leaving the router, or in both directions. Each direction is a separate command.

The following command allows for packets of a size that you specify to arrive into the router:

```
Router(config-if)#x25 ips <packet size in bytes, incoming>
```

To change the size of packets leaving the router, enter

```
Router(config-if)#x25 ops <packet size in bytes, outgoing>
```

IPS stands for Incoming Packet Size, whereas OPS stands for Outgoing Packet Size.

X.25 supports packet fragmentation. If a packet needs to be fragmented in order to send it across the X.25 link, it will be reassembled by the destination X.25 device.

Windowing

Windowing in X.25 is a two-part process. The first part involves specifying the maximum window size. The second part tells the router the actual window size.

The command

```
Router(config-if)#x25 modulo <8 or 128>
```

tells the router that the **modulo** setting will be either 8 or 128 (8 is the default). This value is called the modulus. The **modulo** command tells the router that the maximum window size is one less than the number specified. A **modulo** of 8 indicates that the maximum window size is 7, whereas a **modulo** of 128 means the maximum is 127.

Just as with packet sizes, the actual windowing setup must take place on a per-direction basis—and the abbreviations here are also odd. If you find the default window size of two packets to be insufficient, you can change it.

The following commands tell the router how many packets it may receive from a single source before having to acknowledge receipt or send before having to receive an acknowledgment:

```
Router(config-if)#x25 win # of packets incoming
Router (config-if)#x25 wout # of packets outgoing
```

Remember, the maximum value is one less than the modulus and the default is 2.

Analysis And Troubleshooting

The commands **show x25 map** and **show x25 vc** can be very useful in determining the state of a circuit. Figure 10.2 illustrates both commands, along with other **show x25** options.

Another useful command for displaying X.25 interface information is

```
show interface serial number
```

You'll see all sorts of X.25 information specific to that interface. Figure 10.3 shows that the **modulo** is set to 8, and the window size is set to 2; it also shows the virtual circuit IDs for each type and indicates the largest allowed packet size. You may notice that all the values are set at the defaults.

Example Configuration

Figure 10.4 shows an example configuration for two devices configured back-to-back. This configuration establishes the following:

➤ Which router is in charge of clocking on the link

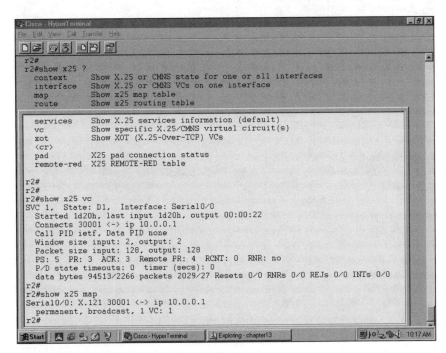

Figure 10.2 Three commands displayed.

➤ IP and X.25 addressing for each interface

➤ A static map for the router when it can see only X.25 out on the WAN and wonders how to send packets to an IP address

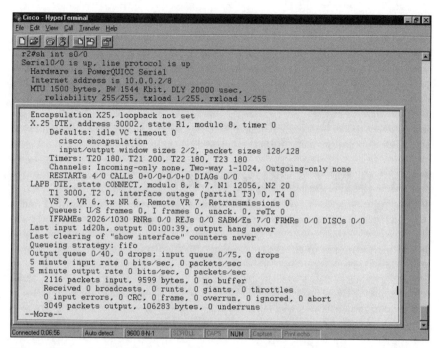

Figure 10.3 Serial interface status.

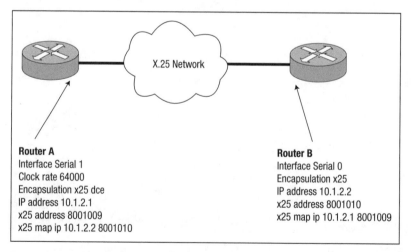

Figure 10.4 Example X.25 diagram.

Practice Questions

Question 1

What does PAD stand for?

○ a. Protocol Assembler Disassembler

○ b. Packet Assembler Disassembler

○ c. Primary Assembler Disassembler

○ d. None of the above

Answer b is correct. PAD stands for Packet Assembler Disassembler. A PAD is an X.25 end point. Therefore, answers a, c, and d are incorrect.

Question 2

What X.25 data networking country code(s) are valid for the U.S.?

○ a. 310 through 316

○ b. 311 through 317

○ c. 311 through 316

○ d. 311

○ e. 316

Answer a is correct. The range of data country codes for the United States is 310 through 316. The fourth digit of an address will be a service provider code. Therefore, answers b, c, d, and e are incorrect.

Question 3

What X.25 data network country code(s) is valid for Japan?

○ a. 440 through 442

○ b. 441 through 443

○ c. 440 through 443

○ d. 440

○ e. 443

Answer c is correct. The range of data country codes for Japan is from 440 through 443. The fourth digit of an address will be a service provider code. Therefore, answers a, b, d, and e are incorrect.

Question 4

What is the highest numbered Virtual Circuit that can exist on an interface?

○ a. 1024

○ b. 2047

○ c. 3072

○ d. 4095

○ e. None of the above

Answer d is correct. An interface can have X.25 Virtual Circuit numbering up to 4095 on an interface. The actual number of virtual circuits allowed on an interface will be determined by the capabilities of the specific router used. Therefore, answers a, b, c, and e are incorrect.

Question 5

How many Layer 3 protocols can share a single Virtual Circuit to a given destination on a Cisco router?

○ a. 10

○ b. 9

○ c. 8

○ d. 7

Answer b is correct. The maximum number of Layer 3 protocols that may be transported across a single Virtual Circuit is nine—the total number of protocols that a Cisco router supports. Therefore, answers a, c, and d are incorrect.

Question 6

How many circuits may a single protocol use to get to a given destination?

○ a. 10

○ b. 9

○ c. 8

○ d. 7

Answer c is correct. The maximum number of Virtual Circuits that a single protocol may use to get to a given destination is eight. Therefore, answers a, b, and d are incorrect.

Question 7

What is the default byte value for incoming and outgoing packet size?

○ a. 16

○ b. 64

○ c. 128

○ d. 512

○ e. 4,096

Answer c is correct. The default value for both incoming and outgoing packet size is a very small 128 bytes. Therefore, answers a, b, d, and e are incorrect.

Question 8

What is the smallest byte value available for incoming and outgoing packet size?

○ a. 16

○ b. 64

○ c. 128

○ d. 512

○ e. 4,096

Answer a is correct. The smallest packet size available is 16 bytes. Therefore, answers b, c, d, and e are incorrect.

Question 9

What is the largest byte value available for incoming and outgoing packet size?

○ a. 16

○ b. 64

○ c. 128

○ d. 512

○ e. 4,096

Answer e is correct. The largest available packet size is 4,096 bytes. Therefore, answers a, b, c, and d are incorrect.

Question 10

What are the available options for the **modulo** command? [Choose the two best answers]

❑ a. 8

❑ b. 16

❑ c. 64

❑ d. 128

Answers a and d are correct. The **modulo** command only has two options: 8 and 128. Therefore, answers b and c are incorrect.

Question 11

A **modulo** setting of 8 would indicate that what value is the maximum setting for both incoming and outgoing window size?

○ a. 7

○ b. 8

○ c. 9

○ d. 10

Answer a is correct. The maximum window size value is one less than the **modulo** setting. Therefore, answers b, c, and d are incorrect.

Question 12

What is the default window size for both incoming and outgoing packets?

○ a. 1

○ b. 2

○ c. 4

○ d. 7

○ e. 8

Answer b is correct. The default window size for both incoming and outgoing is two packets. This means that a reply must be sent after every other packet is received in order to get additional packets in the conversation. Therefore, answers a, c, d, and e are incorrect.

Question 13

X.25 uses what at Layer 2 to ensure data reliability?

○ a. LAPF

○ b. LAPD

○ c. LAPC

○ d. None of the above

Trick! question

Answer d is correct. Link Access Procedure Balanced (LAPB) handles this task. Therefore, answers a, b, and c are incorrect.

Question 14

An X.121 address is entered using what numbering notation?

○ a. Binary

○ b. Octal

○ c. Decimal

○ d. Hexadecimal

Answer c is correct. X.121 addresses are entered using decimal notation, just like IP addresses. Answers a, b, and d are incorrect.

Question 15

An X.25 PAD may be a(n):

○ a. Terminal

○ b. Router

○ c. Frame Relay switch

○ d. Mainframe

Answer b is correct. Routers may be PADs. Therefore, answers a, c, and d are incorrect.

Need To Know More?

 You can find a wealth of information regarding configuring Cisco routers for X.25 at **www.cisco.com/univercd/cc/td/doc/product/software/ios113ed/cs/csprtw/csx25.htm**. This page focuses on the 11.3 version of the IOS since that is what you will be tested on. Support for other versions is available as well.

 The ITU, an international treaty arm of the UN has information regarding the X.25 and X.121 specifications on its Web site. You can find X.25 specs at **www.itu.int/itudoc/itu-t/rec/x/x1-199/x25.html** and the X.121 specs at **www.itu.int/itudoc/itu-t/rec/x/x1-199/x121.html**.

Frame Relay

Terms you'll need to understand:

✓ Data-Link Connection Identifier (DLCI)

✓ Backwards Explicate Congestion Notification (BECN)

✓ Forward Explicate Congestion Notification (FECN)

✓ Committed Information Rate (CIR)

✓ Local Management Interface (LMI)

✓ Inverse-ARP

✓ Non-Broadcast Multi-Access (NBMA)

✓ Traffic shaping

✓ Burst rate

✓ Oversubscription

Techniques you'll need to master:

✓ Ordering correct line speeds

✓ Configuring interfaces for Frame Relay

✓ Configuring a router as a Frame Relay switch

✓ Monitoring Frame Relay operation

Frame Relay is a standard supported by both the American National Standards Institute (ANSI) and the International Telecommunication Union Telecommunication Standardization Sector (ITU-T) that originated from X.25. Unlike X.25, Frame Relay doesn't provide for error correction. The Frame Relay standard defines the connection from your business to the regional provider's switch. Once at the provider, Frame Relay stops and something else—usually Asynchronous Transfer Mode (ATM)—takes over. Frame Relay operates in a Non-Broadcast Multi-Access (NBMA) mode. It can be multi-access like Ethernet but by default does not support broadcast packets.

Frame Relay uses two types of circuits: the Permanent Virtual Circuit (PVC) and Switched Virtual Circuit (SVC). A PVC is a permanent connection to the service provider, like a T-1. An SVC is more like an Integrated Services Digital Network (ISDN) line, in that it connects only when data needs to be transferred. With the adoption of ANSI standard T1.617 and ITU-T q.933 and q.922, Cisco's IOS supports SVCs on Frame Relay as of version 11.2; but many service providers don't offer the service. Because the majority of circuits are PVCs, and because Cisco won't test on SVCs, this chapter won't be discussing SVCs in more detail.

Ordering The Circuit

The concept of Frame Relay revolves around a couple of different threshold levels on an individual link. The first—maximum burst rate—is what you contract for.

Maximum Burst Rate

When you need a new line, you have to figure out the maximum amount of data that you'll need to transfer per second. You call up a service provider and ask it for a Frame Relay link of this size. This amount of data is the maximum that your line can handle; it's your *maximum burst rate*.

Committed Information Rate

The next thing you need to know (which is just as important as your maximum line speed, but often overlooked) is the Committed Information Rate (CIR). The CIR is the guaranteed rate you'll receive. Now, isn't this the same as the maximum burst rate we just discussed? No, which leads us to...

Oversubscription

Service providers will oversell their lines on the assumption that not everyone will be using their full throughput at the same time. Doing so isn't illegal, but many people are confused by all the acronyms and just sign the contract without asking questions. Later they find out that the T-1 they thought they bought really isn't a T-1 at all.

A service provider will add up all the CIRs of its customers on a given wire, and as long as the total doesn't exceed the maximum throughput of the line in question, they're fine. For example, suppose Arctic Bell has a T-1 running into an office park where several subscribers do business. Subscriber A wants a Frame T-1 with a CIR of 256Kbps, subscriber B wants a one-half T (768Kbps) with a CIR of 384Kbps, and subscriber C wants a one-quarter T (384Kbps) with a CIR of 128Kbps. Arctic Bell has total contract rates of one and three-quarter T-1 lines—but it has only one T-1. What it has actually guaranteed each customer so far is one-half T-1.

The end result of this example is that if each customer stays within its CIR, its packets will always be handled. Problems start occurring when customers begin to send more data than they have CIR for. If A, B, and C all start sending data at their maximum burst rate, Arctic Bell's T-1 won't be able to handle the traffic. This oversubscription will result in packets getting lost.

At this time you're probably wondering, "Why would anyone buy Frame Relay?" The answer is that not everyone is going to max out their WAN link at the same time. A WAN connection bandwidth usage chart is filled with peaks and valleys, and Arctic Bell plans to fill in the valleys in subscriber A's traffic with the peaks from subscribers B and C.

When you pay careful consideration to the CIR requirements of your business, Frame Relay is a cost-effective method of WAN access. Be on the lookout, though, for service providers that try to sell you a 0Kbps (zero) CIR. *None* of your packets are guaranteed to get through! By selling a 0Kbps CIR, they can oversubscribe to their heart's content and not be in breach of contract. Their only limit is the number of businesses in the area. At least one large service provider, which shall remain nameless for legal reasons, encourages this practice. Overall, I find a good rule of thumb is that your CIR should equal one quarter of your maximum burst rate.

Attaching To Another Location

After ordering your line, you waited your 90 days, sacrificed a couple of old ISA network cards to the circuit gods, and lo and behold, your circuit is ready a few days early. Now that you have a line, what do you need to know in order to talk to another location?

DLCI

A Data-Link Connection Identifier (DLCI) is needed to talk to the service provider's switch. A DLCI is basically a pointer for the switch, telling it where this particular packet needs to go. Each switch at the service provider's central office (CO) has a configuration it can access. This configuration is like the address on an envelope. The DLCI says, "This packet needs to go to port 8, switch 32, at CO 68 for service provider 3" or wherever your other end is. As the packet moves through the service provider's cloud, the intervening switches just need to look at the service provider information and pass the packet along. Once at the target service provider, the switches forward the packet to the correct CO. (This is an oversimplification, but this book isn't designed to discuss StrataCom switch methods of operation.)

You get the DLCI from the service provider. How you use it depends on how you configure your router, as we'll discuss later.

LMI

The Local Management Interface (LMI) is a signaling standard between your router and the CO switch. LMI is responsible for making sure both devices know the other is there. In addition to acting as keepalives, LMI also acts as a form of Cisco Discovery Protocol (CDP). LMI can provide the router with its DLCI number and IP information regarding the device on the other side of the cloud.

> *Note: Keepalives are packets that each device on a wire generates to verify connectivity. The packets "keep alive" a connection.*

IOS version 11.2 allowed routers to autosense the LMI type the Frame Relay switch is using. With versions prior to 11.2, though, you have to configure the LMI type. You have three options; the thing to remember here is that you want to use the LMI type being used by the Frame Relay switch:

➤ *Cisco*—An LMI type developed by "the Gang of Four": Cisco, StrataCom, Northern Telecom, and Digital Equipment

➤ *Ansi*—Annex D, a standard defined in ANSI standard T1.617

➤ *Q933a*—An ITU-T standard for Annex A

Encapsulation

You'll need to specify Frame Relay encapsulation on the interface, but there are two types: Cisco and Internet Engineering Task Force (IETF). If you don't specify one, the router will default to Cisco encapsulation. This default will cause problems if you aren't connecting to a Cisco router on the other side of the service provider's cloud. If you are connecting to a non-Cisco router, make sure you specify IETF.

Mapping

The router must understand that if it needs to send packets to a given destination, it needs to use the Frame Relay connection. You accomplished this by mapping a Layer 3 address to the DLCI. Think of a static route saying, "In order to get to network www.xxx.yyy.zzz, I need to send packets out interface serial 1." The mapping works the same way, but it says, "In order to get to device www.xxx.yyy.zzz, I need to use Frame Relay DLCI xxx."

You can establish mappings manually or automatically. Both ways require you to tell the interface what DLCI it's connected to. However, something called Inverse-ARP is enabled by default: It takes the LMI information and sends a query across the service provider cloud to find out the address of the device on the other end, and then creates a mapping.

Configuration Commands

You can use several commands to establish Frame Relay. Dynamic address mapping is enabled by default. If for some reason you need to, you can manually configure the map using these commands:

```
Router(config-if)#encapsulation frame-relay {cisco | ietf}
Router(config-if)#frame-relay lmi-type {ansi | cisco | q933a}
Router(config-if)#frame-relay map protocol protocol-address DLCI
    <other options>
```

The options used in these commands are as follows:

➤ *protocol*—The Layer 3 protocol you're mapping to a DLCI. Each Layer 3 protocol you want to use the link needs to be mapped via Inverse-ARP or manually.

➤ *protocol-address*—The Layer 3 address of the interface on the other side of the cloud.

➤ *DLCI*—The DLCI the router uses to talk to the interface across the cloud.

➤ *Broadcast*—An optional command that allows broadcast messages to be sent across the Frame Relay link. Extremely useful if you want routing updates to cross.

➤ *cisco | ietf*—The encapsulation used on this particular configuration. Also optional.

➤ *Payload-compress packet-by-packet*—This optional command establishes compression on the data or payload portion of the packet using the Cisco proprietary STAC compression method. Rather resource-intensive, but often useful for slow WAN links.

Let's say a company has two routers it wishes to connect via Frame Relay: router A and router B. Router A's IP address on its Frame Relay interface is 10.1.2.1 and it connects to the local CO switch with DLCI 100. Router B's IP address is 10.1.2.2 using DLCI 200. The company wants to use static mappings and provide for routing updates and for compression. You'd use these commands:

```
Router A example: frame-relay map ip 10.1.2.2 100 broadcast
  payload-compress packet-by-packet
Router B example: frame-relay map ip 10.1.2.1 200 broadcast
  payload-compress packet-by-packet
```

The two things you *must* remember are, first, that the DLCI is a local identifier between the router and the telco switch. Because the DLCI is local, both routers can be using the same DLCI. This fact is something that people often don't realize. The other thing to remember is that you need to map the remote interface address to the local DLCI address.

Connecting A Single Interface To Multiple Locations

What we have discussed so far is good for small Frame Relay connections, but what about the needs of large organizations? If you have to connect a couple of central routers to hundreds or thousands of remote locations, you don't want to pay for multiple installations, more interface cards for the routers, more channel service units (CSUs), and more serial cables. This is where the subinterface comes in handy. By using subinterfaces, you can logically connect dozens of Frame Relay connections to a single physical interface.

Frame Relay Network Design Types

There are a couple of popular types of design for Frame Relay networks. In addition to point-to-point connections (discussed in the next section), there are the following design types:

➤ *Full mesh*—Each router is connected to every other router in the network. This method costs more than the other two methods, but when properly implemented, it results in faster data access and terrific reliability.

➤ *Partial mesh*—A combination of a full mesh design and point-to-point. Some routers will have full mesh connections between them, whereas other routers will have connections only to other specific routers. For example, a company might have several data centers with a full mesh design between them, with each data center responsible for connection to remote sites within a limited geographic area.

➤ *Hub and spoke (star)*—Every site is connected to only one central router or set of routers. In order for remote site A to talk to remote site B, it has to send packets via the corporate office routers. This design is cost-efficient but doesn't provide any method of routing around down links. If you use this method, keep backhoes away from your property.

Problems With Frame Relay And Multiple Sites

Before we jump into how subinterfaces can solve all your problems, we need to look at why they are used. Primarily, we're concerned with reachability. It involves two different connection types:

➤ *Point-to-point*—Think of a leased line. You have a starting point, a single possible ending point, and nothing you normally need to be concerned about in between. A router at either end of a single serial cable is an example of a point-to-point configuration.

➤ *Multipoint*—Think of some type of shared media, like Ethernet. You can have more than two devices connected to the same wire segment. Ethernet, token ring, and Fiber Distributed Data Interface (FDDI) are all examples of multipoint configurations.

Why do we care about the two different ways that Frame Relay can be configured? Think back to what you know about distance vector routing and routing loops. One method that distance vector routing uses to prevent loops is something called *split horizon*. Split horizon tells the router not to send information about a route out the interface that the update arrived on, which isn't a problem in a true multipoint environment like Ethernet. All routers will send out either broadcasts or multicasts, and each router on that segment will receive and process the update. Because of DLCIs, this arrangement frequently isn't true in Frame Relay networks. Without using subinterfaces, in order to connect a single router interface to multiple sites, you would need to configure an interface as multipoint.

Configuring Subinterfaces

A *subinterface* is, logically, a slice of a physical interface. Let's assume you have a Frame Relay link connecting to physical interface serial 1. The router you're configuring needs to be able to talk to three remote sites via the single physical link. You'll follow these steps:

1. Identify the physical interface to which the Frame Relay link is connected. Because you know it's serial 1, you need to set Frame Relay encapsulation on interface serial 1:

   ```
   Router(config-if)#encapsulation frame-relay {cisco | ietf}
   ```

2. Identify how many connections are needed via this link. For our purposes, you need three. You then create them by typing "interface serial 1.x" where x is a number. Here, you'll use serial 1.1, 1.2, and 1.3. You'll need to specify whether a subinterface is supposed to be point-to-point or multipoint. Typing the command dynamically creates the logical interface in much the same way that typing "interface loopback 0" activates the loopback 0 interface.

3. Make sure that no Layer 3 address exists on the physical interface configuration. This step is very important, because otherwise the router will get confused. You can use the **no** *protocol* **address** command to remove a Layer 3 address without needing to look up the specific address.

4. Specify on each subinterface the DLCI it's connected to by using this command:

   ```
   Router(config-subif)#frame-relay interface-dlci DLCI
   ```

5. Apply Layer 3 addresses to the subinterfaces.

Table 11.1 outlines an example of configuring the router.

Table 11.1 Example walkthrough explained.	
Command	**Explanation**
Router(config)#interface serial 1	Moves the router into interface configuration mode for serial 1.
Router(config-if)#no ip address	Removes an IP address that exists on interface serial 1.

(continued)

Table 11.1   Example walkthrough explained (continued).

Command	Explanation
Router(config-if)#encapsulation frame relay	Establishes Frame Relay encapsulation for physical interface serial 1. All subinterfaces will now be using Frame Relay encapsulation.
Router(config)#interface serial 1.1 point-to-point	Creates the serial 1.1 subinterface, establishes it as a point-to-point interface, and moves the router into subinterface configuration mode.
Router(config-subif)#ip address 10.1.1.0 255.255.255.0	Puts an IP address in subinterface serial 1.1. Remember that the device on the other side of the Frame Relay cloud needs to have a Layer 3 address that is a member of the same network.
Router(config-subif)#frame-relay interface-dlci 100	Tells the router that in order to talk to other devices on network 10.1.1.0 (just one network in this case, because we specified a point-to-point connection), the router needs to send information via Frame Relay DLCI 100.
Router(config-subif)#bandwidth 256	Changes the interface bandwidth value from the default of a T-1 (1.544Mbps) to the actual value, which is 256Kbps in this instance.
Router(config)#interface serial 1.2 point-to-point	Creates the serial 1.2 subinterface, establishes it as a point-to-point interface, and moves the router into subinterface configuration mode.
Router(config-subif)#ip address 10.1.2.0 255.255.255.0.	Puts an IP address in subinterface serial 1.2.
Router(config-subif)#frame-relay x 10.1.2.0 255.255.255.0	Tells the router that in order to talk to other devices on network 10.1.2.0 (just one network in this case, because we specified a point-to-point connection), the router needs to send information via Frame Relay DLCI 200.
Router(config-subif)#bandwidth 384	Changes the interface bandwidth value from the default of a T-1 (1.544Mbps) to the actual value, which is 384Kbps in this instance.

(continued)

Table 11.1 Example walkthrough explained (continued).	
Command	**Explanation**
Router(config)#interface serial 1.3 point-to-point	Creates the serial 1.3 subinterface, establishes it as a point-to-point interface, and moves the router into subinterface configuration mode.
Router(config-subif)#ip address 10.1.3.0 255.255.255.0	Puts an IP address in subinterface serial 1.3.
Router(config-subif)#frame-relay interface-dlci 300	Tells the router that in order to talk to other devices on network 10.1.3.0 (just one network in this case, because we specified a point-to-point connection), the router needs to send information via Frame Relay DLCI 300.
Router(config-subif)#bandwidth 768	Changes the interface bandwidth value from the default of a T-1 (1.544Mbps) to the actual value, which is 768Kbps in this instance.

By using subinterfaces, you're able to connect a single Frame Relay line to a single physical interface and connect to multiple remote locations. Point-to-point subinterfaces allow for routing information to come in from remote location A on a subinterface and be forwarded to remote location B via a different subinterface. This setup allows routing information to be sent out while not sacrificing protection from routing loops.

Frame Relay Traffic Shaping

Traffic shaping is just a fancy term for adjusting the speed on the link. If you have a T-1 talking to a 56Kbps link, there will be times when the T-1 is able to send at full speed. If it does, it will overwhelm the 56Kbps device. When this happens, the Frame Relay switches will notify the T-1 device to stop sending so many packets.

BECNs And FECNs

Backwards Explicate Congestion Notification (BECN), and Forward Explicate Congestion Notification (FECN) packets are how Frame Relay devices tell other Frame Relay devices, "Hey! You're sending me too many packets. Slow down." Frame Relay switches in the service provider cloud normally generate them, which is why they go in both directions.

When a Frame Relay device becomes congested and BECNs and FECNs are generated, problems will arise. If the router doesn't throttle back the number of packets it's sending out per second, packets over the CIR value will be dropped.

For example, suppose a router is connected to a Frame Relay cloud with a T-1 connection with a CIR of 256Kbps. If devices within the cloud become congested, they will tell the router to slow down. The router will slow down its data throughput to 256Kbps. If it doesn't slow down, devices within the cloud will begin dropping packets over the 256Kbps mark.

A second example leads to major problems. Suppose you have two devices: Router A connected to the Frame Relay cloud via a T-1 with a 256Kbps CIR, and Router B connected to the cloud via a 56Kbps line with a 32Kbps CIR. Router A starts sending data and overwhelms the 56Kbps router. Router A receives BECNs and slows down to 256Kbps. This speed continues to overwhelm Router B. Packets will constantly get lost and have to be re-sent.

This problem occurs frequently with multipoint networks in which someone didn't examine the current configurations before adding a new device.

Configuring Traffic Shaping

You can use queuing to prioritize certain types of traffic over others. This way, when the router starts to throttle back the amount of data it sends, the more important types of traffic have a better chance of not being delayed.

The first thing you need to define when determining traffic shaping is a map class. A map class is the go-between for the interface and the queuing configuration. You need to type this command

```
Router(config)#map-class frame-relay map-class-name
```

which puts the router into map class configuration mode.

Next, you need to specify the average rate the interface or subinterface should send at, as well as the maximum rate. Do so by using the command:

```
Router(config-map-class)#frame-relay traffic-rate average maximum
```

where the maximum value is optional. If you want the router to respond to BECNs and modify the amount of data it sends based on that information, use this command:

```
Router(config-map-class)#frame-relay adaptive-shaping becn
```

Once you have decided what type of queuing to use (see Chapter 13 for more information), you need to link the queue configuration to the map class. Use the command:

```
Router(config-map-class)#frame-relay {custom-queue-list |
  priority-group} list-number
```

Once you've built the queuing policy, you need to enable traffic shaping on the appropriate interface. This is accomplished by using the command:

```
Router(config-if)frame-relay traffic-shaping
```

In order to link the map class to all of the virtual circuits on a physical interface, use the command:

```
Router(config-if)frame-relay class map-class-name
```

This command will force all subinterfaces on the physical interface.

Table 11.2 outlines a sample configuration, assuming Frame Relay has already been configured and minus the queuing configuration.

Table 11.2 Traffic shaping example.

Command	Explanation
Router(config)#map-class frame relay *map-class-name*	Puts the router into map class configuration mode, allowing you to configure the map class.
Router(config-map-class)#frame-relay traffic-rate 128000 384000	Tells the router that the average traffic rate is 128,000 bits per second with a maximum possible speed of 384,000.
Router(config-map-class)#frame-relay custom-queue-list *queue-list-number*	Tells the router to use a certain queue configuration in determining which traffic is more important than other types of traffic.
Router(config-map-class)#frame-relay cir *<bytes>*	Establishes the Committed Information Rate (CIR) for the circuit.
Router(config-if)#frame-relay traffic-shaping	Tells the router to be prepared to throttle back sending data if necessary.
Router(config-if)#frame-relay class *map-class-name*	Tells the router that for this specific interface, use the traffic shaping configuration found within the map class name configuration.

Miscellaneous Frame Relay

You'll use a couple of other commands in different scenarios. Although it's unlikely that they will be a part of the exam, we include them here to help you better understand the mechanics of Frame Relay, as well as to aid you in case you want to set up a Frame Relay network in a lab environment.

Back-To-Back Frame Relay

The methods of configuring Frame Relay listed earlier in the chapter assume that you're connecting to a fully configured Frame Relay service provider switch. A couple of other commands are necessary if you wish to attach two routers together via a serial line running Frame Relay.

The reason is the DCE. When you're connecting to a telco switch, your router is the DTE. When creating a Frame Relay connection between two routers, though, one must be the DTE and the other the DCE.

The command

```
Router(config)#frame-relay switching
```

tells the router to accept configuration parameters designating it as a DCE device. The command

```
Router(config-if)#frame-relay intf-type {dce | dte | nni}
```

tells the router what the interface is supposed to act as.

Now that you have set an interface to be the DCE, another command gets around the lack of a real switch. Using the command

```
Router(config-if)#frame relay local-dlci DLCI
```

allows the two routers to route information to each other when there is a lack of LMIs due to the lack of a switch. In some cases, the Frame Relay map command listed earlier in this chapter may also be necessary as an alternative to Inverse-ARP.

Configuring A Frame Relay Switch

In addition to the earlier **frame-relay switching** and **frame-relay intf-type** commands, if you want to build a real Frame Relay switch, you'll have to provide mapping for the way Frame Relay connections move within the cloud. Cisco routers can act as Frame Relay switches, but that doesn't mean they have all the complicated settings that are available on dedicated Frame Relay switches. Figure 11.1 shows an example of Frame Relay switching.

In Figure 11.2, we are concerned with only one command:

```
Router(config-if)#frame-relay route incoming-dlci
  outgoing-interface outgoing-dlci
```

This command tells the router that when packets arrive at an interface on the incoming DLCI, the router needs to send those packets out the outgoing interface using the outgoing DLCI. Table 11.3 shows an example.

EIGRP Over Frame Relay

Enhanced Interior Gateway Routing Protocol (EIGRP) is a routing protocol developed by Cisco. The company calls it a hybrid because it's a combination of a distance vector protocol and a link state protocol. EIGRP is proprietary to

Table 11.3 Frame Relay switch configration example.	
Command	**Explanation**
Router(config)#frame-relay switching	Tells the router that some interfaces may be configured as Frame Relay switch interfaces.
Router(config-if)#frame-relay intf-type dce	Tells the router that this interface provides the clocking for the serial cable to which it's connected. In a back-to-back situation, this command is necessary. The DTE option is the default and tells the router to accept whatever clocking rate is provided. The NNI option is used when configuring two Frame Relay switches back-to-back.
Router(config-if)#no ip address	It's very important not to have Layer 3 addresses on any interface involved with Frame Relay switching. Frame Relay operates at Layer 2, and Layer 3 configuration options just confuse the router.
Router (config-if)#frame-relay route 100 interface serial 2 200	Tells the router that whenever a Frame Relay packet arrives at the configured interface on DLCI 100, it should forward that packet out interface serial 2, DLCI 200. You will also need a similar statement on serial 2 referencing the other serial port and DLCI 100.

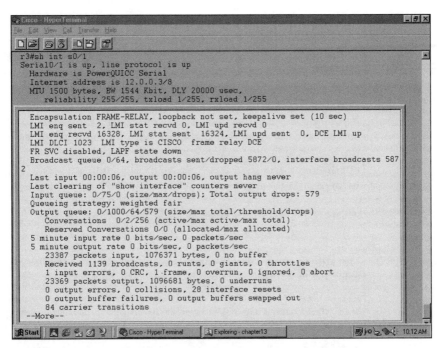

Figure 11.1   Frame Relay switching configuration example.

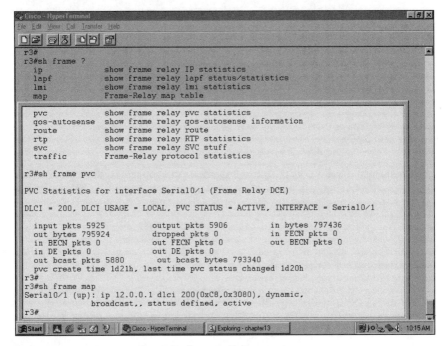

Figure 11.2   Frame relay interface statistics.

Cisco equipment. An in-depth discussion of EIGRP can be found in the *ACRC Exam Cram* published by Coriolis, but one feature of EIGRP interests us here.

A poorly designed network, and an occasional well-designed network, can suffer from routing protocol updates consuming most or all of a slow WAN link and leaving little room for data. If you're using EIGRP, you can tell it not to use more than a certain percentage of the total bandwidth for routing protocol traffic. This limitation makes it very important to set the interface bandwidth to a correct value. The command is as follows:

```
Router(config-if)#ip bandwidth-percentage eigrp
   autonomous-system-number bandwidth-percentage
```

The **autonomous-system-number** is the number that EIGRP is using on that interface, and the **bandwidth-percentage** is the percentage of bandwidth you want to allow EIGRP to consume in a worst-case scenario. This command is also available for IPX and AppleTalk.

Monitoring Frame Relay Operation

Two types of troubleshooting commands are available: configuration troubleshooting and troubleshooting a previously configured connection. Remember that all Frame Relay **show** commands need to be executed in Privileged EXEC mode.

Configuration Troubleshooting

Using the

```
Router#show interfaces serialnumber
```

command will display configuration information about serial devices. You'll be able to tell what encapsulation is set, what DLCI's being used, and so on. Figure 11.2 shows serial 0/1.

You can use the

```
Router#show frame-relay pvc
```

command to show PVC statistics for the circuit. This information includes how long the circuit has been up, traffic in bytes, and traffic shaping alerts. An example is shown in Figure 11.3.

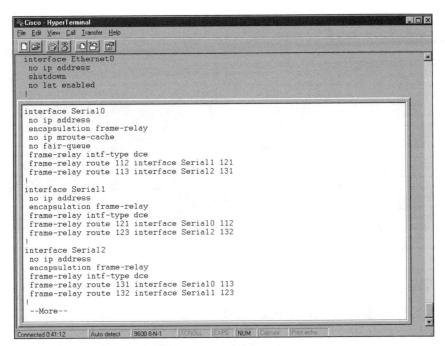

```
Cisco - HyperTerminal
File  Edit  View  Call  Transfer  Help

 interface Ethernet0
  no ip address
  shutdown
  no lat enabled
 !
 interface Serial0
  no ip address
  encapsulation frame-relay
  no ip mroute-cache
  no fair-queue
  frame-relay intf-type dce
  frame-relay route 112 interface Serial1 121
  frame-relay route 113 interface Serial2 131
 !
 interface Serial1
  no ip address
  encapsulation frame-relay
  frame-relay intf-type dce
  frame-relay route 121 interface Serial0 112
  frame-relay route 123 interface Serial2 132
 !
 interface Serial2
  no ip address
  encapsulation frame-relay
  frame-relay intf-type dce
  frame-relay route 131 interface Serial0 113
  frame-relay route 132 interface Serial1 123
 !
 --More--

Connected 0:41:12    Auto detect   9600 8-N-1    SCROLL  CAPS  NUM  Capture  Print echo
```

Figure 11.3   show frame-relay commands and results.

Using the

```
Router#show frame-relay map
```

command will show configuration information regarding both static and dynamic Frame Relay mappings. It displays Layer 3 information, DLCI, and the status of the link. This command is also useful for troubleshooting a previously working connection. If you get configuration information via Inverse-ARP and someone at the telco messes up a configuration, it could change how your router views mappings. An example is shown in Figure 11.3.

Use the

```
Router#show frame-relay route
```

command on a router you have set up as a Frame Relay switch using the **frame-relay route** command. This command displays a list of what interface and DLCI goes to what other interface and DLCI as well as what the state of the link is. See Figure 11.4 for an example.

```
Cisco - HyperTerminal                                              _ □ X
File  Edit  View  Call  Transfer  Help

  01:45:23: %LINEPROTO-5-UPDOWN: Line protocol on Interface Serial2/2, changed sta
  te to up
  01:45:28: %FR-5-DLCICHANGE: Interface Serial2/1 - DLCI 123 state changed to ACTI
  VE
  frame-switch#
  frame-switch#sh frame route
  Input Intf      Input Dlci     Output Intf     Output Dlci     Status
  Serial2/0       112            Serial2/1       121             inactive
  Serial2/0       113            Serial2/2       131             inactive
  Serial2/1       121            Serial2/0       112             inactive
  Serial2/1       123            Serial2/2       132             active
  Serial2/2       131            Serial2/0       113             inactive
  Serial2/2       132            Serial2/1       123             active
  Serial2/4       212            Serial2/5       221             active
  Serial2/4       213            Serial2/6       231             active
  Serial2/5       221            Serial2/4       212             active
  Serial2/5       223            Serial2/6       232             active
  Serial2/6       231            Serial2/4       213             active
  Serial2/6       232            Serial2/5       223             active
Connected 0:02:48     Auto detect   9600 8-N-1    SCROLL   CAPS   NUM   Capture  Print echo
```

Figure 11.4 The **show frame-relay route** output.

Troubleshooting A Previously Configured Connection

The command

```
Router#show frame-relay lmi interface-type interface-number
```

will display LMI information for a specific interface. The interface information is optional, so you can get information regarding all interfaces.

The command

```
Router#show frame-relay pvc interface-type interface-number dlci
```

will display statistics about a specific DLCI on a specific interface. The DLCI and interface are optional, so you can get all PVC information, as well. This is a more-specific command than the **show frame-relay pvc** listed earlier.

The command

```
Router#show frame-relay traffic
```

gives global Frame Relay traffic statistics since the last time the router has been rebooted or the statistics cleared.

The command

```
Router#show frame-relay ip tcp header-compression
```

will give header compression statistics for TCP/IP traffic. This command requires that header compression be established.

Practice Questions

Question 1

> If two routers are connected via Frame Relay and router A is connecting to
> DLCI 100, what DLCIs can router B use?
>
> ○ a. 100
>
> ○ b. 101
>
> ○ c. 150
>
> ○ d. 200
>
> ○ e. 201
>
> ○ f. All of the above
>
> ○ g. None of the above

Answer f is correct. The DLCI is a local configuration between the router and
the central office switch. On the other side of the cloud, it makes absolutely no
difference what DLCI is being used, except in relation to devices connected to
that switch. Because of this, any valid connection will work no matter the numbering. Answers a, b, c, d and e are incorrect because there is not a single correct
answer while answer g is incorrect because any of those values will work if the
service provider sets it up.

Question 2

> What do BECNs do?
>
> ○ a. Share a route.
>
> ○ b. Tell the router what configuration to use when talking to a switch.
>
> ○ c. Tell the switch to send more data.
>
> ○ d. Tell the router to send less data.

Answer d is correct. A Backward Explicate Congestion Notification tells the
router that a device between the two routers can't handle it sending so much
data and that if it continues to do so, packets will be dropped. Answer b refers
to a DLCI, while answers a and c aren't options. Therefore, answers a, b, and c
are incorrect.

Question 3

> Which ANSI standard supports SVCs for Frame Relay?
>
> ○ a. q.933
>
> ○ b. T1.617
>
> ○ c. 232
>
> ○ d. q.922

Answer b is correct. q.933 and q.922 are ITU-T standards for SVCs over Frame Relay, and 232 is a cable standard so answers a, c and d are incorrect.

Question 4

> Which telecommunications vendor was not a member of "the Gang of Four"?
>
> ○ a. Northern Telecom
>
> ○ b. Nippon Telephone and Telegraph
>
> ○ c. Cisco
>
> ○ d. Digital Equipment Corporation
>
> ○ e. StrataCom

Answer b is correct. All of the others were vendors that made up "the Gang of Four" that developed standards for LMI, among other things, making answers a, c, d and e incorrect.

Question 5

> Which is not an option for LMI type selection?
>
> ○ a. **Cisco**
>
> ○ b. **ansi**
>
> ○ c. **ietf**
>
> ○ d. **q933a**

Answer c is correct. All of the others are valid LMI type selections, making answers a, b and d incorrect.

Question 6

> Which two are valid selections for Frame Relay encapsulation type?
>
> ❏ a. **Cisco**
>
> ❏ b. **ansi**
>
> ❏ c. **ietf**
>
> ❏ d. **q933a**

Answers a and c are correct. Cisco is the default encapsulation type, whereas you would use IETF encapsulation if the router on the other side of the cloud isn't a Cisco router. This means that answers b and d are incorrect.

Question 7

> What is wrong with the following configuration? [Choose the two best answers]
>
> Interface serial 1:
>
> ```
> encapsulation frame-relay
> ip address 10.1.0.1 255.255.0.0
> ```
>
> Interface serial 1.1 point-to-point:
>
> ```
> ip address 10.2.0.1 255.255.0.0
> frame-relay interface-dlci 101
> bandwidth 128
> frame-relay cir 64
> ```
>
> Interface serial 1.2 point-to-point:
>
> ```
> ip address 10.3.0.1 255.255.0.0
> frame-relay interface-dlci 201
> bandwidth 256
> frame-relay cir 64
> ```
>
> ○ a. The **frame-relay interface-dlci** statements should be **frame-relay local-dlci**.
>
> ○ b. The CIR values should be one quarter of the available bandwidth.
>
> ○ c. There should not be an IP address on the physical interface.
>
> ○ d. Each subinterface needs the command **encapsulation frame-relay** placed on it.
>
> ○ e. The **frame-relay cir** command goes in a map class configuration.

Answers c and e are correct. When using subinterfaces, you should not place a Layer 3 address on the primary interface, and CIR is specified in a map class. Answer a is incorrect because the frame-relay local-dlci is used to specify a DLCI on a physical interface. This command can be used if the circuit is up but no LMI can be received by the router. Answer b is wrong because there is no such rule. It's a good rule of thumb though. Answer d is just wrong.

Question 8

> At least which Cisco IOS version is needed in order to autosense LMI type?
>
> ○ a. 10.3
>
> ○ b. 11.2
>
> ○ c. 12.0
>
> ○ d. 11.1
>
> ○ e. 11.3

Answer b is correct. Cisco added autosensing to the IOS beginning in version 11.2. All other IOS versions listed in a, c, d, and e are incorrect.

Question 9

> Subinterfaces are used in a routed environment because of what?
>
> ○ a. Split horizon
>
> ○ b. Poison reverse
>
> ○ c. Hold-down timers
>
> ○ d. Routing loops

Answer a is correct. Split horizon tells the router not to send routing updates out the interface it learned that route from. This means that a remote site could send a routing update and our central site router would not forward it out the same interface to other remote sites. Using subinterfaces solves this problem. Answers b and c, while dealing with ways to prevent routing loops like Split Horizon does, have no bearing on Frame Relay. Answer d is why we use the other three. Answers b, c and d are incorrect.

Question 10

Two types of Frame Relay connections are:

- ❏ a. Contention-based
- ❏ b. Point-to-point
- ❏ c. Packet-based
- ❏ d. Multipoint

Answers b and d are correct. These designs reflect how many Frame Relay routers will exist on the subnet. There will be two in a point-to-point scenario and an unspecified number in a multipoint scenario. Answers a and c don't exist.

Question 11

Frame Relay was based on what technology?

- ○ a. X.25
- ○ b. ISDN
- ○ c. ATM
- ○ d. Token ring

Answer a is correct. X.25 is the precursor to Frame Relay. Answers b, c and d are not the precursors to Frame Relay, so those answers are incorrect.

Question 12

What does DLCI stand for?

- ○ a. Dynamic Link Connection Identifier
- ○ b. Dynamic Link Control Identifier
- ○ c. Data Link Control Identifier
- ○ d. Data Link Connection Identifier

Answer d is correct. DLCI is the abbreviation for Data Link Connection Identifier. Because answers a, b, and c are not valid definitions for DLCI, they are incorrect.

Question 13

> Always-up circuits are called:
>
> O a. PVCs
>
> O b. AVCs
>
> O c. NVCs
>
> O d. SVCs

Answer a is correct. Always-up circuits are called PVCs or Permanent Virtual Circuits. Answer d stands for Switched Virtual Circuit, a non-always up circuit. Answers b and c don't exist.

Question 14

> In what ways can a router get a DLCI for a circuit? [Choose the two best answers]
>
> ☐ a. Inverse-ARP
>
> ☐ b. DHCP
>
> ☐ c. An ARP request
>
> ☐ d. Manual configuration

Answers a and d are correct. A router may learn the DLCI for a circuit via both Inverse-ARP and manual configuration. Multiple circuits on a single physical interface need to be manually configured. Answers b and c refer to IP processes and are incorrect.

Question 15

> CIR stands for:
>
> O a. Carry Interface Ratio
>
> O b. Carry Interface Rate
>
> O c. Committed Information Ratio
>
> O d. Committed Information Rate

Answer d is correct. CIR stands for Committed Information Rate, which is the guaranteed portion of the virtual circuit. Answers a, b and c are incorrect.

Need To Know More?

 One of the best all-purpose Web sites about Frame Relay is the Frame Relay Forum, an association of organizations interested in Frame Relay. Visit its site at **www.frforum.com**.

 Explanations of the majority of Frame Relay commands that you can use with a Cisco router can be found at **www.cisco.com/ univercd/cc/td/doc/product/software/ios113ed/cs/csprtw/ csfrelay.htm**. Documentation regarding Frame Relay implementation can be found at **www.cisco.com/univercd/cc/td/doc/product/ software/ios113ed/113ed_cr/wan_c/wcfrelay.htm**.

Enabling A Backup To A Permanent Connection

Terms you'll need to understand:

√ Dial backup

√ Primary

√ Backup

√ Link

√ Interface

√ Load

√ Keepalives

√ Carrier detect

√ Administrative distance (AD)

Techniques you'll need to master:

√ Using the **backup load** command

√ Determining routing protocol preferences

√ Calculating backup delay

Having a second connection that can move data in the event the primary connection fails is a wise move for today's corporate environment. You can back up a permanent connection—or use *dial backup*, as it's usually called—several ways to both alleviate congested conditions as well as provide an alternate route in the event of a link failure.

Dial backup should not be confused with load sharing. *Load sharing* uses multiple paths to the same destination to send packets. Although dial backup can do this, this feature is usually secondary to making sure that data has a means to get to its destination. Because of this need, dial backup is usually performed on much slower links than load sharing tends to be. (You'll find information on load sharing within routing protocol discussions in the Coriolis CCNA and ACRC books.)

Dial backup can use several different types of interfaces. It's normally configured for an ISDN Basic Rate Interface (BRI) or an analog modem attached to an asynchronous interface, but in advanced setups it may be configured to use a dialer pool or another serial interface.

In addition to backing up a primary link in the event it goes down, a backup interface may also be configured to support a primary line in the event of congestion on the primary. The administrator can establish that the backup interface will begin to transport data when a given bandwidth threshold on the primary is reached or exceeded.

Configuring Dial Backup For Primary Link Failure

In order to configure a dial backup link to take over data transport in the event a primary link goes down, you have to do several things. See Figure 12.1 for an example.

➤ Identify the primary link—that is, the link currently carrying traffic that you wish to back up.

➤ Identify the dialup link that will be used to back up the primary.

➤ Configure the primary link (if you haven't already done so) to support the necessary encapsulation, routed protocols, and routing protocols.

➤ Place the

```
backup interface interface-type number
```

command in the interface configuration for the primary interface.

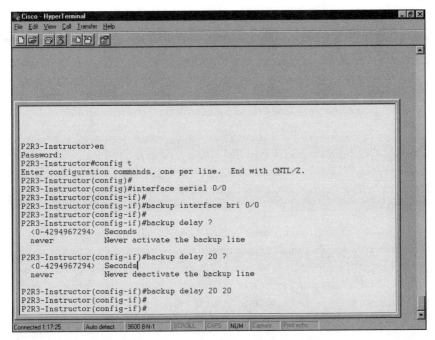

Figure 12.1   Dial backup configuration examples and help.

➤ Configure how long the backup interface should delay coming up when the primary fails and how long it should wait before dropping when the primary comes back up via the command:

```
backup delay {enable-delay | never} {disable-delay | never}
```

The backup interface command options are as follows:

➤ *interface-type number*—Which interface will be used to back up the primary interface? Remember that interface values will vary depending on the router you're configuring. Some routers will use the format **interface serial 1**, whereas a modular router will use the format **interface serial 1/1**, specifying both the slot and port numbers.

➤ *enable-delay*—How many seconds must pass before the backup interface takes over for the primary? A good method to make sure that the primary won't return immediately.

➤ *disable-delay*—How many seconds must pass before the backup link goes down, once the primary has returned? A good method to make sure that the primary won't drop off again.

➤ *never*—Prevents the backup line from being enabled or disabled.

The **enable-delay** and **disable-delay** values are the number of seconds you want the interface to wait before coming up or going down, respectively. These values can be useful in the event your primary line has a tendency to *bounce* or go down for just a few seconds occasionally. Although the **disable-delay never** option has its uses, you'll use the **enable-delay never** option very few times in a production environment.

Once you've configured both the primary and backup interfaces, the backup interface will be placed in a standby mode. The standby mode simulates a down interface until needed. This means that no traffic will pass through the backup interface, and properly configured routes through the interface won't be used.

The router with the backup interface configured will monitor the status of *keepalives*, small packets that networking devices send to each other, and will carrier-detect the presence of keepalive packets on the primary link. If carrier isn't detected on the primary link or if keepalives don't arrive from the neighbor router on a regular basis, then your router will assume the primary link has failed and will activate the backup.

Floating Static Routes

A *static route* is a route that someone has configured. It tells the router, "In order to reach a certain network, you must send data out this interface." See Figure 12.2 for two examples of a static route. Because a router must have a way to determine the best route, it prefers certain routing protocols over others. Cisco routers believe the information provided by static routes is extremely accurate and will prefer those routes over routes learned via dynamic routing protocols.

This preference leads to a problem. If you're running a dynamic routing protocol across the primary link on your router, you need to establish a static route to the other networks via the dial backup interface. But if you do this, then the router will prefer to use the dial backup interface rather than the (probably faster) primary interface. A solution exists in the form of a *floating static route*. In a floating static route, like the one shown in Figure 12.3, the administrative distance (AD) for a static route is changed from 0 or 1 to something higher than the AD for the dynamic routing protocol you're using across the primary.

Table 12.1 lists some routing protocols and their ADs.

If you have a router running OSPF, the administrative distance is 110. If you set up a static route pointing to an IP network that OSPF already knows about, then the router will prefer to use the path specified by the static route. You can

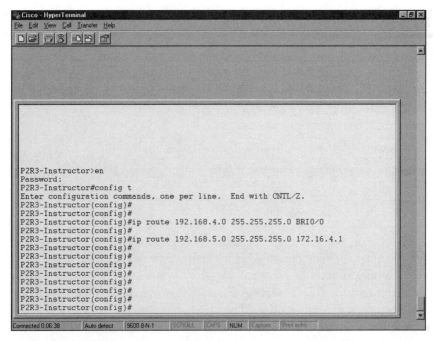

Figure 12.2   Two static route examples.

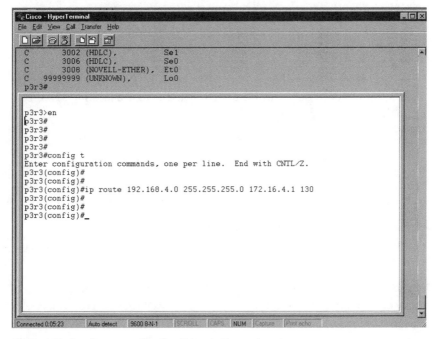

Figure 12.3   An example floating static route.

Table 12.1   Routing protocols and corresponding ADs.

Routing Protocol	Administrative Distance
Directly connected	0
Static route referencing a local interface	0
Static route referencing a remote device	1
Enhanced Interior Gateway Routing Protocol (EIGRP)	90
Interior Gateway Routing Protocol (IGRP)	100
Open Shortest Path First (OSPF)	110
Routing Information Protocol (RIP)	120

fool the router by changing the AD the static route uses to something higher than the value your routing protocol uses. If you establish a static route and tell the router that the AD for this route is 130, then the router will prefer to use OSPF routes if they are available. This technique allows you to run a dynamic routing protocol across the primary link but have an alternate route via the backup link. The command used is as follows:

```
ip route <destination-network> <destination-network mask>
    {local-interface | remote device address} <AD>
```

The **ip route** command's options are as follows:

➤ *destination-network*—The remote network that this static route refers to. In order to get to the network, we send packets to the location specified by the rest of the command.

➤ *destination-network mask*—Generally an IP subnet mask. Helps the router choose between subsets of the same classful IP network number.

➤ *local-interface*—The local interface by which data needs to leave the router, if you want the data sent to this network. This option has an AD of 0.

➤ *remote device address*—Much the same as **local-interface**. Specifies the remote device address you need to send data to if you want the data sent to this network. This option has an AD of 1.

➤ *AD*—The administrative distance for the route you're creating. The AD should be higher than that of your regularly used routing protocol. 130 is a good value, because it's higher than the AD of the four primary routing protocols and thus will be used only when the dynamic routing protocol doesn't have an active route.

An example is **ip route 10.1.2.0 255.255.255.0 BRI0 130**. This command tells the router that in order to send routes to network 10.1.2.0, it should use interface BRI0. By adding the AD of 130, you make the router compare this route to its existing routing table. In the event of multiple paths to the 10.1.2.0 network, the router will use the active route with the lowest AD. The command **ip route 10.1.2.0 255.255.255.0 192.168.1.4 130** also makes the router check its routing table—but instead of sending packets out of the BRI0 interface, the router will forward packets to the device 192.168.1.4. To keep things simple, this should be a neighboring device.

Activating Dial Backup To Support A Primary Link

You can configure dial backup to activate an interface when the amount of traffic on the primary link reaches or exceeds a certain amount. Once you have selected and configured the primary link interface as in Figure 12.4, you need to add this command:

```
backup load {enable-threshold | never} {disable-threshold | never}
```

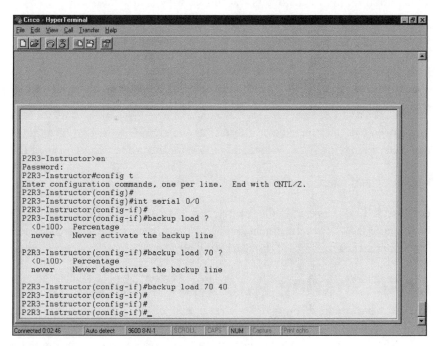

Figure 12.4   Dial backup to help out another line.

The **backup load** command's threshold options are as follows:

➤ *enable-threshold*—Percentage of use on the primary link at which the backup link will be enabled and start load sharing traffic

➤ *disable-threshold*—Percentage of use on the primary link at which the backup link will be disabled

➤ *never*—Prevents the backup link from being enabled or disabled

Unlike many Cisco interface references, the **backup load** command doesn't use a portion of 255 in the command. The value referenced is a straight percentage of the link's capability.

Do not use values of 0 or 100 in this command. The activation and deactivation values are based on a floating five-minute average, and setting either value to 0 will result in a backup link that either always stays up or never comes up.

Using Dial Backup With Dialer Profiles

A physical interface may be either an active interface *or* a dial backup interface. This limitation led to customers wanting to fully utilize all of the interfaces they were purchasing. The solution was to allow a **backup interface** command to map to a dialer pool. Because a dialer pool is attached to a virtual interface called a *dialer interface*, and a physical interface may be a member of multiple dialer pools, this arrangement lets you use a physical interface in the normal course of business even though it may someday be called on to serve as a backup to a primary interface.

You'll need to configure a dialer interface as shown in Chapter 8. Once that is complete, go into interface configuration mode for the primary link and enter the

```
backup interface dialer number
```

command. This command tells the primary link to use the dialer pool as the backup interface. When the primary link goes down, the router will use a physical interface that is a member of the specified dialer pool to serve as a backup link.

Load Sharing And Dial Backup

Using the **backup load** command enables one link to be activated and help out the primary link. Routing protocols, though, tend to have their own ideas about what paths traffic should take. For example, if you previously configured a router to bring up an ISDN connection to help out a T-1 when the T-1 had a certain load, a routing protocol such as OSPF isn't going to make use of the

ISDN line without a little bit of help. OSPF determines the best path by looking at the bandwidth of the link. Because a T-1 has greater bandwidth than ISDN, OSPF will prefer to send all data across the T-1 and ignore the ISDN line.

You use load sharing with dial backup on an OSPF routed network by using the

```
ip OSPF cost cost
```

command in interface configuration mode for the dial backup interface. Doing so tricks OSPF into thinking that a 128Kbps ISDN line is really a 10Mbps Ethernet link, or whatever you need to simulate. OSPF will then load-share data across both lines.

IGRP and EIGRP aren't as difficult to work with. They both support load sharing across links of different speeds, although with a few additional commands. The problem most people have with load sharing with IGRP and EIGRP is the number of factors these protocols take into account when determining the best path. (You can find more detail regarding the path selection attributes of these two routing protocols in the Coriolis books for the CCNA and ACRC exams. Here, we will assume all factors are equal except for the possible bandwidth of each link.)

Assume that you want to back up a T-1 with an ISDN connection. A T-1 has a bandwidth of 1.544Mbps, whereas an ISDN line has a bandwidth of 128Kbps. It would take 12 ISDN lines to equal one T-1. This gives you a variance of 12. Using the command

```
variance multiplier
```

in routing protocol configuration mode tells the router to use the ISDN line even though it isn't nearly as fast as the T-1. Doing so creates a problem, because the router will load balance equally across both lines. This arrangement is undesirable—either the ISDN line will become saturated or the T-1 will be underutilized. To fix this issue, you have the

```
traffic-share {balanced | min}
```

command, which you also configure in routing protocol configuration mode. The *balanced* option in this command tells the router that for every packet sent across the ISDN line, it should send 12 across the T-1.

The load sharing options for the commands discussed in this section are as follows:

➤ *cost*—In OSPF, the wire's bandwidth in bits per second divided into 100 million. Thus, a 10Mbps Ethernet link has a cost of 10. The **cost** command tricks the OSPF protocol into thinking that the link is a different speed than it really is.

➤ *multiplier*—Determines the range of wires that may be used for load sharing. Each load sharing link must be within a range of x to y, where x is the value of the primary link, and y is x divided by the variance value.

➤ *balanced*—Tells the router to load share according to the capabilities of each line.

➤ *min*—Tells the router to divide traffic only among routes with the best metrics.

Verifying A Dial Backup Configuration

The command

```
show interface type number
```

will display the status of the configured interface. Displayed will be information on which device is serving as a backup, the delay before the backup is enabled, and the delay before the backup is disabled once the primary is restored.

Practice Questions

Question 1

In order to create a floating static route when you're running the RIP routing protocol, what administrative distance would work best?

○ a.   120

○ b.   100

○ c.   140

○ d.   80

○ e.   1

Answer c is correct. When creating a floating static route, you need to make sure that the specified administrative distance is *higher* than that of the routing protocol you're using. This way, the router will only use this route when it doesn't have a route to the specified network in its routing table. Since RIP has an Administrative Distance of 120, you need an AD that is higher than 120. Therefore, answers a, b, d, and e are incorrect.

Question 2

What command allows IGRP to load share across links of unequal bandwidth?

○ a.   **split**

○ b.   **variance**

○ c.   **load-share**

○ d.   None of the above

Answer b is correct. The **variance** command tells IGRP and EIGRP to use a specified value in determining what links are available for load sharing. Answers a and c are not valid options, thus incorrect; since a valid answer exists, answer d is also incorrect.

Question 3

What type of configuration allows an interface to both back up another link and be used on a regular basis?

- ○ a. Dialer pool
- ○ b. Dialer interface
- ○ c. Serial interface
- ○ d. BRI interface

Answer a is correct. A dialer pool acts as a go-between for a physical interface and a dialer interface. Answer b, the dialer interface, is referenced in the **backup interface** command; when needed, it will select a physical interface out of those available in the pool. Answers c and d are physical interfaces. Answers b, c, and d are all incorrect.

Question 4

In the command **backup delay 20 30**, when the primary link drops, how long will it take before the backup link is activated?

- ○ a. 30 seconds
- ○ b. 20 seconds
- ○ c. 30 minutes
- ○ d. 20 minutes

Answer b is correct. The first number in the command states how long the interface will wait before becoming active. Therefore, answers a, c, and d are not correct. This value is in seconds.

Question 5

The maximum value for the disable-threshold portion of the **backup load** command is:

- ○ a. 1000
- ○ b. 255
- ○ c. 128
- ○ d. 100

Answer d is correct. The values used in the **backup load** command are percentages of the capacity of the primary link. Thus, the maximum value that can be used is 100. Therefore, answers a, b, and c are not correct. However, using 100 is not recommended because the load sharing will be removed very quickly in most cases.

Question 6

The administrative distance for OSPF is:

○ a. 90

○ b. 100

○ c. 110

○ d. 120

Answer c is correct. The administrative distance for OSPF is 110. Answers a, b, and d, are the administrative distance for, in order, EIGRP, IGRP, and RIP.

Question 7

In the command **backup delay 10 50**, how many seconds after the primary comes back online will the backup link wait before dropping?

○ a. 10 seconds

○ b. 40 seconds

○ c. 50 seconds

○ d. 60 seconds

○ e. None of the above

Answer c is correct. The delay value being referenced is the second value, which says "when the primary comes back online, wait 50 seconds before dropping the backup link." Therefore, answers a, b, d, and e are not correct. The delay is used to make sure that the primary is going to remain online.

Question 8

In the command **ip ospf cost** *cost*, what does the *cost* variable refer to?

○ a. The cost of the link in dollars. We use expensive links more often to get our money's worth.

○ b. The cost of the link in bandwidth. We can trick OSPF routing with this command.

○ c. The cost of the link in bandwidth. We can trick OSPF spanning tree with this command.

○ d. The additional cost of this link to take into account additional processing overhead from another process, like route redistribution.

Answer b is correct. This command tells OSPF to ignore the bandwidth values it knows for this link and instead substitute the given value. Therefore, answers a, c, and d are incorrect. This command can really mess up a routing table if it used incorrectly.

Need To Know More?

 Cisco Systems. *Cisco IOS Dial Solutions*. Cisco Press. ISBN: 1-57870-055-8. This book discusses Dial Backup in Chapters 46 through 49. While the information is valuable, most of it can also be found at the following URLs.

 Several configuration examples with explanations can be found at: **www.cisco.com/univercd/cc/td/doc/product/software/ ios113ed/113ed_cr/dial_c/dcprt5/index.htm**.

 Explanations of configuration options may be found at: **www.cisco.com/univercd/cc/td/doc/product/software/ ios113ed/113ed_cr/dial_r/drprt5/index.htm**.

Traffic Queues

. . . .

Terms you'll need to understand:

√ Weighted fair queuing

√ Priority queuing

√ Custom queuing

√ List number

√ Byte count

√ Queue limits

√ STAC compression

√ Predictor compression

√ Microsoft Point-to-Point Compression (MPPC)

Techniques you'll need to master:

√ Queuing

√ Determining traffic importance

√ Configuring compression

Traffic queuing is done by the router to handle arriving traffic in such a way that it benefits the organization more than the default configuration does. Traffic queuing can be used to place certain types of traffic ahead of other types when the router decides what packet to route next. This queuing can be very useful when an organization uses some protocols that are more sensitive to delay than others. Cisco routers offer three types of queuing strategies: weighted fair queuing, priority queuing, and custom queuing. This chapter explains when to use each of the three types of queuing, how to configure the router for each type, and potential pitfalls.

The Three Types Of Queuing

Weighted fair queuing raises the priority level of small packets above the priority level of large packets. This approach tends to benefit traffic generated by applications in which the user will notice a lag. An example would be Telnet traffic. Telnet sends small TCP packets containing a single character. Once the packet has been returned to the user, the character is placed on the screen. A user will notice the delay if this doesn't happen quickly, and in many cases, productivity will suffer.

Priority queuing places traffic in groups according to the configured priority of the traffic in question. It's possible to place Internetwork Packet Exchange (IPX) traffic in a higher priority grouping than IP and vice versa.

Custom queuing is an extension of priority queuing. The administrator has more options available and is able to differentiate the flow of individual packets to a greater degree than with priority queuing.

Traffic queuing is most effective on slow, "bursty" links. Generally, these links are Wide Area Network (WAN) serial lines. If a link experiences a small amount of congestion, traffic queuing may be an option to improve the user's perception of increased traffic throughput. If a link doesn't ever become congested or is always congested, then it's unlikely that traffic queuing will be of much benefit.

The first thing to determine when it comes to traffic queuing is which type of traffic deserves priority. This decision will vary depending on the needs of your organization. Typically, any traffic generated by some sort of terminal or terminal emulator is a prime candidate to benefit from traffic queuing. These applications are very susceptible to perceived delays from the user. In other cases, you may decide that all IPX traffic has priority because it's mission critical, whereas IP traffic isn't. The types of traffic the administrator determines are important will have a big impact on the appropriate selection of a queuing strategy.

In order to determine which type of queuing is correct for the traffic involved, you should ask the following questions:

➤ *Are the links congested?* If not, then no queuing strategy is necessary, because traffic isn't being delayed by bandwidth. If there is a delay but the links aren't congested, then the problem may be caused by upstream or downstream links. A router that isn't robust enough for the job at hand could also cause this problem.

➤ *Does the administrator require strict control over the order of traffic?* If not, then in most cases, weighted fair queuing is the answer.

➤ *Can all traffic handle a delay?* If not, then see the section on priority queuing. If so, see the section on custom queuing.

The following three sections will describe each type of queuing in detail and provide examples of Priority and Custom Queuing.

Weighted Fair Queuing

Weighted fair queuing follows a modified *first in, first out* strategy. Normally, a router will route traffic based on the standard definition of first in, first out. Unfortunately, this approach often means that a router spends its time waiting for a large packet to finish arriving when a small packet is sitting there, waiting its turn.

The modified first in, first out strategy tells the router to route the first packet that arrives completely. When a small packet and a large one head toward the router and they begin arriving at close to the same time, the small packet will finish arriving long before the large packet. Rather than waiting for the large packet to finish arriving, the router will route the small packet.

Weighted fair queuing will also break up streams of packets into *conversations*. Because packet streams can hog the available bandwidth, the router will break up the stream and insert other packets that need to be routed. An example of a packet stream would be an FTP transfer. Weighted fair queuing will break up the megabytes associated with the download and allow time-sensitive traffic to be routed. The router can break up streams into several different types of conversations, including:

➤ Source or destination Media Access Control (MAC) address

➤ Source or destination network address

➤ Source or destination port or socket address

➤ Frame Relay Data-Link Connection Identifier (DLCI)

➤ Quality of service values

Weighted fair queuing is enabled by default on all physical interfaces that have bandwidth of 2,048Mbps *and* do not use Synchronous Data Link Control (SDLC), Point-to-Point Protocol (PPP) with compression, X.25, or Link Access Procedure, Balanced (LAPB) encapsulation. Weighted fair queuing can't be enabled on interfaces that have these items configured.

Weighted Fair Queuing Configuration

The **fair-queue** command is used to establish weighted fair queuing on an interface. In addition, this command sets a congestive-discard-threshold value:

```
Router(config-if)#fair-queue congestive-discard-threshold-number
```

This value controls how many packets in a given conversation will be queued before the router begins discarding new packets. This queuing helps alleviate the effects of packet streams.

If the *congestive-discard-threshold-number* is set to 128, like the following,

```
Router(config-if)fair-queue 128
```

then up to 128 packets will be placed in the queue for a given conversation. Once the 128-packet limit has been reached, packets arriving for that conversation will be discarded until the number of packets queued for that conversation has fallen below one quarter of the value, in this case 32. The default value for the *congestive-discard-threshold-number* is 64. The range that it may be configured in is 1 through 512, inclusive.

Figure 13.1 shows an example of changing the values for weighted fair queuing. (There are two other values shown in the figure, but they're not important for our purposes here.) The middle value of 256 is the default for "best effort conversations" or packet streams that don't require special services. The last value of 0 is the default for "reservable queues"—queues used with the RSVP feature.

Priority Queuing

Priority queuing allows you to tell the router to send all packets of a certain type before moving on to other packets. For example, an administrator may configure priority queuing to send all Telnet traffic before sending any other type. Priority queuing consists of four queues in which packets may be placed while waiting to be routed. These queues and how many packets they can hold by default are:

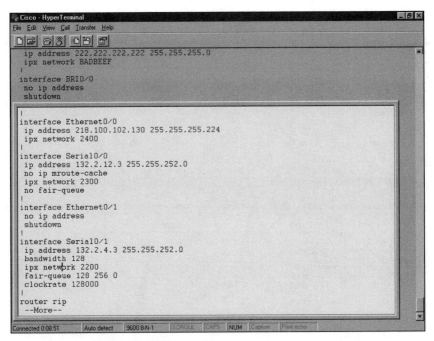

Figure 13.1   Weighted fair queuing.

➤ *High*—20 packets

➤ *Medium*—40 packets

➤ *Normal*—60 packets

➤ *Low*—80 packets

The more important queues don't require as large a buffer because the router will always service those queues before servicing lower queues. Once the High queue is empty, the router will move on to the lower queues. When the router examines a queue, if it contains a packet whose time to live has not yet expired, that packet is routed. The router then checks the High queue again and works its way down the list. If too much traffic is placed in the High queue, there is a risk that the router won't service the lower-level queues.

Priority Queuing Configuration

Once you've decided to use priority queuing, you must also decide which protocols go to which queues. More than one protocol may inhabit a queue, and a default queue must be assigned to capture any traffic not specified. You do so via a *priority list*. An example of a priority list and interface application are shown in Figure 13.2, and Figure 13.3 shows a more advanced configuration

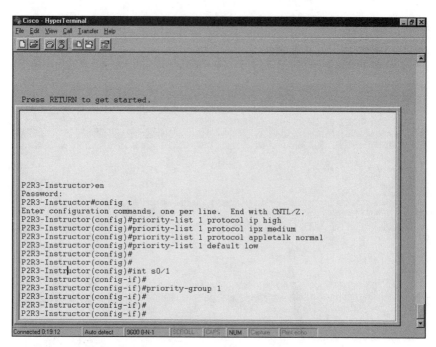

Figure 13.2   Priority queuing.

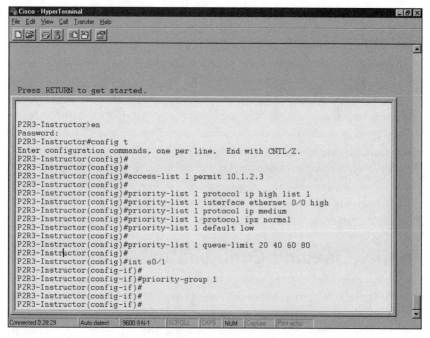

Figure 13.3   A more extensive priority queue specifying the incoming interface.

including filtering based on the incoming interface. A priority list may be configured by both interface and protocol; thus a single list may state that all TCP/IP traffic goes to the High queue whereas all traffic coming in from interface Ethernet 2 goes to the Medium queue. The following command strings, in order, show how to configure a priority list by protocol and by interface:

```
Router(config)#priority-list list-number protocol protocol-name
  (high | medium | normal | low) queue-keyword keyword-value
Router(config)#priority-list list-number interface interface-type
  interface-number (high | medium | normal | low)
```

The priority queuing configuration parameters are as follows:

➤ *list-number*—In Internetwork Operating System (IOS) versions 11.2 and higher, this value is from 1 through 16, inclusive. In IOS versions 11.1 and earlier, this value is 1 through 10, inclusive.

➤ *protocol-name*—This value can be **aarp, arp, apollo, appletalk, bridge** (transparent), **clns, clns_es, clns_is, cmns, compressedtcp, decnet, decnet_node, decnet_router-l1, decnet_router-l2, ip, ipx, pad, rsrb, stun, vines, xns,** or **x25.** Please note that with regards to the **decnet_router** types, the last character is a number, whereas the character preceding the number is a lowercase *L.*

➤ *queue-keyword and keyword-value*— The queue keywords have the following values:

  ➤ *byte-count*—**gt:** (greater than) or **lt:** (less than)

  ➤ *list*—An access list number

  ➤ *(tcp | udp) port*—A port number or name

  ➤ *fragments*—An IP only option

➤ *interface-type*—The type of interface, such as Ethernet or Serial.

➤ *interface-number*—The number of the specified interface.

The following commands, in order, show how to specify which queue is the default, change the queue sizes, and attach the priority list to an interface:

```
Router(config)#priority-list list-number default
  (high | medium | normal | low)
Router(config)#priority-list list-number queue-limit
  high-queue-limit medium-queue-limit normal-queue-limit
  low-queue-limit
Router(config-if)#priority-group list-number
```

The queue sizes are as follows:

➤ *high-queue-limit*—Number of datagrams that can be stored in the High queue. The default is 20.

➤ *medium-queue-limit*—Number of datagrams that can be stored in the Medium queue. The default is 40.

➤ *normal-queue-limit*—Number of datagrams that can be stored in the Normal queue. The default is 60.

➤ *low-queue-limit*—Number of datagrams that can be stored in the Low queue. The default is 80.

Cisco has put a lot of effort into making the default queue values efficient. Think carefully before changing the values: A change may leave lower queues not serviced as often or at all.

A Priority Queuing Example

The following example of priority queuing demonstrates the additional flexibility that this type of queuing gives you over weighted fair queuing. Figure 13.4 shows a router being configured with the following commands:

```
1)  Router (config)#priority-list 1 protocol ip high tcp 23
2)  Router(config)#priority-list 1 protocol ip high list 1
3)  Router(config)#priority-list 1 protocol ip medium
4)  Router(config)#priority-list 1 interface serial 0/0 normal
5)  Router(config)#priority-list 1 protocol appletalk low
6)  Router(config)#priority-list 1 protocol ipx low
7)  Router(config)#priority-list 1 default low
8)  Router(config)#priority-list 1 queue-limit 20 50 60 80
9)  Router(config)#access-list 1 permit 192.168.72.6
10) Router(config)#interface Serial 0/1
11) Router(config-if)#priority-group 1
```

The code works like this:

➤ Line 1 places all Telnet traffic into the High queue.

➤ Line 2 places all IP traffic allowed by access list 1 into the High queue.

➤ Line 3 places all other IP traffic into the Medium queue.

➤ Line 4 places all non-IP traffic arriving from Serial 1 into the Normal queue.

➤ Line 5 places all AppleTalk traffic into the Low queue.

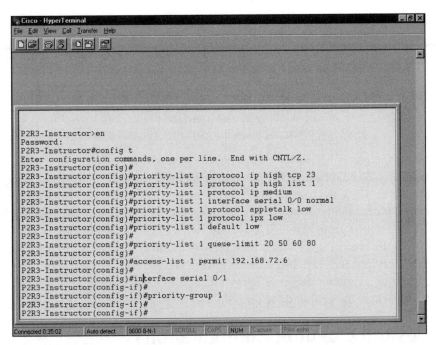

Figure 13.4 Priority queuing.

➤ Line 6 places all IPX traffic into the Low queue.

➤ Line 7 establishes the Low queue as the queue where all unspecified traffic will go.

➤ Line 8 changes the default settings for how many packets each queue can hold from 20 for the High, 40 for the Medium, 60 for the Normal, and 80 for the Low to 20 for the High, 50 for the Medium, 60 for the Normal, and 80 for the Low.

➤ Line 9 is the access list referenced in line 2.

➤ Line 10 moves from Global configuration mode to Interface configuration mode for Ethernet 0.

➤ Line 11 applies the priority group to interface Ethernet 0.

Custom Queuing

Custom queuing allows you to prioritize traffic so that important traffic is serviced more frequently. At the same time, this queuing strategy doesn't ignore certain protocols because it's too busy handling others. Whereas priority queuing will handle all traffic in an upper queue before moving to a lower queue, custom queuing will handle a certain amount of bandwidth in a given queue and then move on to the next queue.

 Custom queuing allocates traffic to up to 16 queues via a queue list, or 10 queues if you're using an IOS version prior to 11. The list will specify which queue a particular packet goes to by the protocol involved, the interface the packet arrived from, the TCP/IP application the packet is for, or other methods.

When the router begins handling queued packets, it looks in the first queue available. The first queue is queue 0; it handles router system traffic like keepalives. Once the first queue is empty, certain rules take over. The first rule is that traffic will be handled in a "round robin" fashion. Once the router is finished with a given queue, it moves on to the next. The router doesn't start over at the beginning as it does with priority queuing. The second rule is that the router is done servicing a queue once it has pulled a certain number of packets or a certain number of bytes out of that queue, regardless of whether more packets are waiting to be serviced.

Custom Queuing Configuration

The following commands show how to configure custom queuing based on protocol and interface, respectively:

```
Router(config)#queue-list list-number protocol protocol-name
   queue-number queue-keyword keyword-value
Router(config)#queue-list list-number interface interface-type
   interface-number queue-number
```

Figure 13.5 shows an example of custom queuing. The custom queuing parameters are as follows:

➤ *list-number*—The number of the queue list from 1 to 16, as shown in priority queuing.

➤ *protocol-name*—The name of the protocol, as shown in priority queuing.

➤ *queue-number*—The number of the custom queue from 1 to 16. These queues do not have to be configured in any specific order, and gaps may be left between queues.

➤ *queue-keyword keyword-value*—Possible values are **gt** (greater than), **lt** (less than), **list**, **tcp**, **udp**, and a port value.

➤ *interface-type*—The name of the interface referenced.

➤ *interface-number*—The number of the interface referenced.

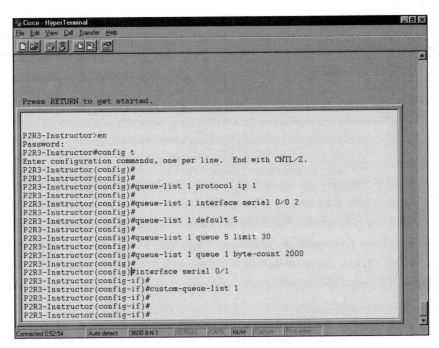

Figure 13.5   Custom queuing.

The administrator must assign a default queue for packets that aren't covered by the queue list. You can also change the number of packets each queue will hold. Those commands are as follows:

```
Router(config)#queue-list list-number default queue-number
Router(config)#queue-list list-number queue queue-number
   limit limit-number
```

The custom queue numbering and size parameters are as follows:

➤ *list-number*—The number of the queue list from 1 to 16.

➤ *queue-number*—The number of the custom queue from 1 to 16.

➤ *limit-number*—The maximum number of packets that a queue may hold at any one time. Values range from 0 through 32,767, inclusive, with a default value of 20.

You can specify how long the router forwards packets from any one queue. You do so by configuring how many bytes the router may forward before moving on to the next queue. Assuming that more packets are contained within a queue than the router has been configured to forward at any one time, the router will forward enough packets to take it to the configured limit, even if the last packet forces the router over that limit. Once the limit has been reached, the router moves on to the next queue.

 When you're customizing how many packets the router may forward from any one queue, it's a good idea to pay attention to the packet size of the topology in question. If the first queue is configured for 2,000 bytes and all remaining queues are configured for 1,500 bytes, Ethernet packets that reside in the first queue will get twice the attention of Ethernet packets residing in any other queue. This happens because Ethernet packets are slightly larger than 1,500 bytes. The router will forward one packet from each queue with a limit of 1,500 bytes, but it will forward two packets from the first queue.

The command to configure how many bytes will be transferred from each queue every time the router accesses that queue and the command to set the queue list on an interface follow:

```
Router(config)#queue-list list-number queue queue-number
  byte-count byte-count-number
Router(config)#custom-queue-list list
```

The custom queue throughput and interface application parameters are as follows:

➤ *list-number*—The number of the queue list from 1 to 16.

➤ *queue-number*—The number of the custom queue from 1 to 16.

➤ *byte-count-number*—The minimum number of bytes the router is to forward from a specific queue. The default for all queues is 1,500 bytes.

➤ *list*—The queue list number created to place packets in queues.

A Custom Queuing Example

This example shows how you can give Telnet traffic the highest priority, followed by other IP traffic, anything entering the router via interface Serial 1 with AppleTalk, IPX, and all other traffic being considered less critical. It's important to note that when a packet fits more than one queue, it's placed in the queue mentioned first. Figure 13.6 shows a router experiencing this activity. The command lines to specify these priorities are as follows:

```
1) Router (config)#queue-list 1 protocol ip 1 tcp 23
2) Router(config)#queue-list 1 protocol ip 2
3) Router(config)#queue-list 1 interface serial 0/0 3
4) Router(config)#queue-list 1 protocol appletalk 4
```

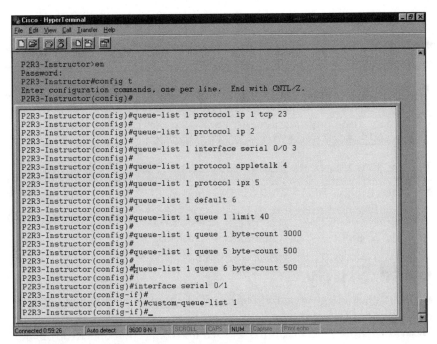

Figure 13.6   Setting custom queuing priorities.

```
5) Router(config)#queue-list 1 protocol ipx 5
6) Router(config)#queue-list 1 default 6
7) Router(config)#queue-list 1 queue 1 limit 40
8) Router(config)#queue-list 1 queue 1 byte-count 3000
9) Router(config)#queue-list 1 queue 5 byte-count 500
10) Router(config)#queue-list 1 queue 6 byte-count 500
11) Router(config)#interface serial 0/1
12) Router(config-if)#custom-queue-list 1
```

The code works like this:

➤ Line 1 puts all Telnet (TCP port 23) traffic in queue 1.

➤ Line 2 places all other IP traffic in queue 2.

➤ Line 3 puts all traffic that isn't IP traffic but is traffic arriving from Serial 1 in queue 3.

➤ Line 4 puts all AppleTalk traffic in queue 4.

➤ Line 5 puts all IPX traffic in queue 5.

➤ Line 6 creates a default queue for all other traffic that the router may be configured to support.

➤ Line 7 raises the number of packets that queue 1 can store from 20 to 40.

➤ Line 8 raises the number of bytes that the router can forward when handling queue 1 from 1,500 to 3,000.

➤ Line 9 reduces the number of bytes that the router will forward for AppleTalk traffic in queue 5 from 1,500 to 500. This setting can be useful if an administrator doesn't want the router to spend much time forwarding many small packets used for network informational purposes.

➤ Line 10 is a duplicate of line 9, but affecting IPX packets in queue 6.

➤ Line 11 moves from Global configuration mode to Interface configuration mode for Ethernet 0.

➤ Line 12 applies the list to interface Ethernet 0.

Case Study

Acme Corp. is a large organization with offices throughout the southwest. Its major client is Desert Predators, Inc. Due to the large volume of orders that Desert Predators generates, it has a leased line connection directly to Acme's network. Because Acme has set up Internet connectivity, the traffic generated by employees using the Internet for business purposes has caused some unacceptable delays in filling orders from Desert Predators as well as other customers.

Desert Predators accesses the Acme network via a TCP/IP Telnet connection. Orders are placed on a server on the Acme network, which then converts the information into a format that the Acme backend systems can process. Acme's problem is that customers entering data often experience many short delays in seeing data on their screens. To ensure that data is entered correctly, the order entry people often wait several seconds to make sure the system is accepting their information. Acme wants to correct this problem. Acme management wants all customer traffic to receive top priority and also wants to ensure the least amount of delay possible. They look at Internet access as a convenience to their employees and, as such, performance in this area may be permitted to suffer if it makes their customers happier.

To summarize, the important points in this situation are as follows:

➤ Customer order entry times are unacceptable.

➤ Although the Internet is used, it's regarded as less important than customer data.

➤ Acme uses protocols beyond TCP/IP.

The proposed solution is to allow Telnet traffic to have priority over all other traffic and to use priority queuing to accomplish this routing. By placing all outside-generated Telnet traffic in the High queue, you ensure that customers get the top priority. Place all Telnet traffic generated by Acme in the Medium queue, and then place all other IP traffic in the Normal queue. The Low queue is set up to capture all remaining traffic.

Data Compression

In addition to the queuing methods mentioned previously, Cisco routers also support several forms of compression. *Compression* increases the efficiency of WAN links by making packets smaller, thus reducing the amount of bandwidth they use. This comes at a cost of increased processor usage on the routers on either side of the WAN link. The types of compression supported are:

➤ Link compression (also known as per-interface compression)

➤ Payload compression (also known as per-virtual circuit compression)

➤ TCP header compression

➤ Microsoft Point-to-Point Compression (MPPC)

In addition, a hardware compression card is available on some Cisco devices. This chapter doesn't cover hardware compression features.

Link Compression

Link compression, also called *per interface compression*, involves compressing both the header portion of the packet as well as the data portion. Although link compression is Layer 3 protocol independent, it isn't encapsulation independent. You can use link compression when using PPP or LAPB encapsulation utilizing either Predictor or STAC compression. If you're using High-Level Data Link Control (HDLC) encapsulation, you can only use STAC compression.

The best time to use link compression is on slow, point-to-point WAN links. A 56Kbps Frame Relay link or an ISDN line are good examples.

Predictor Compression

Predictor compression attempts to predict a sequence of characters by examining a sequence in a dictionary. Predictor then looks at the next string of bits in the data portion to see if there is a match. If there is a match, then the new character sequence replaces the old. If it doesn't match, Predictor starts the process again with the next set of characters.

STAC Compression

An offshoot of one of the first desktop compression algorithms, *STAC* was developed by STAC Electronics and is a Lempel-Ziv compression algorithm. STAC examines data strings for redundant characters and replaces them with a smaller token. For example, if a data string contained the characters *2345678* several times, STAC could replace that string with the notation *@3*. This notation, being smaller than the original string, would reduce bandwidth usage. The notation is converted back to the original string on the other side of the WAN.

MPPC

The Microsoft Point-to-Point Compression protocol allows Cisco routers to communicate with Microsoft clients using a compressed data stream. When enabled on an Access Server interface, this method allows the client to gain increased bandwidth. This type of compression is highly recommended for corporate dial-in customers where the clients have to dial through an 800 number and are using a Microsoft operating system.

Use the following command to configure point-to-point software compression for an LAPB, PPP, or HDLC link:

```
compress predictor | stac | mppc
```

Figure 13.7 shows an example of this command. Using a *lossless* compression algorithm (an algorithm that exactly recreates the original data streams without degradation), routers are able to reliably transport data across a WAN. If you're using PPP encapsulation across a point-to-point connection, you can use the following interface configuration command instead of the **compress** command:

```
ppp compress predictor | stac
```

See Figure 13.8 for an example.

Payload Compression

Sometimes known as *per-virtual circuit compression*, *payload compression* compresses only the data portion of the data stream, leaving the header intact. This method leaves the header readable to all devices and is primarily used in networks that can't guarantee that a packet will always be crossing a particular point-to-point link. Payload compression is well suited for switched and cell-based networking topologies like Frame Relay, X.25, Switched Multimegabit Data Service (SMDS), and Asynchronous Transfer Mode (ATM). You can

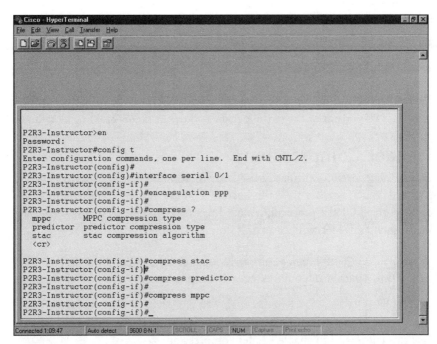

Figure 13.7   Options for the **compress** command.

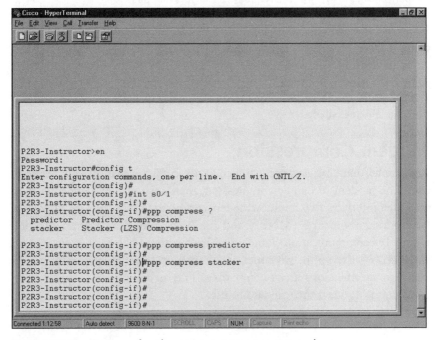

Figure 13.8   Options for the **ppp compress** command.

use the following command to enable STAC compression on a Frame Relay point-to-point interface or subinterface:

```
frame-relay payload-compress
```

Payload compression is also very effective with packets when the data portion is at least 80 percent of the entire packet and the packet is crossing slow links.

Header Compression

Header compression is primarily used in situations where the payload of the packet is much smaller than the header. TCP/IP header compression works only on the TCP/IP protocol; it's used primarily on packets with small payloads, such as Telnet, while crossing slow WAN links.

 TCP/IP header compression leaves the Layer 2 portion of the packet uncompressed—it compresses only the TCP/IP headers.

Use this command to enable header compression:

```
Router(config-if)# ip tcp header-compression passive
```

If you use the *passive* option, the router will compress outgoing packets only when it has received an incoming packet that is compressed. If you're using X.25, use the following command to map compressed TCP headers to an X.121 address for a given link:

```
X25 map compressdtcp
```

Modem Compression

In dial environments, compression can occur in the modem. If you decide to allow the modem to handle compression, then don't enable compression on the router interface. Two common modem compression standards are Microcom Networking Protocol 5 (MNP5) and the International Telecommunication Union Telecommunication Standardization Sector (ITU-T) V.42*bis*. MNP5 and V.42*bis* offer up to two times and four times compression, respectively. The two specifications aren't compatible. The modems at both ends of the connection negotiate the standard to use.

Encrypted Data

Attempting to compress encrypted data is a bad idea. By design, when data is encrypted, there are few patterns for the compression algorithm to examine. Thus when you attempt to compress an encrypted packet, bandwidth usage generally increases. This is the same phenomenon seen when you try to compress an already compressed packet.

Don't use compression if a majority of your traffic is encrypted packets.

CPU Cycles Vs. Memory

The amount of memory that a router needs depends on a number of factors. How many circuits are attached? How many and what kind of access lists are running? Even when you're running a single Layer 3 protocol, the memory and CPU usage can vary widely, especially if more than one routing protocol is running. Thus, it's almost impossible to say how much of a hit a router will receive when you run compression on an interface.

You'll find that, in general, Predictor uses more memory than STAC, and that payload compression uses more memory than link compression. The flip side is that link compression uses more CPU time than payload does. In general, the most important aspect to determining how compression will affect your router is how many packets are being compressed. The more packets you have that are being compressed/decompressed, the larger a performance hit your router will take.

Practice Questions

Question 1

What transport protocol will not support weighted fair queuing?

○ a. Frame Relay

○ b. X.25

○ c. ISDN

○ d. AppleTalk

Answer b is correct. Weighted fair queuing will not operate with X.25 or compressed PPP. It will operate with other serial protocols, including Frame Relay, ISDN, and AppleTalk, as long as those protocols aren't using X.25 or compressed PPP and they operate at 2.048MB or slower. Therefore, answers a, c, and d are incorrect.

Question 2

The default number of packets that the Normal queue in priority queuing can hold is:

○ a. 20

○ b. 40

○ c. 60

○ d. 80

Answer c is correct. The Normal queue can hold 60 packets by default. Therefore, answers a, b, and d are incorrect.

Question 3

> The default data transfer rate in bytes per queue with custom queuing is:
>
> ○ a. 4,500
> ○ b. 4,000
> ○ c. 3,000
> ○ d. 1,500
> ○ e. 500

Answer d is correct. The default transfer rate in bytes per queue is 1,500. There-fore, answers a, b, c, and e are incorrect.

Question 4

> Payload compression is suited to what type of traffic? [Choose the two best answers]
>
> ❏ a. Telnet
> ❏ b. FTP
> ❏ c. ATM
> ❏ d. ISDN

Answers b and c are correct. Payload compression works well with packets where the data portion is large compared to the header portion: ATM and FTP traffic. The header portion of Telnet traffic is larger than the payload. Therefore, answer a is incorrect. Just because a link is slow doesn't mean pay-load compression should be used. Look at the type of traffic first. ISDN is slow, but that alone isn't a valid reason for payload compression. Therefore, answer d is incorrect.

Question 5

> The compression option that allows compression for Microsoft OS clients is:
>
> ○ a. **mppc**
> ○ b. **msppc**
> ○ c. **ppc**
> ○ d. **mpc**

Answer a is correct. The **compress mppc** command allows compression to Microsoft clients. Answers b, c, and d don't exist as options for compression.

Question 6

How many queues does custom queuing support?

○ a. 4

○ b. 8

○ c. 10

○ d. 16

Answer d is correct. Custom queuing supports the use of 16 queues with IOS version 11. Before 11, the limit was 10. Therefore, answer c is incorrect. Answers a and b are invalid choices, and are therefore incorrect.

Question 7

The default congestive discard threshold value for weighted fair queuing is:

○ a. 16

○ b. 32

○ c. 64

○ d. 128

○ e. 256

Answer c is correct. The default congestive discard threshold value for weighted fair queuing is 64 packets. The other values are valid settings but must be manually configured. Therefore, answers a, b, d, and e are incorrect.

Question 8

What Layer 3 protocol supports header compression?

○ a. AppleTalk

○ b. IPX

○ c. SNA

○ d. TCP/IP

Answer d is correct. Only TCP/IP supports header compression. You can use header compression when tunneling IP packets across an X.25 network. The other protocols don't include TCP headers to compress. Therefore, answers a, b, and c are incorrect.

Question 9

The **compress** command has three options you can use. Which of these are *not* options? [Choose the two best answers]

- ❏ a. **stac**
- ❏ b. **stacker**
- ❏ c. **predict**
- ❏ d. **predictor**
- ❏ e. **mpc**
- ❏ f. **mppc**

Answers b, c, and e are correct. The options available with the **compress** command are **stac, predictor,** and **mppc.** Therefore, answers a, d, and f are incorrect. The **stacker** option exists, but with the command **ppp compress stacker,** not the **compress** command. The IOS and Cisco exams can get finicky.

Question 10

What is the default number of packets that a custom queue can hold?

- ○ a. 20
- ○ b. 40
- ○ c. 60
- ○ d. 64
- ○ e. 80

Answer a is correct. The default number of packets that a custom queue can hold is 20, with a range of 0 through 32,767. Therefore, answers b, c, d, and e are incorrect.

Need To Know More?

 More information about queuing commands can be found in the Performance Management section of the documentation area of the Cisco Web site at: **www.cisco.com/univercd/cc/td/doc/ product/software/ios113ed/113ed_cr/fun_r/frprt4/frperfrm.htm.**

 The Lempel-Ziv compression algorithm has quite a bit of controversy relating to its use on software. To learn more about the LZ algorithm check out the Indiana University Knowledge Base at **http://kb.indiana.edu/data/aghf.html.**

 Information regarding the MPPC compression scheme can be found in RFC 2118, information about the Predictor compression scheme can be found in RFC 1978, and info on the Stacker compression scheme can be found in RFC 1967 at **www.faqs.org/rfcs/.**

Network Address
Translation

. . . .

Terms you'll need to understand:

√ Socket

√ Port

√ Network Address Translation (NAT)

√ Port Address Translation (PAT)

√ Overloading

√ Overlapping

√ Transmission Control Protocol (TCP) load distribution

Techniques you'll need to master:

√ Configuring a simple (one-to-one) IP address translation

√ Configuring an overloaded (many-to-one) IP address translation

√ Configuring an overlapped network

√ Configuring TCP load balancing using NAT

√ Configuring static and dynamic NAT

√ Configuring PAT on a 700 series router

The basic uses of Network Address Translation (NAT) are to allow a non-registered IP address to be used inside a private network and also to gain access to a public network such as the Web. The edge router connected to the public network uses NAT to translate the private network addresses to a registered public address. The translation can be performed statically or dynamically. In the case of a simple translation, each non-registered IP address will be translated to a unique public address. This translation would allow access from networks that are using unregistered addressing (or the private address space) to the Web. In this scenario, you would first have to find an Internet Service Provider (ISP) to supply a block of addresses for use. Doing so may be difficult for all but the largest of companies with money to pay for public address space.

To conserve the use of address space, the private space can be *overloaded* to a single or small number of addresses by using the source port of the packet to further distinguish the sending address. To put this in picture form, the packet header is shown in Figure 14.1.

The disadvantages to NAT implementation are the increased latency, address accountability, and loss of certain application functionality:

➤ *Latency*—An increased latency is due to the introduction of a translation step in the switching path.

➤ *Accountability*—You may think it's advantageous to hide the internal addresses from the external world. However, doing so can be problematic when you're trying to determine which internal IP address is responsible for what traffic. Constantly monitoring the NAT connections or providing *only* static NAT translations would detract from the ease of use provided by a dynamic NAT implementation.

➤ *Functionality*—Some applications that require a specific source port or source address would not be able to function in a NAT environment that provides randomly selected address and port assignments. An example would be a specialized database that uses specific, known (to the database) IP addresses for access to specific records. Functionality could be

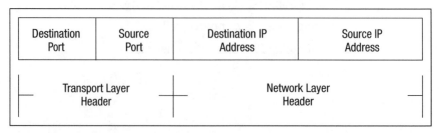

Figure 14.1 Packet header information.

restored using statically mapped translations, but again the dynamic functionality of NAT would be lost.

The advantages of NAT provide for the conservation of legal addresses, reduction of overlap dysfunctionality, increased Internet flexibility, and elimination of network renumbering in a changed environment:

➤ *Conservation*—Legally registered addresses can be conserved using the private address space and NAT to gain access to the Internet.

➤ *Overlap dysfunction*—In an overlapped network situation (described later in the chapter), NAT can provide a means for immediate connectivity without renumbering.

➤ *Flexibility*—Connecting to an Internet provider or changing providers can be accomplished with only minor changes to the NAT configuration.

➤ *Eliminates renumbering*—As network changes are made, the cost of immediate renumbering can be eliminated by using NAT to allow the existing address scheme to remain. The renumbering effort can be gradually implemented or relegated to a Dynamic Host Configuration Protocol (DHCP) server in a stepped fashion rather than all at once.

 The benefits and drawbacks to NAT are featured on both the CMTD and BCRAN exams.

The ubiquitous use of the private space and the proficiency of NAT/PAT have greatly reduced the short supply of address space available on the Internet. This fact hasn't stopped the development of IP version 6 (or IP Next Generation [IPNG]), but it seems to have slowed the implementation of IPNG dramatically.

NAT Definitions

The addresses used for NAT translation can be summed up in four categories:

➤ *Inside local*—IP addresses that are unique to the host inside the network, but aren't globally significant. They're generally allocated from RFC 1918 or randomly picked.

➤ *Inside global*—IP addresses that are assigned by the Internet Addressing-North America (IANA) or service provider and are legitimate in the global address space or Internet. The inside local addresses are translated to the inside global address for Internet use.

➤ *Outside local*—IP addresses of a host on an outside network that is presented to the inside network and is legitimate to the local network. These addresses *do not* have to be globally significant. They're generally selected from RFC 1918 or randomly picked.

➤ *Outside global*—IP addresses that are globally routable on the Internet space.

To make the thought process easier, consider the following definitions:

➤ *Inside*—Addresses that are inside my network

➤ *Outside*—Addresses that are outside my network

➤ *Local*—Addresses that are legitimate inside my network

➤ *Global*—Addresses that are legitimate outside my network

Now, in an effort to totally confuse the issue, simple NAT translation replaces the inside local IP address with an inside global address. In other words, your made-up-not-legitimate-RFC-1918 addresses are converted to real-legitimate-globally-routable-on-the-Internet addresses—and both are valid inside your world.

The use of overloading is the same as simple NAT translation; however, the same inside global address is used again and again by maintaining the translation using the port address.

For TCP load distribution, your network presents an inside global address to the Internet; when this virtual address is called, it's translated to an inside local address. The translation here could also be to an inside global address (the translation is done purely for load distribution purposes).

Last, you need the outside local address category when two networks (an outside and an inside network) are using the same IP address space. In the case of overlapping network numbering, the network that's using an outside global address must be translated to an outside local address if the inside network is to be unique in the outside (Internet) space. This would be the case where an organization elected to use an arbitrary IP range without consideration to a connection to the Internet.

Conversely, an outside address, could be the same as the address that's being used on the inside, because the outside global address is not-on-your-network-but-okay-where-it-is. This would be the case where two organizations have merged using the same address space. Because this network address is okay-where-it-is-but-not-okay-on-your-network, it must be translated to an outside local address—an address that's outside of your network but okay-when-it-gets-in. Figure 14.2 shows each category of address and its location relative to

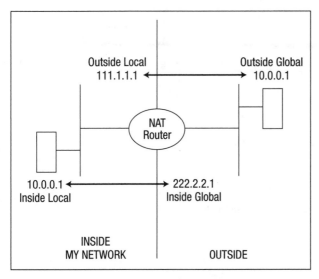

Figure 14.2   Overlapping address definitions.

your network. The terms *inside* and *outside* are relative to the network being discussed; hence, what is outside your network is inside from the far side's perspective.

In this case, both networks are using the 10.0.0.0/24 network. My Network is being translated to the 222.2.2.0/24 network and the Other Network is being translated to 111.1.1.0/24 network.

NAT Configurations
In this section, we will cover the four basic applications of NAT Configurations.

Simple NAT Configuration
NAT translation in its original form replaced the source IP address with a publicly legitimate address. The replacement address came from a pool of addresses that were defined on the NAT device. These replacement addresses were, of course, publicly valid in the Internet address space. NAT is an application layer process that inserts the legitimate address into the packet header and maintains a table of translated addresses, as shown in Figure 14.3.

The simplest form of configuration is a one-to-one translation where the IP address of the inside local address in the network header is replaced by an inside global address. The replacement can be done statically or dynamically. The following example shows a simple NAT translation:

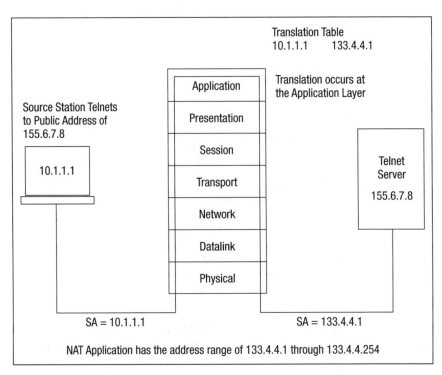

Figure 14.3   NAT in operation.

```
!define what addresses are to be converted
access-list 1 permit 10.0.0.1 0.0.0.255

!define the pool of addresses to use for translation and
!what interfaces and addresses to use
ip nat pool my-natpool 222.2.2.1 222.2.2.254 netmask 255.255.255.0
ip nat inside source list 1 pool my-natpool

!declare inside interfaces
interface e0
  ip address 10.0.0.1 255.255.255.0
  ip nat inside

!declare outside interface
interface s0
  ip address 133.4.4.1 255.255.255.0
  ip nat outside
```

The **access-list** defines what addresses to translate using the **permit** statement. The two key commands are **ip nat pool** and **ip nat inside**. The **ip nat pool** statement can be read as "**ip nat** use the **pool** called **my-natpool** which has the addresses **222.2.2.2.1** through **222.2.2.254** using a **network mask** of **255.255.255.0.**"

Each address that is matched in the access list will use the pool of addresses specified in the previous statement. In order to decide which addresses are to be translated, the **ip nat inside** (or **outside**) statement is used. This statement can be read as "**ip nat** if an interface is declared as **inside** and the **source** address of a packet matches the access-**list 1** use the **pool** called **my-natpool** to replace the ip address."

The following conditions dictate the use of NAT translation:

➤ Only interfaces that are declared inside or outside will be translated.

➤ Only traffic from an outside interface to an inside interface (or vice versa) will be translated.

➤ Packets received on an outside interface destined for an outside interface *will not* be translated.

➤ Packets received on an inside interface destined for an inside interface *will not* be translated.

The definition of *inside* and *outside* can be arbitrary. You can declare the S0 interface to be an inside interface and E0 to be the outside interface—the **ip nat inside** command is simply changed to **ip nat outside**. The question then would be, why? The entire concept of NAT is direction-based, so why confuse the issue?

A key concept to keep in mind is that *only* traffic from an inside interface to an outside interface (or vice versa) will be translated. A packet that is inbound to an inside interface and has as a routed destination an outside interface is a candidate for translation. The command

```
ip nat inside source list 1 pool my-natpool
```

states that if the source address is on list 1, use the declared pool. The selection of inside versus outside and source versus destination is up to the administrator. The examples in the following sections will use inside and outside in relation to the owned network, which is the preferred methodology.

Static NAT Configuration

It's possible, and sometimes desirable, to configure NAT statically. A classic example would be a resource on the inside of a network that must be accessed from the outside world at a specific location. The advertised location of the resource is propagated to the world through DNS. In this example, the inside resource must *always* carry in the outside world the same translated address, and the inside resource must *always* be reachable at the same inside global address.

Static translation is performed using the following command:

```
Ip nat inside source static 10.0.0.1 222.2.2.1
```

This command says, "**ip nat** if the packet is inbound to an **inside** interface destined for an **outside** interface always (**statically**) change the address 10.0.0.1 to the address **222.2.2.1**."

Using the previous example, in which a group of requestors are being translated using a pool and one of the internal devices is a resource (10.0.0.1), the configuration is changed to the following.

```
access-list 1 permit 10.0.0.0 0.0.0.255

ip nat pool my-natpool 222.2.2.2 222.2.2.254 netmask 255.255.255.0
ip nat inside source static 10.0.0.1 222.2.2.1
ip nat inside source list 1 pool my-natpool

!declare inside interfaces
interface e0
  ip address 10.0.0.1 255.255.255.0
  ip nat inside

!declare outside interface
interface s0
  ip address 133.4.4.1 255.255.255.0
  ip nat outside
```

You should notice that the range of available addresses doesn't contain the statically assigned address. The resource has a uniquely defined address in the outside world.

NAT Overloading Configuration

The concept of *overloading* uses the source port to further distinguish which sending station is being transmitted. In this fashion, a single legitimate IP address can be used for many senders. The source port is a number greater than 1,024; it's a software-addressable port at the Transport layer. The first 1,024 port numbers are considered well-known ports (WKP) assigned by Request For Proposal (RFP) 1400.

The terms *socket* and *port* are often used interchangeably; however, this is incorrect. A socket is the IP address: Portnumber pair that is unique to an IP addressable device. The port refers to a numbered entity that is addressable by software. For example, every device has a port number of 23 for Telnet (whether it's in use or not). Only one device has the socket 155.6.7.8:23. The socket refers to a specific location on the network, whereas a port is simply a reference point that could exist on any device.

The overloading feature of NAT uses the entire socket to track the sender—thus, the same IP address can be substituted for many sending addresses. This feature is shown in Figure 14.4.

Each of the devices (sending through the NAT device) is translated and given a new socket number. The new socket number has a unique port number and a common IP address for each translation. In this fashion, only one legitimate address is required for the translation. The use of the port to make the translation unique is called Port Address Translation (PAT). With PAT, the entire socket is replaced, which means that it's really Socket Address Translation (SAT). (If the translation is done only on weekends, then you have PAT using SAT on SAT and SUN. Most Dr. Seuss books were written by highly skilled technical people.)

To convert the configuration for simple NAT translation to overload, the administrator has to be able to type the command **argument overload**. Overloading an inside global address uses the same syntax, but with the extra argument, the router knows to track the port numbers for the translation table. The following configuration extends simple NAT translation to an overload implementation:

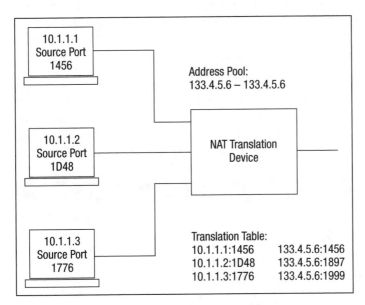

Figure 14.4   Overloading of substitute addresses.

```
!define what addresses are to be converted
access-list 1 permit 10.0.0.1 0.0.0.255

!define the pool of addresses to use for translation and
!what interfaces and addresses to use
ip nat pool my-natpool 222.2.2.1 222.2.2.2 netmask 255.255.255.0
ip nat inside source list 1 pool my-natpool overload

!declare inside interfaces
interface e0
  ip address 10.0.0.1 255.255.255.0
  ip nat inside

!declare outside interface
interface s0
  ip address 133.4.4.1 255.255.255.0
  ip nat outside
```

The change to the configuration is extremely minor: An extra argument was added to the simple NAT translation. However, in an overload configuration, only a single IP address is needed to front for a large number of clients.

NAT Overlapping Configuration

The merger of two companies using the same private address space can be accommodated with the NAT *overlapping network* feature. Essentially, each network is translated to the other. This double translation can take place on a single router. This NAT functionality is *not* something that should be designed into a network. It's offered as an aid to merge two entities without renumbering each end station, while a plan is formed for renumbering the network so that this NAT Band-Aid can be taken off.

The overlapping of network numbering will probably continue to be a problem with the current merger mindset in the business world. Many companies have chosen to use the private address space defined by RFC 1918, which reserves the address ranges for the private network space as shown in Table 14.1.

Table 14.1 Private address ranges.		
Class	**Range**	**Number Of Networks**
A	10.0.0.0	1
B	172.16.0.0 through 172.31.0.0	16
C	192.168.0.0 through 192.168.255.0	255

The use of this limited number of addresses in the private space increases the odds dramatically that an overlap will occur if two private networks are merged which both use the private numbering system. For this reason, most design guidelines dictate that if you're using the private space, *do not* start with the 10.1.0.0 network because others are likely to do the same thing. The recommended practice is to start in the middle—such as 10.128.0.0—and work from there. The drawback to this guideline is that most technical people read the same literature and go to the same classes and talk to the same pundits. Therefore, the next time a merger occurs, they won't have to worry about the overlap of the 10.1.0.0 network—they will have to worry about the overlap of the 10.128.0.0 network.

Overlapping can also occur when a company elects to use a non-private address for its own purposes with the idea that the company will never connect to the Internet. Once a connection is contemplated, a translation can be put in place while the internal renumbering takes place.

The concept of overlapping networks is one that NAT can deal with. It isn't desirable to create an overlapped network. As we discussed earlier, overlapping networks would typically occur during a merger of two companies that were using the same private address space. The overlap configuration can be put into place as a stopgap while renumbering takes place.

The following configuration uses the addresses designated as outside global and outside local with reference, albeit arbitrary, to one or the other network. One network is declared as the inside space, and one is declared as the outside space. Figure 14.5 shows a scenario in which two networks that are both using

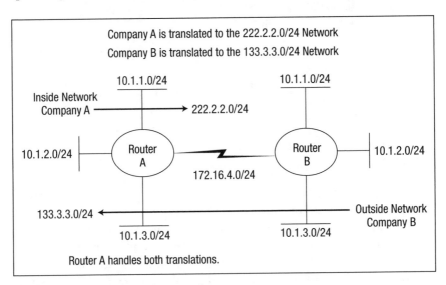

Figure 14.5 Overlapped networks.

the 10.0.0.0 address space can be merged using an overlap configuration. We should point out that you could accomplish the same overall effect by doing a simple translation on the edge router, leaving each of the networks; however, with the overlap configuration the translation is done on one router platform. This approach provides a single point for the configuration and a single point for maintenance of the address space.

The following configuration in Listing 14.1 accomplishes the double translation on Router A:

Listing 14.1 Double translation on Router A.

```
!declare the address pools
ip nat pool coming-in 133.3.3.1 133.3.3.254 prefix-length 24
ip nat pool going-out 222.2.2.1 222.2.2.254 prefix-length 24

!declare the translations
ip nat outside source list 1 pool coming-in
ip nat inside source list 1 pool going-out

!specify which addresses will use the pool
access-list 1 permit 10.1.0.0 0.0.255.255

!specify the interfaces
interface serial 0
   ip   address 172.16.4.1 255.255.255.0
   ip nat outside
!
interface ethernet 0
   ip address 10.1.1.1 255.255.255.0
   ip nat inside
!
interface ethernet 1
   ip address 10.1.2.1 255.255.255.0
   ip nat inside
!
interface ethernet 2
   ip address 10.1.3.1 255.255.255.0
   ip nat inside
```

The configuration declares that all addresses beginning with 10.1 will be translated. The key is which pool shall be used. For those source addresses that arrive on an outside interface and are destined for an inside interface, the translation will use the pool called **coming-in**. The source addresses that arrive on an inside interface destined for the outside interface will use the pool called **going-out**. The access list that dictates which addresses are matched and must use the designated pool is the same for both the inside and outside translations, because all 10.1 addresses require translation before crossing from an inside to an outside interface or vice versa.

NAT TCP Load Distribution Configuration

Finally, NAT can be used for *TCP load distribution*. This technique works in a somewhat reverse form than the other translations. In the other three uses of NAT, the sender was using a non-legitimate source address in a packet destined for the outside world. Load distribution takes advantage of the NAT functionality by allowing a site to advertise an address—but when you send a packet to the advertised address, it's rerouted to another address.

An example would be a large hardware company with multiple mirrored servers on its internal Web site. The company advertises through DNS that to access its server, you should attach to 155.7.7.7; but in reality, the servers are addressed as 155.7.7.1, 155.7.7.2, and so on. As requests come in, they're sent in a round-robin fashion to each of the mirrored servers. Figure 14.6 shows an example of this configuration.

You can use Network Address Translation as a simple tool for TCP load balancing. A classic example is shown in Figure 14.7. Company A has four mirrored Web servers. The company advertises that users can download beta copies of its software for testing from **www.companya.com**, which can be found at 188.88.88.88 on the Internet. The address 188.88.88.88 is a legitimate address that Company A obtained from its service provider. NAT provides a way to

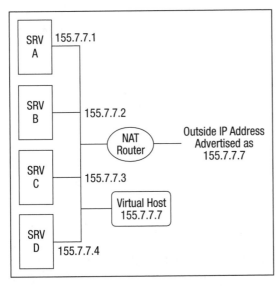

Figure 14.6   TCP load distribution using NAT.

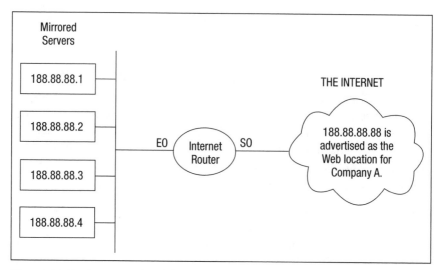

Figure 14.7 NAT TCP load distribution.

translate incoming requests for 188.88.88.88 in a round-robin or rotary fashion to balance the requests across the mirrored servers.

The configuration is straightforward. Any packet that arrives at Company A's Internet router and has a destination for the 188.88.88.88 host is translated in a rotary fashion to one of the four mirrored servers. The following configuration shows the syntax for this implementation:

```
!declare the pool
ip nat pool company-A 188.88.88.1 188.88.88.4 prefix-length 24

!declare the translation
ip nat outside destination list 1 pool company-A rotary

!declare the access-list for translation candidates
access-list 1 permit 188.88.88.88 0.0.0.0

!declare the interfaces
interface S0
  ip nat outside

interface E0
  ip nat inside
```

You should note that the declaration statement for the translation specifies that the **destination** address should be checked against list 1, not the source address as in previous configurations. In addition, the argument **rotary** is placed at the end of the declaration. This way, each incoming packet is translated to one of the pool members in a recurring sequential fashion, and a load distribution is achieved over the four servers.

Verification Of NAT Translation

There are few commands to verify and troubleshoot the NAT configuration. The **show** commands are **show ip nat translation** and **show ip nat statistics**. The translation table is the same format for simple, overload, overlapped, and load distribution, but the information provided is different depending upon the configuration. The following shows the output for a simple translation:

```
Router#show ip nat translation
Pro  Inside global  Inside local  Outside local  Outside global
--   133.3.3.1      10.1.0.1      --             --
--   133.3.3.2      10.1.0.2      --             --
--   133.3.3.3      10.1.0.3      --             --
```

Because this is a simple translation, only the relevant information is put into the table. The concept of outside local and outside global isn't used, and therefore, this information isn't presented when a simple NAT translation is configured. If an overloaded translation has been configured, the output from the **show ip nat translation** command would be as follows:

```
Pro  Inside global     Inside local     Outside local   Outside global
tcp  133.3.3.1:1098    10.1.0.1:1098    173.4.5.6:23    173.4.5.6:23
tcp  133.3.3.2:1345    10.1.0.2:1345    173.4.5.6:23    173.4.5.6:23
tcp  133.3.3.3:1989    10.1.0.3:1989    173.4.5.7:21    173.4.5.7:21
```

You should notice that the outside local address and the outside global address are the same. Because the router isn't performing an overlapped configuration, the outside global address isn't known.

When an overlapping configuration is being used, the router has knowledge of the outside global address. So, the output from a **show ip nat translation** command would appear as follows:

```
Pro  Inside global     Inside local     Outside local    Outside global
tcp  133.3.3.1:1098    10.1.0.1:1098    173.4.5.6:23     10.1.0.23:23
tcp  133.3.3.2:1345    10.1.0.2:1345    173.4.5.6:23     10.1.0.23:23
tcp  133.3.3.3:1989    10.1.0.3:1989    173.4.5.7:21     10.2.0.45:21
```

Because the router is performing both translations, the outside global address is known. The **show ip nat statistics** command may also be useful in troubleshooting a NAT installation. The following output is an example of this command:

```
Router#show ip nat statistics
Total translations: 1 (0 static, 1 dynamic; 0 extended)
Outside interfaces: Serial0Inside interfaces:
                    Ethernet0Hits: 1  Misses: 0
Expired translations: 2Dynamic mappings:-- Inside Source
access-list 1 pool my-pool refcount 2 pool my-pool:
                    netmask 255.255.255.0
    start 172.3.4.1 end 172.3.4.7
    type generic, total addresses 7,
                    allocated 1 (14%), misses 0
```

The **statistics** command shows which interfaces are inside or outside, what the pool name is, and what the addresses are with the mask. The hits and misses refer to the number of times a translation lookup succeeded or failed.

To troubleshoot NAT, you can use the **debug ip nat** command. The output from this command shows the translated addresses and, for a TCP connection, the transaction numbers. The following shows a sample output from a NAT debug:

```
Router#debug ip nat
NAT: s=10.1.0.1->12.1.3.2, d=155.5.5.5 [1]
NAT: s=155.5.5.5, d=12.1.3.2->10.1.0.1 [1]
NAT: s=10.1.0.1->12.1.3.2, d=155.5.5.5 [2]
NAT*: s=155.5.5.5, d=12.1.3.2->10.1.0.1 [2]
Additional output omitted..............
```

The translation is clearly shown from the source address to the destination and the reverse communications. The * indicates that the translation was done in the fast path or using cache. (To watch and debug this output in realtime would be daunting, at best.) The number in brackets indicates the sequencing number for a TCP session, which could be useful for debugging a protocol analyzer trace of the session.

An additional command that's available is the **clear** command for **ip nat**. You can shut down a translated session using this command. The syntax for clearing a simple NAT translation is

```
clear ip nat translation inside global-ip-address local-ip-address
```

It's incumbent upon you to type the addresses without error, to clear the correct address. A small typographical error in the command syntax may clear the wrong session! It's also possible to clear *all* current translated sessions on the router using the command:

```
clear ip nat translation *
```

The use of the * as a wildcard will clear *all* currently established NAT sessions. (This could be a career move on your part.)

> In the documentation for both the CMTD and BCRAN courses, the **clear ip nat translation** command is shown without a space before the *. The CMTD exam asked the question, "How do you clear all NAT translations?" The answer is, "Without a space between the argument and the wildcard character!"

Port Address Translation

PAT is a form of NAT in which the port is also replaced at the translating device. PAT is the only address translation feature in the Cisco 700 series router. We didn't discuss it in Chapter 9, so we need to cover some additional 700 series commands here.

> Only a minor treatment of the PAT syntax is discussed in both the CMTD and BCRAN course material.

The PAT concept is the same as NAT. A pool of addresses isn't needed, because only one address will service all devices.

The two commands associated with PAT on the 700 are

```
SET IP PAT ON
```

which is a global command and requires no arguments, and

```
SET IP PAT PORTHANDLER   port ip-address
```

where *port* is the Transport layer port for the application and *ip-address* is the local address of the device.

The **port handler** command can use the following text arguments in place of the *port* above.

```
Default / Telnet / FTP / SMTP / WINS / HTTP
```

The **Telnet, FTP, SMTP, WINS,** and **HTTP** arguments declare the well-known ports for those protocols and are translated by the router from RFC 1400. The key arguments are **Default** and *port*. The **Default** argument specifies *any* port that isn't declared by another **SET IP PAT PORTHANDLER** command.

The **Port-number** argument is used when the administrator must specify a port other than Telnet, FTP, SMTP, WINS, or HTTP, the defined ports.

Once you've set **IP PAT ON**, the single address that is used for the PAT translation is used in the port handler assignment(s). The port handler, which is unique to the 700 series, declares which ports will be translated. Earlier in this chapter, for the IOS routers an access list declared which traffic would be translated. Here, the selection is made on a port basis. If the port is declared by a port handler, it will be translated. The 700 router can have up to 15 port-handler statements. Figure 14.8 shows the port handler in use.

The FTP and HTTP servers will be translated when they're sent using the Router profile. They will be translated to the address of the interface in use at the time. In this example, FTP packets from the outside world that are destined for 155.5.5.2 (the 700's ISDN interface address) will be translated to 10.0.0.22 (the inside FTP server). Likewise, HTTP packets addressed to the 155.5.5.2 address will be translated to 10.0.0.25 (the HTTP server).

Turning PAT on is a system-wide command to the 700. The definition for the port-handler function is done within a profile.

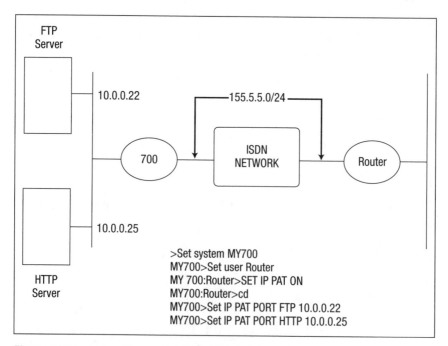

Figure 14.8 Using the port handler for PAT.

You must keep in mind a number of limitations when using the 700 series router:

➤ A ping from an outside host ends at the router. Hence, end-to-end connectivity testing isn't possible.

➤ Only one inside Web server, FTP server, Telnet server, and so forth, is supported, because all port traffic is defined by a single **IP PORTHANDLER** command.

➤ Only 15 port handler addresses are supported in a single configuration.

➤ 400 PAT entries are allocated for sharing among the inside machines.

➤ A maximum of 1,500 MAC addresses can be supported.

These limitations shouldn't deter you from using PAT on a 700. We caution you to remember the market positioning of this device: Small remote offices could take advantage of the translation function to share resources on a larger network. The limiting numbers for the 700 series router are:

➤ 400 PAT entries are allocated for sharing among the inside machines.

➤ 15 Port handler addresses can be used.

➤ 1,500 maximum MAC addresses can be supported.

The bottom line is that the 700 series can be configured for a lot more than a 128Kbps ISDN line can handle. The limitation isn't what the device can do, but more what can be done on the resource that the device uses.

Practice Questions

Question 1

The basic use of NAT:

○ a. Allows registered IP addresses to be used in a private network.

○ b. Allows unregistered IP addresses to be used in a private network.

○ c. Allows registered IP addresses to be used in a public network.

○ d. Allows unregistered IP addresses to be used in a public network.

Answer d is correct. This question is two-fold and requires that the reader understand what is meant by a registered and unregistered address and what is meant by public and private networking.

Question 2

The translation table entry for an inside global address that shows 198.3.3.4:1567 declares the:

○ a. Port translation of the address.

○ b. Socket translation of the address.

○ c. Unique pool address used for the translation.

○ d. None of the above.

Answer b is correct. The socket is the full address IP:PORT assignment. It is *not* the unique pool address, because overloading is obviously in use and the pool address will be used again and again. The key here is to recognize that what has been translated is the entire socket.

Question 3

The use of NAT on a Cisco router can provide for the following needs [Choose the two best answers]:

❑ a. Networks that have overlapping IP addresses

❑ b. Networks that are overloaded with IP traffic

❑ c. Networks that use only registered IP addresses

❑ d. Networks that use the RFC 1918 address space

❑ e. Networks that require ISP connections

Answers a and d are correct. The fact that a network is connected to an ISP does *not* require NAT. In addition, a network that is overloaded with IP traffic is a different problem!

Question 4

The private address range includes:

○ a. 172.1.0.0 through 172.16.0.0

○ b. 144.1.0.0 through 144.16.0.0

○ c. 172.16.0.0 through 172.32.0.0

○ d. 192.168.0.0 through 192.168.32.0

Answer c is correct. The information in this question should be studied for all Cisco tests. Knowledge of the private network numbers is key to any installation, troubleshooting or design issue. The private networks are:

➤ *Class A*—10.0.0.0, 1 network

➤ *Class B*—172.16.0.0 through 172.32.0.0, 16 networks

➤ *Class C*—192.168.0.0 through 192.168.255.0, 255 networks

Question 5

To always map the inside local address 10.0.0.1 to an inside global address of 188.9.9.1, the following command is used:

○ a. **ip nat inside source static 10.0.0.1 188.9.9.1**

○ b. **ip nat static 10.0.0.1 188.9.9.1**

○ c. **ip nat inside source 10.0.0.1 188.9.9.1 static**

○ d. **ip nat static inside local 10.0.0.1 inside global 188.9.9.1**

Answer a is correct. The issue here is the syntax. You should take note that for *all* NAT syntax, the commands begin with **ip nat [inside or outside]** and **[source or destination]**. Using that logic, you're left to remember whether the **static** argument comes at the end or beginning of the declaration. The point to keep in mind is that, in this case, general syntax eliminated the second and fourth choices immediately.

Question 6

To allow a router to perform overlapping address translation, the keyword _____ is used as an argument to the translation command.

○ a. **overlapping**

○ b. **overload**

○ c. **remap**

○ d. None of the above

Answer d is correct. Overlapping addresses are handled by a two-way translation. No keyword is required.

Question 7

Given the following output, what function is the router performing?

```
Pro  Inside global    Inside local    Outside local  Outside global
tcp  133.3.3.1:1098   10.1.0.1:1098   173.4.5.6:23   173.4.5.6:23
tcp  133.3.3.2:1345   10.1.0.2:1345   173.4.5.6:23   173.4.5.6:23
tcp  133.3.3.3:1989   10.1.0.3:1989   173.4.5.7:21   173.4.5.7:21
```

○ a. Simple NAT translation

○ b. Complex NAT translation

○ c. Overlapping NAT translation

○ d. Overloaded NAT translation

Answer d is correct. It's apparent from the output that the translation used is overloaded. Both the outside local and outside global addresses are being reported as the same. This being the case, the router doesn't know what the outside global addresses really are. It can't be simple NAT translation, because the outside addresses are shown. If we had overlapping networks, where the router was performing both translations, the outside local and global addresses would be different.

Question 8

The command to disconnect all current NAT translations is:

○ a. **clear ip nat translation all**

○ b. **clear ip nat translation ***

○ c. **disconnect ip nat translation all**

○ d. **disconnect ip nat translation ***

Answer b is correct. This command is similar to **clear ip route ***. Keep in mind that if the only selection that makes sense doesn't have a space before the *, it's probably okay.

Question 9

The disadvantages to NAT are [Choose the three best answers]:

- ❏ a. Increased latency due to translation
- ❏ b. Program functionality due to required IP addressing
- ❏ c. Overlap dysfunction due to addressing
- ❏ d. Larger route table descriptions
- ❏ e. Increased route table sizes
- ❏ f. End user accountability

Trick! question

Answers a, b, and f are correct. This question requires some thought since it requires a general knowledge of how NAT operates on the router. NAT does not impinge upon the route table size or function. Overlap dysfunction due to addressing is an *advantage* of NAT. The latency is a given because NAT is an application layer function. Certain programs that are hard-coded for specific IP addresses won't function in a NAT environment, hence NAT isn't an option for them. The end user's address is hidden from the world, and if a dynamic pool is being used, it isn't easy to trace what packets come from what workstation.

Question 10

An inside global address is:

- ○ a. Locally and globally routable
- ○ b. Globally routable only
- ○ c. Locally routable only

Answer a is correct. The global addresses are both locally and globally routable.

Question 11

Which of the following commands are correct to declare a NAT translation pool? [Choose the two best answers]

❑ a. **Ip nat pool company-a 188.188.188.1 188.188.188.2 prefix-length 24**

❑ b. **Ip nat pool company-a 188.188.188.1 188.188.188.188 netmask 255.255.255.0**

❑ c. **Ip nat pool company-a 188.188.188.1 188.188.188.2 255.255.255.0**

❑ d. **Ip nat pool company-a 188.188.188.1 255.255.255.0 188.188.188.188 255.255.255.0**

❑ e. **Ip nat pool company-a 188.188.188.1/24 188.188.188.188/24**

Answers a and b are correct. The thrust of this question is that there are two ways to declare the mask. Each of the other choices declares the netmask incorrectly.

Question 12

The benefits to NAT are [Choose the three best answers]:

❑ a. Reduced latency during packet translation

❑ b. Conservation of IP addresses

❑ c. ISP connectivity flexibility

❑ d. Increased accountability for end users

❑ e. Ability to handle overlapped network dysfunction

❑ f. Address block consolidation

❑ g. TCP port handling

Answers b, c, and e are correct. Latency is not a *benefit;* it is a deterrent. User accountability is lost because the addresses are "hidden" from the outside world *as well as the administrator.* Address block consolidation and port handling are *not* functions of NAT.

Question 13

The network address 172.28.9.0/24 can be used in:

○ a. The globally routable space

○ b. Only the locally routable space

○ c. Both the local and global routable space

○ d. Only the global routable space

Answer b is correct. The 172.28.9.0 network is part of the private address space defined by RFC 1918.

Question 14

Up to _____ port handler definitions can be created on a 700 series router.

○ a. 12

○ b. 10

○ c. 15

○ d. 32

Answer c is correct. The answer is 15, by definition.

Question 15

The pool of addresses for a 700 series router can contain:

○ a. A full class C

○ b. Up to 400 addresses

○ c. Any address range within a subnet

○ d. None of the above

Answer d is correct. The 700 doesn't use a pool, per se. It uses the port handler addresses on a one-to-one basis.

Need To Know More?

 Cisco Systems. *Cisco 700 Series Installation and Configuration Guide.* This book is the standard documentation set that comes with the 700 series and is the most informative source for explanations. Text Part number 78-2412-03.

 Cisco Systems. *Cisco 700 Command Reference: Text Part number 78-2413-03.* This book compiles and explains in some detail the syntax and usage for PAT configurations on the 700 series router.

 Cisco Systems. Documentation CD-ROM. Any recent version of the CD-ROM has much background information on the various technologies discussed here. The search engine will allow the user to look specifically at white paper information in lieu of a command search. This gives the user a quick way to find a discussion of the search issue, not just the command to use it.

 Visit the official Cisco Web site at **www.cisco.com** for information and links to all technologies employed by Cisco. Specifically for the 700 series documentation and information you can access **www.cisco.com/univercd/cc/td/doc/product/access/acs_fix/ 750/index.htm.**

Authentication, Authorization, And Accounting (AAA)

Terms you'll need to understand:

√ AAA

√ Authentication

√ Authorization

√ Accounting

√ Packet mode

√ Character mode

√ TACACS

√ RADIUS

√ Virtual profiles

Techniques you'll need to master:

√ Enabling AAA on the Remote Access Server (RAS) device

√ Enabling authentication

√ Declaring authorization levels

√ Establishing accounting tracking

√ Understanding the creation of a virtual profile

Introduction To AAA

Authentication, Authorization, and Accounting (AAA) provides a method for setting up access control on the router. You use access control to provide a means to declare who (authentication) can access the network, dictate what (authorization) the users can do, and track (accounting) what the user has done. AAA provides a method to control and configure these three independent security functions.

CiscoSecure Access Control Server (ACS) provides authentication, authorization, and accounting and is used in many of the BCRAN classes as the AAA server. This does *not* mean that CiscoSecure is the only AAA server—it's one of the available AAA servers. CiscoSecure comes bundled with the following:

➤ *AAA server*—The server provides basic AAA functionality for authentication, authorization, and accounting.

➤ *Netscape Fastrack Server*—This piece provides an interface function to the GUI Admin Client. The Admin Client allows the administrator to manage the CiscoSecure ACS database through Netscape or Internet Explorer. The Web-based interface allows login to the ACS database to perform system administrator tasks. ACS will store these modifications in its relational database management system (RDBMS), or in another supported RDBMS.

➤ *RDBMS*—The ACS server can operate with an external RDBMS or the Oracle and Sybase Enterprise database applications, because it uses the open database connectivity (ODBC) interface. The RDBMS used in CiscoSecure is SQLAnywhere, which is a non-scalable RDBMS.

Authentication

Authentication provides a method of identifying users. During the authentication process, the user login (name) and password are checked against the AAA database. Also, depending on the protocol, some of the protocols will encrypt the username and/or password to prevent capturing this information during transmission. .

Authentication determines who the user is prior to the user being allowed into the network. The process is only the first piece of the puzzle of access. Once the user ID and password are accepted, the user is then authorized.

Authorization

Authorization allows the administrator to control authorization on a one-time basis: per service, per user list, per group, or per protocol. AAA lets you create attributes that describe what the user is allowed to do. The attributes are compared to the database for a given user, and the capabilities are returned to the AAA server. This assembled set of attributes describes what tasks the user is authorized to perform. Prior to each user task the database is sent a query for authorization.

Accounting

Accounting allows you to collect information such as start and stop times for user access, executed commands, traffic statistics, and the like, for storage in the RDBMS. Accounting lets you track services and resources that are consumed by the user. The thrust is that this information can be used for client billing, internal billing, network management, or audit trails.

Interfaces: Character Vs. Packet Mode

Understanding the communication method on each port or port definition is an important step toward understanding the configuration of AAA. Character mode sends keystrokes to the router through the teletype (TTY), Virtual Terminal (VTY), Auxiliary (AUX), and Console (CON) ports for configuration or query commands. These are the *control* ports on the router. Packet mode is used on the async, group-async, Basic Rate Interface (BRI), Primary Rate Interface (PRI), serial, dialer profile, and dialer rotary ports. These are the *communication* ports on the router. Packet mode uses interface mode or a link protocol session to communicate with a device other than the router. This becomes important as you read on. The concept of control versus communication involves a fine distinction. The use of the term *control* indicates a character communication connection that allows control or configuration of the router. On the other hand, *communication* indicates that the port is being used to access a source other than the router.

Each authentication and authorization is tied to one of these interfaces. Syntax is the key. The AAA authentication and authorization pieces are presented in the following sections. During this discussion, the concept of which interface is being used becomes germane.

Communication ports are used to access a source other than the router and include the async, group-async, BRI, PRI, serial, dialer profile, and dialer rotary ports. Console ports are used to access the router for configuration purposes. The console ports include the TTY, VTY, AUX, and Console.

AAA Configuration

To enable AAA on the router, the command is as follows:

```
aaa new-model
```

The **no** form of this command disables AAA on the router. Once AAA is enabled, you must point the router to the source of the AAA server. For a Terminal Access Control Access Control Server (TACACS), the command is:

```
tacacs-server host ip-address [single-connection]
```

The IP address is the location of the CiscoSecure server or another TACACS server. The optional **single-connection** parameter tells the router to maintain a single connection for the duration of the session between the router and the AAA device. The alternative is to open and close a TCP connection for each session; opening and closing a connection is the default. Cisco recommends the single-connection feature for improved performance.

A shared password is used between the access router and the AAA server for security. The command to establish this password on the router is as follows:

```
tacacs-server key password
```

The password must be configured on the AAA server also. The passwords are case-sensitive.

The first steps for configuring AAA on a Remote Authentication Dial In User Service (RADIUS) are similar. The **tacacs** argument is replaced by **radius**. The following example is the initial command set for a RADIUS implementation:

```
aaa new-model
radius-server host 115.55.43.1
radius-server key bigdog
```

Here the IP address is 115.55.43.1, and the shared password is *bigdog*.

AAA Authentication

The next piece of the configuration requires the administrator to declare the methods by which authentication will take place. The key issue is to ensure that you have a way to gain access to the router if the AAA server is downed. Failure to provide a back-door interface can result in lost communications to the router and the necessity to break in via the console port. You should take care to *always* configure a local access method during implementation of AAA.

The syntax for configuring AAA on the router can be daunting. The global configuration commands allow you to declare which method will be used for authentication. These methods are checked in the order in which they are specified in the command. The generic form for the **authentication** command is as follows:

```
aaa authentication [login | enable | arap | ppp | nasi]
```

This syntax *does not* include the arguments for the command: The arguments specify the methods. It's clearer to show each of the commands and then discuss the arguments that you can add to the command. The command could be **aaa authentication login, aaa authentication enable,** or **aaa authentication arap,** and so on. To be clear, each command can stand alone. The next five subsections declare each of the command definitions for the **authentication** command. Each command is used for a specific purpose:

➤ **aaa authentication login**—How do I authenticate the login dialog box?

➤ **aaa authentication enable**—Can the user get to the privileged command prompt?

➤ **aaa authentication arap**—The AppleTalk Remote Access Protocol (ARAP) users must use RADIUS or TACACS+.

➤ **aaa authentication ppp**—What method should be used if a user is coming over a Point-to-Point Protocol (PPP) connection?

➤ **aaa authentication nasi**—What method should be used if a user is coming over a NetWare Asynchronous Services Interface (NASI)?

AAA Authentication LOGIN

What method of authentication will be used during the login procedure? The answer to this question is defined by this command:

```
aaa authentication login [default | listname]
```

The declaration of **default** tells the router what to do if no listname has been declared on the interface. If a listname has been declared, then that listname will control the login. For example, the global command

```
aaa authentication login mypeople
```

declares how the list called **mypeople** will be interpreted. On each interface that is declared as a **mypeople** interface, one or more of the following arguments will be used for the authentication:

```
[enable | line | local | none | tacacs+ | radius | guest]
```

Each of the arguments declares a method of authentication, and they can be listed one after another on the command line. Not all methods are valid for all authentication methods. For instance, login cannot take guest as an argument. The guest argument is related to the ARAP authentication only. Each of the main commands is detailed below for the available arguments. The following example shows this concept:

```
Router(config)#aaa auth login mypeople tacacs+ radius local
Router(config)#aaa auth login default tacacs+
Router(config)#line 1 12
Router(config-line)#login authentication mypeople
```

The first statement declares that the list **mypeople** will use TACACS+, then RADIUS, and then local username/password pairs, in that order, for authentication. The fourth statement declares that on lines 1 through 12, anyone attaching to these interfaces will be authenticated in **mypeople** order. If someone attaches to the console port, he or she will be authenticated by TACACS+ only, because that is the default.

The term *listname* refers to the list of methods that will be used, not to a list of people that will be authenticated. In our example, you can interpret *listname* as "My people will use this list for authentication."

The order of the authentication arguments is important. In the same example, if the *user* fails authentication with TACACS+, he will be denied access. If the *router* fails to access TACACS+, then the router will try to contact a RADIUS server. The key issue is that a secondary method will be used only if a previous method is unavailable to the router.

This is important to remember, because if TACACS+ is the only option to verify a login and the TACACS+ service is unavailable or down, then *nobody* can log in. If the authentication methods are set as TACACS+ and local, then administration username/password pairs could be placed on the router; that way, even if TACACS+ is down, an administrator will still be able to gain access to the router.

It's important to maintain a proper order for the methods. We suggest that local be a last resort method if all else fails, so that access to the router is maintained by at least a local username/password pair.

Each of the methods for login authentication is described in the following list. You should memorize these definitions for the exam.

> *Enable*—Use the enable password for authentication on the interface. The authentication is compared against the enable password on the router.

> *Line*—Use the password on the line that is being attached to. You do so using the line command login (ask for a password) and the command **password xxx**, where *xxx* is the password for the line.

> *Local*—Use the username *yyyy* password *xxxx* pairs that are on the router for authentication.

> *None*—Don't use an authentication method.

> *Tacacs+*—Use the TACACS server declared by the **tacacs-server host ip-address** statement on the router.

> *Radius*—Use the RADIUS server declared by the **radius-server host ip-address** statement on the router.

AAA Authentication ENABLE

What method will be used if a user tries to access privileged mode on the router? If no AAA methods are set, then the user must have the enable password as the IOS would demand. If AAA is being used and *no* default is set, then the user will also need the enable password for access to the privileged mode. The construct for AAA is similar to the login authentication commands. The following example shows the implementation of **aaa authentication enable**:

```
Router(config)#aaa authentication enable thefolks tacacs+
```

This command declares that to gain access to privilege mode, the router must first check TACACS+; if TACACS+ returns an error or is unavailable, the router should then use the enable password. With all the lists that are set for AAA, the secondary methods are used only if the authentication methods return an error or are unavailable.

Each of the methods for enable authentication is described in the following list. You should memorize these definitions for the exam:

> *Enable*—Use the enable password for authentication on the interface. The authentication is compared against the enable password on the router.

> *Line*—Use the password on the line that is being attached to. This is done using the line command login (ask for a password) and the command **password xxx**, where *xxx* is the password for the line.

> ➤ *None*—Don't use an authentication method.

> ➤ *Tacacs+*—Use the TACACS server declared by the **tacacs-server host ip-address** statement on the router.

> ➤ *Radius*—Use the RADIUS server declared by the **radius-server host ip-address** statement on the router.

AAA Authentication ARAP

The **aaa authentication arap** command is used in conjunction with the **arap authentication** line configuration command. The **aaa authentication arap** statement describes the methods that are tried when AppleTalk Remote Access (ARA) users attempt to gain access to the router. The **arap authentication** command points back to the **aaa authentication arap** global command.

An example for this configuration is as follows:

```
Router(config)#aaa authentication arap dudes tacacs+ local
Router(config)#line 1 12
Router(config-line)#arap authentication dudes
```

The first statement declares that TACACS+ will be used first; then local username/password pairs will be used if TACACS+ returns an error or is unavailable. On lines 1 through 12, the list **dudes** points back to the AAA declaration in the first statement.

The methods for enable authentication are described in the following list. You should memorize these definitions for the exam:

> ➤ *Line*—Use the password on the line that is being attached to. This is done using the line command login (ask for a password) and the command **password xxx**, where *xxx* is the password for the line.

> ➤ *Local*—Use the username *yyyy* password *xxxx* pairs that are on the router for authentication.

> ➤ *Tacacs+*—Use the TACACS server declared by the **tacacs-server host ip-address** statement on the router.

> ➤ *Guest*—Allow a login if the username is guest. This option is only valid using ARAP.

> ➤ *Auth-Guest*—Only allow the guest login if the user has already logged into the command executive process (EXEC mode) process on the router, and has now started the ARAP process.

Note that, by default, guest logins through ARAP are disabled when you initialize AAA. The **aaa authentication arap** command with either the **guest** or **auth-guest** keyword is required for guest access when using AAA.

AAA Authentication PPP

The **aaa authentication ppp** command is used in conjunction with the **ppp authentication** line configuration command. The **aaa authentication ppp** command describes the methods that are tried when PPP users attempt to gain access to the router.

An example for this configuration is as follows:

```
Router(config)#aaa authentication ppp dudettes tacacs+ local
Router(config)#line 1 12
Router(config-line)#ppp authentication dudettes
```

The same type of syntax is used throughout all the AAA commands. With the **ppp** command, you set the interface command **is ppp authentication** *option(s)*, where the options can be the standard non-AAA options of **pap, chap, pap chap, chap pap, or ms-chap**. In addition, you can use the AAA command methods. In the previous example, the authentication will be TACACS+; it will then use local username/password pairs if TACACS+ is unavailable or returns an error.

The methods for authentication using AAA for PPP are described in the following list. You should memorize these definitions for the exam:

➤ *Local*—Use the username *yyyy* password *xxxx* pairs that are on the router for authentication.

➤ *None*—Don't use an authentication method.

➤ *Tacacs+*—Use the TACACS server declared by the **tacacs-server host ip-address** statement on the router.

➤ *Radius*—Use the RADIUS server declared by the **radius-server host ip-address** statement on the router.

➤ *Krb5*—The Kerberos release 5 (krb5) method is available only for PPP operations, and communications with a Kerberos security server must be established. Kerberos login authentication works with PPP Password Authentication Protocol (PAP) only. (The name *Kerberos* comes from mythology and is the name of the three-headed dog that guarded the river Styx.)

> ➤ *If-Needed*—This is another PPP-only option. It stops
> authentication if the user has been authenticated previ-
> ously on the TTY line.

AAA Authentication NASI

The **aaa authentication nasi** command is used with the **nasi authentication**
line configuration command to specify a list of authentication methods that
are tried when a NASI user attempts to gain access to the router.

An example for this configuration is as follows:

```
Router(config)#aaa authentication nasi people tacacs+ local
Router(config)#line 1 12
Router(config-line)#nasi authentication people
```

As with the other access methods, when a user is using NASI, this example
would require TACACS+ authentication and then use the username/password
pair if TACACS+ was unavailable.

The methods for authentication using AAA with NASI are
described in the following list. You should memorize these
definitions for the exam:

> ➤ *Line*—Use the password on the line that is being attached
> to. This is done using the line command login (ask for a
> password) and the command **password xxx**, where *xxx* is
> the password for the line.

> ➤ *Enable*—Use the enable password for authentication on
> the interface. The authentication is compared against the
> enable password on the router.

> ➤ *Local*—Use the username *yyyy* password *xxxx* pairs that
> are on the router for authentication.

> ➤ *None*—Don't use an authentication method.

> ➤ *Tacacs+*—Use the TACACS server declared by the **tacacs-
> server host ip-address** statement on the router.

When AAA is turned on, *all* lines/ports on the router will use AAA—hence
the default group should be configured for any access method that the router
will see.

AAA Authorization

Once users have been authenticated, you can further restrict what they're allowed to do. You do so using the **aaa authorization** command. These restrictions

can be applied to activities or services offered on the router. As with the authentication, it's easier to see an example before diving into each option available. The syntax is quite simple: It declares which activity or service (**network, exec, command level, config-commands, and reverse-access**) is being attempted and what method of authorization is to be used (local, none, RADIUS, TACACS, or krb5). The following is an example of the syntax:

```
Router(config)#aaa new-model

    Router(config)#aaa authentication login dudes tacacs+ local
    Router(config)#aaa authorization exec tacacs+ local
    Router(config)#aaa authorization command 1 tacacs+ local
    Router(config)#aaa authorization command 15 tacacs+ local
```

In this example, AAA is turned on with **aaa new-model**, and the authentication method is declared for the list called **dudes**. The third line declares that if one of the logged-in users wants to gain access to the EXEC mode, TACACS+ will be contacted to see if the user is allowed to perform that function. The last two lines are similar, and the logged-in user will be tested against the TACACS database for authorization to run level 1 and level 15 commands.

The router IOS commands are either level 1 or level 15 commands. It's possible to change the level of each command on the router to allow for a much more controlled access environment for the users. This is the power of AAA, but the administration overhead to accomplish this may be daunting to most administrators. In addition, this level of control may be unnecessary for most installations. Can it be done? Yes. Should it be done? Maybe.

The generic form of the authorization command is as follows:

```
Aaa authorization do-what? check-how?
```

The **do-what** arguments can be:

➤ **network**—Uses the **check-how** method for authorization to perform all network-related service requests, such as the Serial Line Internet Protocol (SLIP), PPP, and ARAP protocols.

➤ **exec**—Uses the **check-how** method for authorization to determine if the user is allowed to create and run the router EXEC shell. If TACACS+ or

RADIUS is being used, it's possible that the database could return autocommand information such as the menu system for the user.

➤ **command** *level*—Uses the **check-how** method for authorization for all commands at the specified privilege level. The level can be set to values of 1 through 15.

➤ **reverse-access**—Uses the **check-how** method for authorization for reverse access connections, such as reverse Telnet.

The **check-how** arguments are the same as those used for authentication and are listed here. The **check-how** simply points to where the authentication should be done:

➤ **tacacs+**—TACACS+ authorization is done by associating attribute-value (AV) pairs to individual users. The AV pair associates a function that the user is authorized to do. When a user attempts to do a **do-what**, the TACACS database is checked.

➤ **if-Authenticated**—If the user has been authenticated, then he is allowed to perform this function. Notice that you aren't checking authorization, but whether the user is in the database and is valid.

➤ **none**—The router doesn't request authorization information for this **do-what**. Authorization isn't performed, and a query isn't sent to the database.

➤ **local**—The router or access server consults its local database, as defined by the **username** *xxx* **password** *yyy* global router command.

➤ **radius**—RADIUS authorization is done by associating attributes to a username on the RADIUS server. Each username and the associated attributes are stored within the RADIUS database.

➤ **krb5-instance**—The router will query the Kerberos server for authorization. The authorizations are stored on the Kerberos server.

In general, you can implement authorization in many ways. The issues are what database or resource has the AV pair, attribute, or map to provide the router with the answer to the authorization query.

AAA Accounting

Finally, AAA accounting can supply information back to the database concerning user activity. This concept was especially helpful in the early days of Internet service when many ISPs billed users according to 20 or 40 hours per week at a fixed cost and assessed hourly or minute charges in excess of the specified timeframe. Today, it's much more common for the ISP to allow unlimited access time for a fixed monthly fee. This does not, however, minimize the power of accounting to supply you the capability to track unauthorized attempts and provide proactive security for system resources. In addition, you can use accounting to track resource usage, to better allocate system usage.

Accounting is generally used for billing and auditing purposes and is simply turned on for those events that are to be tracked. As with authentication and authorization, an example is a good way to start. Syntactically, the commands follow this syntax:

```
aaa accounting what-to-track how-to-track
    where-to-send-the-information
```

The following example shows a simple accounting setup:

```
Router(config)#aaa accounting command 15 start-stop tacacs+
Router(config)#aaa accounting connection start-stop tacacs+
Router(config)#aaa accounting system wait-start tacacs+
```

In the first line, accounting has been activated for all level 15 commands, to show when the command was begun and when it ended for the user who initiated the command. The second line logs to the database when the user's connection began and when it ended. The last statement tracks any system level event—such as a reload or configuration change—by start and end times. The **wait-start** argument assures that the logging of the start of the system event is acknowledged before the event is allowed to start. The key issue here is that if a reload of the router is issued, it's imperative that the event be logged and acknowledged before the router reloads. If the message is missed or lost in transmission, the event would go unrecorded.

Accounting records can be sent to a TACACS+ server or a RADIUS server, and the records that are to be tracked are recorded to the router with the AAA accounting commands.

The **what-to-track** arguments are as follows:

➤ **network**—Network accounting logs the information, on a user basis, for PPP, SLIP, or ARAP sessions. The accounting information provides the time of access and the network resource usage in packet and byte counts.

➤ **connection**—Connection accounting logs the information about *outbound* connections made from the router or RAS device, including Telnet and rlogin sessions. The key word is *outbound*, which allows tracking of connections made from the RAS device and where those connections were established.

➤ **exec**—EXEC accounting logs the information when a user creates an EXEC terminal session on the router. If it's a dial-in user, the IP address and telephone number are recorded along with the time and date of the access. This information can be particularly useful for tracking unauthorized access to the RAS device.

➤ **system**—System accounting logs the information about system-level events. System level events include AAA configuration changes and reloads for the device. Again, this information would be useful to track unauthorized access or tampering with the router.

➤ **command**—Command accounting logs information regarding which commands are being executed on the router. The accounting record contains a list of commands executed for the duration of the EXEC session, along with the time and date information.

As you can see, the amount of information you can track is substantial. It's incumbent upon you to track only the information that will be useful. Unwanted tracking of information can create a large overhead to the network resource.

The **how-to-track** argument can be any of the following:

➤ **start-stop**—The **start-stop** function sends an accounting record when the process has begun. It's sent as a background process, and the user request is begun without delay. When the user process is completed, the stop time and information are sent to the AAA database. You use this option when you need an elapsed time of usage.

➤ **stop-only**—The **stop-only** function sends the aggregated information based on the **what-to-track** at the end of the user process. You can use this option when you need only the **what-to-track** information.

➤ **wait-start**—As we mentioned previously, the **wait-start** option won't allow the user process to start until an acknowledgement is received by the RAS device from the accounting database engine. **Wait-start** is particularly important when the tracked event may cause a loss of connectivity with the accounting database.

The last piece of information needed for the router or RAS is where to send the information that is being tracked. The **where-to-send-the-information** can be in either of the following locations:

➤ **tacacs+**—The information is sent to the TACACS+ server defined by the **tacacs-server** host *ip-address* command.

> **radius**—The information is sent to the RADIUS server database defined by the **radius-server host i***p-address* command. The current Cisco implementation doesn't support the command accounting feature.

 Accounting is a powerful tool for proactive management of network resources; however, it's a double-edged sword. The more accounting, the more resources are used to accomplish the accounting. It's generally recommended that you use the **stop-only** argument if an elapsed time isn't needed. The format of accounting records will depend upon the AAA software that you're using. The treatment of AAA within the confines of the BCRAN class is intended to give the student a basic understanding of AAA. All AAA software engines can provide the same or similar functionality; it's impossible to describe the intricacies of an individual software suite as the standard for AAA.

Virtual Profiles

The next evolution of a dialer profile is the creation of a virtual profile. Virtual profile information can be kept on a AAA server and associated with a user. The key elements to the virtual profile are:

> *The physical interface specification*—This information is maintained on the router or RAS device and is generic for any outbound connection.

> *The generic information about a connection that is stored in a template on the router or access device*—This information allows the physical interface to be divorced from the connection-specific information.

> *The user-specific information that is stored on the AAA server*—This information is specific to the user and the connection and can be managed and maintained in a central location.

When a user has gained access to the RAS device and initiates an outbound connection, the AAA server can provide the detailed information on how to handle the user-specific connection. The evolution is complete. The router maintains the resource, and the AAA server provides the information about a connection on a user by user basis. In this way, the router administrator only has to provide a resource and not the details regarding the use of it.

Once the user has gained access to the remote access server by passing authentication, the user then requests an interface to create a session. If the authorization is passed, the AAA server provides the virtual template on behalf of the user, and the connection is established with the user-specific connection information.

Virtual profiles provide the latest evolution for remote access. Throughout this book, the connections made from an access server have gone from a unique phone number assigned to an interface, to a group of numbers associated with an interface with the **dialer-map** command, to dialer profiles. The last step—virtual profiles—completely disassociates the router from maintaining the information about a remote connection.

Practice Questions

Question 1

> AAA defines which functions? [Choose the three best answers]
>
> ❑ a. Authentication
>
> ❑ b. Accounting
>
> ❑ c. Auditing
>
> ❑ d. Authorization
>
> ❑ e. Access

Answers a, b, and d are correct. This question asks for a basic understanding of the acronym itself. Answers c and e are not correct.

Question 2

> Which of the following are packet-mode ports on the router? [Choose the two best answers]
>
> ❑ a. BRI
>
> ❑ b. Serial 1
>
> ❑ c. AUX
>
> ❑ d. CON 0
>
> ❑ e. TTY

Answers a and b are correct. The AUX, CON, and TTY ports support character mode or control mode and allow configuration or access to the RAS device. Therefore, answers c, d, and e are not correct. Packet mode is used to connect to a remote device off the router.

Question 3

> To enable AAA on a router, the command is:
>
> ○ a. **enable aaa**
>
> ○ b. **aaa enable**
>
> ○ c. **aaa new-model**
>
> ○ d. **router aaa**

Answer c is correct. The syntax to turn on AAA is unique. Although a guess might be answer a **enable aaa**, answer b **aaa enable** or answer d **router aaa**, only the command **aaa new-model** is correct.

Question 4

> To capture the commands used during an EXEC session on the router to a TACACS+ database, the following command would be needed:
>
> ○ a. **router(config)#aaa accounting exec stop-only tacacs+**
>
> ○ b. **router(config)#aaa authorization exec start-stop tacacs+**
>
> ○ c. **router(config-line)#aaa accounting exec stop-start tacacs+**
>
> ○ d. **router(config-line)#aaa accounting exec stop-only tacacs+**

Answer a is correct. The accounting commands are issued in Global configuration mode; hence c and d are eliminated. Answer b declares (incorrectly) an authorization command, not an accounting command.

Question 5

> To declare TACACS+ as the primary authentication method and the username/password pairs defined on the router as a secondary authentication method for a NetWare Asynchronous Service Interface login on an interface with no AAA definition, the command is:
>
> ○ a. **aaa authentication login default tacacs+ username**
>
> ○ b. **aaa authentication nasi default tacacs+ username**
>
> ○ c. **aaa authentication login default tacacs+ local**
>
> ○ d. **aaa authentication nasi default tacacs+ local**
>
> ○ e. None of the above

Answer d is correct. The keyword is **nasi** to declare a NetWare Asynchronous Service Interface connection, and because there is *no* AAA definition on the interface, the default list is used. The **login** keyword is used for local logins to the interface not using the NASI protocol. Therefore, answers a and c are incorrect. The keyword to declare the use of username/password is **local**, not **username**. Therefore, answer b is incorrect.

Question 6

The accounting keyword **wait-start**:

○ a. Will not allow a command to be processed until the user is authenticated

○ b. Will not allow a command to be processed until the database has been notified

○ c. Will not allow a command to be processed until the router has been notified

○ d. Will not allow a command to be processed until the user is authorized

Answer c is correct. The **wait-start** option is generally used for the tracked commands that may disturb the communication between the router and the AAA database. Therefore, answers a, b, and d are incorrect.

Question 7

Virtual profiles:

○ a. Can override the configuration of a dialer interface

○ b. Are configured on the router

○ c. Can only be used on a BRI interface

○ d. Are specific to an authenticated user

Answer d is correct. An authenticated user, when using an interface, will "download" the interface setup from the AAA server. Answer a is tempting; however, if a specific interface is configured for only one number when it's accessed, it won't be superceded by a virtual profile. Answers b and c are simply incorrect.

Question 8

> Authorization is the method by which AAA allows user access to a RAS.
>
> ○ a. True
>
> ○ b. False

Answer b is correct. Authorization is used to permit or deny specific functions once the user has been *authenticated*.

Question 9

> Given the router script
>
> ```
> Router(config)#aaa authentication nasi people
>         tacacs+ local
>         Router(config)#line 1 12
>         Router(config-line)#nasi authentication
>             people
> ```
>
> any user who establishes a connection to the router on lines 1 through 12 will be authenticated by the declared TACACS server, unless it's down.
>
> ○ a. True
>
> ○ b. False

Answer b is correct. *Only* those users who are accessing lines 1 through 12 using NASI will use the TACACS+ database. If a user is coming in with any other protocol, the default authentication method will be used. This question requires more than simple syntax understanding—a grasp of each argument to the **aaa authentication** command is needed.

Question 10

Authorization determines:

○ a. Who the user is

○ b. What the user can do

○ c. When the user did it

○ d. Where the user is

○ e. Why the user is logged in

Answer b is correct. The question may seem obvious, but it reinforces the concept of which piece is being tested. Answer a is incorrect because it is authentication that determines who you are. Authorization determines what you can do. Accounting tracks what you did, so answer c is incorrect. Answers d and e were not discussed in this chapter.

Need To Know More?

 Cisco Systems: *Cisco IOS Dial Solutions*. Cisco Press. ISBN 1-578-70055-8. A resource book not designed as a good read, but as a useful command reference. It has many examples and reference tables in one location.

 Shimomura, Tsutomu and John Markoff: *Takedown: The Pursuit and Capture of Kevin Mitnick, America's Most Wanted Computer Outlaw—By the Man Who Did It*. Warner Books. ISBN 0-786-88913-6. Another good book to add dimension to the concept of security.

 Stoll, Clifford: *The Cuckoo's Egg: Tracking a Spy Through the Maze of Computer Espionage*. Pocket Books. ISBN 0-671-72688-9, 1995. This book is a good read to gain an appreciation of why AAA is important.

 Cisco Systems: Documentation CD. Any recent version of the CD has much background information on the various technologies discussed here. The search engine will allow you to look specifically at white paper information in lieu of a command search. Doing so gives you a quick way to find a discussion of the search issue, not just the command to use it.

 Visit the official Cisco Web site at **www.cisco.com** for information and links to all technologies employed by Cisco.

Sample Test

In this chapter, we provide pointers to help you develop a successful test-taking strategy, including how to choose proper answers, how to decode ambiguity, how to work within the Cisco testing framework, how to decide what you need to memorize, and how to prepare for the test. At the end of the chapter, we include 62 questions on subject matter that pertains to Cisco Exam 640-505, "Remote Access." In Chapter 17, you'll find the answer key to this test. Good luck!

Questions, Questions, Questions

There should be no doubt in your mind that you're facing a test full of specific and pointed questions. The version of the Remote Access exam you'll take is a fixed-length exam; it will include 62 questions, and you'll be allotted 90 minutes to complete it. You'll be required to achieve a score of 706 points (out of 1000) or better to pass the exam.

For this exam, questions belong to one of six basic types:

➤ Multiple-choice with a single answer

➤ Multiple-choice with multiple answers

➤ Multipart with a single answer

➤ Multipart with multiple answers

➤ Simulations (that is, you must answer a question based on Cisco IOS command output)

➤ Fill in the blank (you must type out your answers without using the abbreviations that many Cisco administrators are used to using)

Always take the time to read a question at least twice before selecting an answer, and always look for an Exhibit button as you examine each question. Exhibits include graphics information that's related to a question. An exhibit is usually a screen capture of program output or GUI information that you must examine to analyze the question's contents and to formulate an answer. The Exhibit button brings up graphics and charts used to help explain a question, provide additional data, or illustrate program behavior.

Not every question has only one answer; many questions require multiple answers. Therefore, you need to read each question carefully to determine how many answers are necessary or possible and to look for additional hints or instructions when selecting answers. Such instructions often occur in brackets immediately following the question itself (as they do for all multiple-choice, multiple-answer questions). Unfortunately, some questions do not have any right answers and you're forced to find the "most correct" choice.

Picking Proper Answers

Obviously, the only way to pass any exam is to select enough of the right answers to obtain a passing score. However, Cisco's exams are not standardized like the SAT and GRE exams; they're far more diabolical and convoluted. In some cases, questions are strangely worded, and deciphering them can be a real challenge. In those cases, you may need to rely on answer-elimination skills. Almost always, at least one answer out of the possible choices for a question can be eliminated immediately because it matches one of these conditions:

➤ The answer does not apply to the situation.

➤ The answer describes a nonexistent issue, an invalid option, or an imaginary state.

After you eliminate all answers that are obviously wrong, you can apply your retained knowledge to eliminate further answers. Look for items that sound correct but refer to actions, commands, or features that are not present or not available in the situation that the question describes.

If you're still faced with a blind guess among two or more potentially correct answers, reread the question. Try to picture how each of the possible remaining answers would alter the situation. Be especially sensitive to terminology; sometimes the choice of words ("remove" instead of "disable") can make the difference between a right answer and a wrong one.

Only when you've exhausted your ability to eliminate answers, but remain unclear about which of the remaining possibilities is correct, should you guess at an answer. An unanswered question offers you no points, but guessing gives you at least some chance of getting a question right; just don't be too hasty when making a blind guess.

Decoding Ambiguity

Cisco exams have a reputation for including questions that can be difficult to interpret, confusing, or ambiguous. In our experience with numerous exams, we consider this reputation to be completely justified. The Cisco exams are tough, and they're deliberately made that way.

The only way to beat Cisco at its own game is to be prepared. You'll discover that many exam questions test your knowledge of things that are not directly related to the issue that a question raises. This means that the answers you must choose from—even incorrect ones--are just as much a part of the skill assessment as the question itself. If you don't know something about most aspects of Remote Access, you might not be able to eliminate obviously wrong answers because they relate to a different area of Remote Access than the area the question at hand is addressing. In other words, the more you know about the Cisco IOS and troubleshooting Cisco internetworks, the easier it will be for you to tell a right answer from a wrong one.

Questions often give away their answers, but you have to be Sherlock Holmes to see the clues. Often, subtle hints appear in the question text in such a way that they seem almost irrelevant to the situation. You must realize that each question is a test unto itself and that you need to inspect and successfully navigate each question to pass the exam. Look for small clues, such as access-list modifications, problem isolation specifics (such as which layers of the OSI model are not functioning correctly), and invalid Cisco Internetwork Operating System (IOS) commands. Little things like these can point at the right answer if properly understood; if missed, they can leave you facing a blind guess.

Another common difficulty with certification exams is vocabulary. Be sure to brush up on the key terms presented at the beginning of each chapter. You may also want to read through the glossary at the end of this book the day before you take the test.

Working Within The Framework

The test questions appear in random order, and many elements or issues that receive mention in one question may also crop up in other questions. It's not uncommon to find that an incorrect answer to one question is the correct answer to another question, or vice versa. Take the time to read every answer to each question, even if you recognize the correct answer to a question immediately. That extra reading may spark a memory or remind you about a Cisco router or Catalyst switch IOS feature or function that helps you on another question elsewhere in the exam.

Deciding What To Memorize

The amount of memorization you must undertake for an exam depends on how well you remember what you've read and how well you know the Cisco IOS by heart. The tests will stretch your recollection of the router's commands and functions.

At a minimum, you'll want to memorize the following kinds of information:

➤ The resources and tools available to administer and troubleshoot a Cisco internetwork

➤ A standard troubleshooting technique for adequately diagnosing network problems

➤ Configuration commands for PPP, DDR, Frame Relay and Queuing

➤ Troubleshooting commands for PPP, DDR, Frame Relay and Queuing. The **show** and **debug** commands are heavily tested on.

If you work your way through this book while sitting at a Cisco router (actually, you may need a group of routers) and try to manipulate this environment's features and functions as they're discussed throughout the book, you should have little or no difficulty mastering this material. Also, don't forget that The Cram Sheet at the front of the book is designed to capture the material that's most important to memorize; use this to guide your studies as well.

Preparing For The Test

The best way to prepare for the test—after you've studied—is to take at least one practice exam. We've included one here in this chapter for that reason; the test questions are located in the pages that follow (and unlike the preceding chapters in this book, the answers don't follow the questions immediately; you'll have to flip to Chapter 17 to review the answers separately).

Give yourself 90 minutes to take the exam, keep yourself on the honor system, and don't look at earlier text in the book or jump ahead to the answer key. When your time is up or you've finished the questions, you can check your work in Chapter 17. Pay special attention to the explanations for the incorrect answers; these can also help to reinforce your knowledge of the material. Knowing how to recognize correct answers is good, but understanding why incorrect answers are wrong can be equally valuable.

Taking The Test

Relax. Once you're sitting in front of the testing computer, there's nothing more you can do to increase your knowledge or preparation. Take a deep breath, stretch, and start reading that first question.

There's no need to rush; you have plenty of time to complete each question. Both easy and difficult questions are intermixed throughout the test in random order. Don't cheat yourself by spending too much time on a hard question early on in the test, thereby depriving yourself of the time you need to answer the questions at the end of the test.

That's it for pointers. Here are some questions for you to practice on.

Question 1

With asynchronous signaling, the:

○ a. Timing is maintained between the modems over a carrier network.

○ b. Transmitting device signals the start of each byte.

○ c. Receiving device clocks the line.

○ d. Transmitting device clocks the line.

Question 2

What is the defined standard for the DCE/DTE interface?

○ a. RS-232-C

○ b. EIA/TIA-232

○ c. IETF DCE/DTE interface specification

○ d. RFC 232

Question 3

The _____ command allows for both incoming and outgoing calls on an interface.

Question 4

Using even parity, the last bit transmitted after 1100110 would be:

○ a. 1

○ b. 0

Question 5

For the DTE to terminate an existing connection, it must:

○ a. Drop DTR

○ b. Drop CTS

○ c. Send ATH to the DCE

○ d. Drop CD

Question 6

A user is connected to the console port of a router where the Ethernet 0 interface is configured as 144.5.5.5. The **telnet 144.5.5.5 2003** command will create an 8-N-1 connection to the third asynchronous port on this router.

- ○ a. True
- ○ b. False

Question 7

The _____ command allows the processing of any protocol on the line.

Question 8

To configure a modem using the **modemcap** database entry **hayes_optima**, the command is:

- ○ a. **modem autoconfigure type hayes_optima**
- ○ b. **modem autoconfigure modemcap hayes_optima**
- ○ c. **modem autoconfigure hayes_optima**
- ○ d. **modem autoconfigure entry hayes_optima**

Question 9

IP unnumbered interfaces are used:

- ○ a. To conserve IP addresses.
- ○ b. Only on point-to-point connections.
- ○ c. When SNMP management isn't an issue.
- ○ d. All of the above.

Question 10

The DTE device sends data on pin 2 and receives data on pin 3.

○ a. True

○ b. False

Question 11

On a 2522 router with an A/S interface, to use the interface for asynchronous communication, the _____ command is used.

Question 12

What is the correct order of steps for the following D channel signaling release procedure steps?

a. Release

b. Release complete

c. Released

d. Disconnect

○ a. a, c, d, b

○ b. d, a, c, b

○ c. a, c, b, d

○ d. d, b, a, c

Question 13

What command is used to declare the CO device to which the router BRI port is connected?

○ a. **switch**

○ b. **ISDN type**

○ c. **switch-type**

○ d. **switch-model**

Question 14

The common framing for a North American T1 is:

○ a. AMI

○ b. B8ZS

○ c. ESF

○ d. SF

Question 15

What are the four components of a dialer profile? [Choose the four best answers]

❏ a. Dialer interface

❏ b. Dialer map

❏ c. Map class

❏ d. Rotary group

❏ e. Dialer pool

❏ f. Physical interfaces

❏ g. Dialer string

Question 16

The PRI D channel is _____ Kbps.

○ a. 8

○ b. 32

○ c. 64

○ d. 128

Question 17

The BRI D channel [Choose the two best answers]:

❑ a. Is used for setup and signaling

❑ b. Uses out-of-band signaling

❑ c. Uses common-channel signaling

❑ d. Is byte-oriented

Question 18

The _____ command changes the **dialer idle-timeout** when a call is pending.

Question 19

What command is used to display the D channel information about the BRI interface on a 1600 series router?

○ a. **show interface bri0**

○ b. **show interface bri0 d-channel**

○ c. **show ISDN D**

○ d. **show interface bri0 1**

Question 20

What does the R designation in the ISDN documentation refer to?

○ a. Registration reference point

○ b. Rate reference point

○ c. Reference point

○ d. Carrier return point

Question 21

What signaling is used on the D channel at the data-link layer?

○ a. Q.931

○ b. LAPB

○ c. PPP

○ d. Q.921

Question 22

What **interface** command is used to enable the nonproprietary aggregation of additional links?

○ a. **multilink ppp**

○ b. **set bod**

○ c. **ppp multilink**

○ d. **enable multilink**

Question 23

What command is used to determine whether the first B channel on BRI0 is in use?

○ a. **show interface bri0**

○ b. **show interface bri0 b1**

○ c. **show interface bri0 1**

○ d. **show interface bri0 b**

Question 24

The clock source for a T1/E1 controller can be set to _____ or _____, and it's usually set to _____.

○ a. Internal; external; internal

○ b. External; internal; external

○ c. Line; external; internal

○ d. Line; internal; line

Question 25

What does the PAD provide for?

○ a. Fragmentation and defragmentation of IP to X.25 packets

○ b. Extra buffer area for asynchronous interfaces

○ c. Fragmentation and defragmentation of IP to PPP packets

○ d. The X.25 equivalent of an ISDN S interface

Question 26

The Data Networking Country Code(s) is comprised of how many digits?

○ a. 3

○ b. 4

○ c. 11

○ d. 10

Question 27

What is the highest numbered X.25 virtual circuit that can be configured on an interface?

○ a. 1,024

○ b. 2,048

○ c. 4,095

○ d. Limited to the memory of the device

Question 28

How many layer 3 protocols can share a single virtual circuit to a given destination on a Cisco router?

○ a. 10

○ b. 9

○ c. 8

○ d. 7

Question 29

The default values for the X.25 are _____ for the packet size and _____ for the modulo.

○ a. 1,024; 128

○ b. 1,024; 8

○ c. 128; 128

○ d. 128; 8

Question 30

What protocol uses LAPB to ensure data reliability?

○ a. ISDN

○ b. PPP

○ c. X.25

○ d. SDLC

Question 31

Which of the following is an X.121 pubic address for North America?

○ a. 3001123456

○ b. 3001FE0008

○ c. 10005a123456

○ d. 129.128.123.180

Question 32

Two routers are connected through a Frame Relay cloud. Router A has an assigned DLCI of 100. Router B must map Router A's IP address to what number if the two routers are to establish a PVC?

○ a. 100

○ b. 101

○ c. 100 and 101

○ d. None of the above

Question 33

What is a router being told when a frame switch sends a BECN packet?

- ○ a. A beacon condition has occurred, and all parties should back off and perform a lobe test.
- ○ b. BECome kNown again or reestablish the SVC.
- ○ c. The switch will be sending more data.
- ○ d. The router should send less data.

Question 34

What standard is used to support the router to switch setup for ISDN?

- ○ a. Q.931
- ○ b. T1.617
- ○ c. Q.921
- ○ d. Q.933

Question 35

The local management interface selection for Frame Relay on a Cisco router can be configured as which of the following? [Choose the two best answers]

- ❏ a. Cisco
- ❏ b. ANSI
- ❏ c. IETF
- ❏ d. ITU-T

Question 36

From the perspective of distance vector route protocol convergence, subinterfaces are used for frame and X.25 circuits because:

- ○ a. of NBMA.
- ○ b. Poison reverse would poison the whole interface.
- ○ c. Split horizon is on by default.
- ○ d. Routing loops could be created.

Question 37

The precursor to Frame Relay was based on what technology?

○ a. ISDN

○ b. X.25

○ c. T1/E1

○ d. Leased lines

Question 38

What does DLCI stand for?

○ a. Dynamic Link Connection Identifier

○ b. Dynamic Link Control Identifier

○ c. Data Link Control Identifier

○ d. Data Link Connection Identifier

Question 39

How can a router obtain a DLCI for a circuit? [Choose the two best answers]

❑ a. Inverse-ARP

❑ b. Manual configuration

❑ c. ARP request

❑ d. From the LMI

Question 40

Which of the following could create a floating static route to network 10.0.0.0/16 if the current routing protocol is IGRP?

○ a. **ip route 10.0.0.0 255.255.0.0 interface s 0 120**

○ b. **ip route 10.0.0.0 255.255.255.0 122.3.4.0 135**

○ c. **ip route 10.0.0.0 133.4.5.6 135**

○ d. **ip route 10.0.0.0 255.255.255.0 144.5.5.5 10**

Question 41

Which of the following commands is used to instruct a router to use only the lowest-cost route when using the command variance for IGRP?

○ a. **traffic-share balanced**

○ b. **load-share none**

○ c. **no load-share**

○ d. **traffic-share minimum**

Question 42

What type of interface can be used for backup and does not restrict resource usage when all primary links are functional?

○ a. Serial interface

○ b. Dialer interface

○ c. BRI pool interface

○ d. DDR

Question 43

If the **backup delay 20 30** command on a serial interface fails, how long will it take before the backup link is activated?

○ a. 30 seconds

○ b. 20 seconds

○ c. Depends on the link failure

○ d. Depends on the routing protocol

Question 44

The command **backup load 128 128**:

○ a. Brings up a secondary link when the primary link is approximately 50 percent busy, and drops the secondary link when the secondary link goes below approximately 50 percent busy.

○ b. Brings up a secondary link when the primary link is approximately 50 percent busy, and drops the secondary link when the aggregation of the primary and secondary link goes below approximately 50 percent busy.

○ c. Brings up a secondary link when the primary link is above 128Kbps, and drops the link when the aggregation of the primary and secondary links goes below 128Kbps.

○ d. Is an invalid command.

Question 45

The administrative distance for EIGRP is:

○ a. 90

○ b. 100

○ c. 110

○ d. 120

Question 46

Which of the following protocols supports weighted Fair Queuing? [Choose the three best answers]

❑ a. Frame Relay

❑ b. X.25

❑ c. ISDN

❑ d. PPP

Question 47

What is the number of queues that can be configured for Priority Queuing?

○ a. 4

○ b. 16

○ c. 8

○ d. As many as needed

Question 48

Header compression is best suited to what type of traffic?

○ a. Telnet

○ b. FTP

○ c. ATM

○ d. TFTP

Question 49

With 56Kbps modem technology, the maximum upload speed to a provider is:

○ a. 56Kbps

○ b. 33.6Kbps uploads

○ c. 115.2Kbps, if compression is used

○ d. 53Kbps

Question 50

There are _____ DS0s used in a T1 circuit.

○ a. 12

○ b. 16

○ c. 24

○ d. 32

Question 51

When a T1 link is configured for B8ZS, what is the maximum bandwidth of a DS0?

○ a. 64Kbps

○ b. 33.6Kbps

○ c. 64Mbps

○ d. 56Kbps

Question 52

High-speed "last-mile" options available to consumers include:

○ a. Digital local loop

○ b. VPDN

○ c. DSL

○ d. DSN

Question 53

On a Cisco 700 series router, which of the following is considered a permanent profile?

○ a. System

○ b. Internal

○ c. Core

○ d. Ethernet

Question 54

Any protocol routed in the User profile must be routed in the Internal profile.

○ a. True

○ b. False

Question 55

The **set default** command on a Cisco 700 series router will:

○ a. Reset the router to factory defaults

○ b. Reset the router to factory defaults and reboot the router

○ c. Restore the system-profile settings

○ d. Declare the profile that will be used as a last resort

Question 56

The translation table entry for an outside global address that shows 198.3.3.4:1567 declares the:

○ a. Port translation of the address

○ b. Socket translation of the address

○ c. Unique pool address used for the translation

○ d. None of the above

Question 57

Network address translation can be used in which of the following scenarios? [Choose the two best answers]

❑ a. Networks that have overlapping IP addresses

❑ b. Networks that use RFC1918 addressing and require Internet access

❑ c. Networks that don't use RFC 1918 addressing and require Internet access

❑ d. Networks that require Internet access

❑ e. Networks that use registered addresses on their firewall devices

Question 58

The private address range includes:

○ a. 172.1.0.0 through 172.16.0.0

○ b. 144.1.0.0 through 144.16.0.0

○ c. 172.16.0.0 through 172.32.0.0

○ d. 192.168.0.0 through 192.168.32.0

Question 59

What is one of the disadvantages associated with the use of NAT?

○ a. Overlap dysfunction due to addressing

○ b. Larger route table descriptions

○ c. Increased route table sizes

○ d. End user accountability

Question 60

An outside global address is:

○ a. Locally and globally routable

○ b. Must be a registered IP address with the IANA.

○ c. Locally routable but not globally routable.

○ d. Globally routable but may not be locally routable.

Question 61

PPP uses which of the following protocols for negotiation prior to a connection being established?

○ a. NCP

○ b. LCP

○ c. PAP

○ d. TCP

Question 62

Which of the following statements is true concerning a remote control solution for dialup access?

○ a. The end user is provided better security.

○ b. A host connection at the central site is required.

○ c. Applications are limited by modem speeds.

○ d. It cannot be supported through the router.

Answer Key

1. b	22. c	43. c
2. b	23. c	44. d
3. modem inout	24. d	45. a
4. b	25. a	46. a, c, d
5. a	26. b	47. a
6. a	27. c	48. a
7. transport input all	28. b	49. b
8. a	29. d	50. c
9. d	30. c	51. a
10. a	31. a	52. c
11. physical-layer async	32. d	53. b
12. b	33. d	54. a
13. c	34. a	55. b
14. c	35. a, b	56. b
15. a, c, e, f	36. c	57. a, b
16. c	37. b	58. c
17. a, b	38. d	59. d
18. dialer fast-idle	39. b, d	60. d
19. a	40. a	61. b
20. b	41. d	62. b
21. d	42. b	

Question 1

Answer b is correct. The term *asynchrony* refers to the lack of concurrence with time. The transmitter must signal the start of the characters. Answer a is incorrect and is a bit tricky because modems use asynchronous signaling. The timing is not maintained between the modems but between the devices at each end of the point-to-point circuit. Answer a clearly states that the two modems are communicating over a carrier network. Each modem is maintaining timing with the carrier device that it is attached to. Answers c and d are incorrect because they refer to a synchronous method of signaling.

Question 2

Answer b is correct. The EIA/TIA-232 is the defined standard that was developed from the RS-232-C standard. Answer a is incorrect because the *RS* in the answer means *recommended standard*. Answer c is incorrect because the IETF is the Internet Engineering Task Force, which maintains and recommends standards at a higher level than the physical layer. Answer d is incorrect because RFC is the acronym for "Request for Comment"and does not specify a standards release.

Question 3

The correct answer is **modem inout,** which is one of the key line parameters for a router.

Question 4

Answer b is correct. Because there are already four 1 bits, the last bit would be a 0. For even parity, the number of 1s must be even for the byte. Because there are four 1 bits in the first seven bits, the parity bit is set to 0. If this question asked for odd parity, the parity bit would be set to 1 so that the number of 1 bits would be odd.

Question 5

Answer a is correct. For the DTE to terminate, it will drop Data Terminal Ready (DTR). Answer b is incorrect because Clear To Send (CTS) is a flow-control pin and not used to terminate a connection. Answer c is incorrect. Answer c will definitely close the connection, because the modem command "ATH" calls for the modem to "hang up." However, the ATH command sequence is not generated by the DTE— ATH is generated by a command-line entry or script. Answer d is incorrect. Dropping the CD would be correct if the question asked how the DCE device terminates the connection.

Question 6

Answer a is correct. Cisco reserves the 2003 port number for the third asynchronous port on a router. The 2000 family of port numbers is specific to setting up a Telnet or character-based 8-1-N connection to a port. Each reserved series—2000, 3000, 4000, and so forth—is specific to a type of connection and whether an individual port or the next available port in a rotary is selected. Answer b is incorrect because the statement is true.

Question 7

The correct answer is **transport input all**. This command takes the argument of **none** in Version 12 code. Other arguments to the **transport input** command are **lat, mop, nasi, none, pad, rlogin, telnet,** and **v120**. You must specify an incoming transport protocol before a line will accept incoming connections. In earlier releases, the default was **all**, but, in the current code, the lines are unusable for incoming traffic until a protocol (or protocols) is specified.

Question 8

Answer a is correct. The correct syntax uses the keyword type before the argument. The general syntax is **modem autoconfigure type** followed by the name of the modemcap entry. Answers b, c, and d are incorrect because they do not follow the syntax rules. Answer c is tempting because it provides all the information, but it does not follow the syntax.

Question 9

Answer d is correct. The use of unnumbered interfaces won't allow for SNMP management, because the physical interface doesn't have an address to query. Furthermore, eliminating the need for a network address on the link will save one network number, and only point-to-point links can be used. On a multipoint link, each interface would be required to have an address. Finally, if the interface has no IP address it cannot be managed.

Question 10

Answer a is correct. Transmit data is on pin 2, and receive data is on pin 3. The question includes the DTE device information to add confusion. The DCE and the DTE devices transmit on pin 2. Pins 2 and 3 are crossed on the cables, so each device listens on pin 3 and transmits on pin 2.

Question 11

The correct answer is **physical-layer async**. Remember that the argument for the command is **async**—*not* **asynch**. For the fill-in-the-blank questions, spelling counts! By default, a router that has an interface marked as A/S (asynchronous/synchronous) has a synchronous interface. In that case, the **physical-layer async** command is needed.

Question 12

Answer b is correct. The disconnect message begins the process, and the three-part message follows. The disconnect is issued by the end station that is terminating the call followed by the release message, then the switch responds with released, and the end station (or router) sends the release complete message, thereby ending the process. Answers a and c are incorrect. Both answers start with the release, which seems correct after reading the question; however, to release a connection, the disconnect is the first message issued. Answer d is incorrect. It starts with the disconnect, but it's followed by the release complete, which is out of order.

Question 13

Answer c is correct. The correct argument is the **switch-type**. Answers a, b, and d are incorrect because they are not syntactically proper.

Question 14

Answer c is correct. ESF, or Extended Super Frame, is the common framing for a North American T1 line. Answers a and b are incorrect. A common mistake in this type of question is to quickly recognize the B8ZS or AMI as a proper line coding method and neglect to see that the question is asking for the framing. Answer d is incorrect because SF (Super Frame) is not commonly used for framing in North America. SF has been replaced by ESF.

Question 15

Answers a, c, e, and f are correct. By Cisco's definition the *dialer interface* which can include a *map class* uses a *dialer pool* which is made up of *physical interfaces*. This question should be precisely understood because any number of test questions can be derived from the components of a dialer definition. Answers b, d, and g are incorrect; while they may or may not be used in a profile, they do not constitute a component of a dialer profile. For example, the dialer map, rotary group, and dialer string can be used in (or with) a profile, but they are not considered one of the components of a profile.

Question 16

Answer c is correct. The PRI is comprised of 24 DS0s, each of which is 64Kbps, including the D channel. Each answer provides a legitimate "computer type number" with an octal base, but only 64 is correct. Answer a is incorrect. 8 may be a good "computer" number but it is not used as a definition in any ISDN bandwidth other than 8 bits are transmitted for a byte. Answer b is incorrect; 32 channels is correct for an E1 signal, but incorrect when talking about a T1. Answer d is incorrect, and it can be confused with the user bandwidth of a BRI, which is 2 B channels (128). The question is asking about the D channel; however, every channel on a T1 is the same. What the channels do might be different (D versus B), but the bandwidth is the same.

Question 17

Answers a and b are correct. The BRI D channel is used for setup, signaling, and out-of-band signaling. Out-of-band signaling uses a seperate channel to send the setup and signaling messages. Answer c is incorrect because the BRI D channel doesn't use common-channel signaling; the D channel is "set aside" to perform signaling for the B or bearer channels. ISDN uses the D channel for signaling to allow the B (bearer) channels to use all their bandwidth for data. Answer d is incorrect because the PRI D channel is byte-oriented and the BRI D channel is bit-oriented.

Question 18

The correct answer is **dialer fast-idle**. This command changes the idle time parameter to a lower value so that a pending call will force a quicker timeout.

Question 19

Answer a is correct. If the B channel information is wanted, the channel number must be added (for example, **show interface bri0 1**). This question can be asked several ways. The key point is that the **show interface** command takes three arguments (three for a basic rate interface). Namely, the three arguments specify the type of interface, in this case a **bri**; number of the interface, in this example it is the first or **0** interface; and the B channel number or numbers that are to be displayed. If the B channel is left off the command, only the D channel information is supplied. Answers b, c, and d are incorrect because all three carry an argument after the show interface *physical-interface*, which would call for B channel information.

Question 20

Answer b is correct. This is simply a memorization question. Each reference point R, S, T, U, and V is defined to have meaning. The R is called the *rate* reference point. Cisco assigned "meaning" to the letter designations, and this type of information cannot be found in the ISDN specification documentation.

Question 21

Answer d is correct. Answer a is incorrect because Q.931 is the network layer protocol for D channel signaling. Answers c and b are incorrect, because LAPB and PPP are B channel protocols. Answer d specifies the Q.921 protocol, which is the data-link layer protocol for D channel setup.

Question 22

Answer c is correct. PPP is an interface command that takes the argument **multilink**. Answer a is incorrect, because multilink (which is an argument for the ppp command) is shown as the command where ppp is the argument. Answer b is incorrect for a router interface, but the **set BOD** command could be confused with the 700 commands where **set** is used quite frequently. Answer d is incorrect; while it seems likely, it is syntactically incorrect.

Question 23

Answer c is correct. The **show interface bri0 1** command will give the status of the first B channel on the BRI0 interface. Answers a, b, and d are incorrect because each has an incorrect syntax. Answer a does not have a B channel argument and will show the status of the D channel. Answer b uses the argument **b1**, and although it may sound "nice," it is incorrect. Answer d uses the argument "b" which is simply incorrect from a syntactical perspective.

Question 24

Answer d is correct. The two choices for the clock source are line and internal. Normally, the clock source is set for line because the provider, or telephone company, clocks the line. Answers a and c are incorrect. Both answers offer the **external** argument, and, while the clocking is provided by an external source, the setting is for line. Answer b is incorrect; even though the clock is provided externally, it is configured as line on the router, not external. This question is representative of some of the more inventive questions on the exam, where one often finds two questions for the price of one.

Question 25

Answer a is correct. The packet assembler disassembler (PAD) receives a character stream and converts it to data packets and vice versa on the output. The fact that the PAD is converting IP is irrelevant, but the fact that the PAD is converting it to X.25 packets is germane. Answer b is incorrect, and it sticks out like a sore thumb. Answer b refers to asynchronous communication, which X.25 is surely not. Answer c is incorrect; it correctly identifies the fragmentation and defragmentation processes, but it incorrectly specifies that the conversion is to PPP packets. X.25 reliably carries packets using LAPB as the protocol. Answer d is incorrect even though it might be a tempting selection. Answer d represents the 2-wire/4-wire conversion point for ISDN, but the packets are not altered (assembled or disassembled) at the interface.

Question 26

Answer b is correct. For example, the range of Data Country Codes for the United States is from 310 through 316 with the fourth digit providing the service-provider code. Answer a is incorrect because country codes are three digits. However, the *entire* Data Networking Country Code includes the service-provider designation. Answers c and d are incorrect because they refer to the *entire* X.121 address space, which includes a terminal identifier as well as the DNCC. These values are assigned by the ITU-T.

Question 27

Answer c is correct. An interface can have X.25 virtual circuit numbering up to 4,095 on an interface. Answers a and b are incorrect, although they are good "computer" numbers. Answer d is incorrect, although it's almost correct because the actual number of VCs that can be created depends on the device. However, the number 4095 is not a limit to the available memory. It is a programmed number based on the "capability" of the device as perceived by Cisco. The genuine answer can only be 4,095 because the question asks for the highest number of the VC, not the largest total number of VCs.

Question 28

Answer b is correct. Each VC can support up to nine protocols (the total number of protocols supported) or up to eight virtual circuits can be combined for a single protocol. Nine protocols can be configured for a single circuit, and eight circuits can be configured for a single protocol. Answer a is incorrect because Cisco only supports 9 protocols, hence it would be physically impossible to send more than that. Answer c is wrong, but 8 *is* the maximum number of channels that are supported for multilink. Answer d is simply wrong.

Question 29

Answer d is correct. The default value for the packet size is 128, which gives the provider a very small packet for transmission. The modulo is 8, which is generally used for all terrestrial links. Answers a and c are incorrect because a modulo of 128 is generally reserved for a satellite link, where any acknowledgment is a costly overhead and the transmission delay is high. Answer b is incorrect; 1,024 is wrong for the default packet size. 1,024 is a common U.S. carrier packet size, but not the default on the router. The focus is on the default values for the packet size and modulo parameters. A service provider for X.25 will specify the packet size and modulo for a network.

Question 30

Answer c is correct. X.25 uses LAPB to ensure data reliability. Answer a is incorrect because ISDN uses LABD for reliability. Answers b and d are incorrect because PPP and SDLC are, by definition, their own data-link encapsulation methods. The key point here is to recognize the correct layer of the OSI model that is being addressed. ISDN and X.25 operate at the network layer (layer 3), while PPP and SDLC operate at the data-link layer (layer 2).

Question 31

Answer a is correct. An X.121 address is entered in decimal. Answer b, while it has the correct number of digits, is in hexadecimal notation and cannot be correct. Answer c is incorrect because it is a layer 2 address, whereas X.121 addresses are layer 3. Answer d is incorrect because X.121 addresses do not use periods as part of the address format.

Question 32

Answer d is correct. The DLCI is only locally significant. The Router B must map the IP address of Router A to the DLCI that Router B is using to gain access to the PVC that is connected to Router A. Answers a, b, and c could be correct *if* that is the local DLCI to Router B. Nonetheless, the most correct answer is d because *any* DLCI could be correct. All in all, it makes no difference what Router A's DLCI is from the perspective of Router B.

Question 33

Answer d is correct. The router is being told that the switch is congested and to send less data. Answer a is incorrect because it refers to a Token Ring condition where a break in communications has occurred and the signal is a beacon. Answer b is incorrect because it is a fictitious command. Answer c is incorrect because the question wants to know what the router is being told. Because a Backward Explicate Congestion Notification (BECN) has been sent out, the switch might be sending more data but that is not what the BECN is telling the router.

Question 34

Answer a is correct. Q.931 is an ISDN standard. Answer b is incorrect because T1.617 is an ANSI Frame Relay standard. Answer c is incorrect because Q.921 is the ITU-T standard for ISDN link layer messaging. Answer d is incorrect because Q.933 is an ITU-T standard for Frame Relay.

Question 35

Answers a and b are correct. Cisco and ANSI are valid arguments for the **frame-relay lmi-type** command. Answer c is incorrect because the IETF standards body is the Internet Engineering Task Force, which has little to do with the Frame Relay development. Answer d is incorrect because ITU-T is not an argument for the **lmi-type** command. The ITU-T developed a frame standard called Q.933 Annex A as an LMI type; however, the question asks what can be configured. The three options for the LMI type are Cisco, ANSI, and q933.

Question 36

Answer c is correct. Split horizon tells a router not to send routing updates out the interface it learned a route from. This means that a remote site could send a routing update to a central router, and the central router would not propagate that information out the same interface to another remote router. Using subinterfaces solves this problem. Answer a is incorrect because nonbroadcast multiaccess (NBMA) is a special type of Frame-Relay implementation where all devices connected share a common network number and do not use subinterfacing. NBMA is generally only used when the number of IP network numbers is a critical issue. Answer b is incorrect. Poison reverse only poisons a route; however, this is not why subinterfaces are used. Answer d is incorrect because routing loops are not a function of subinterfaces.

Question 37

Answer b is correct. Frame Relay was developed as a lower-overhead alternative to X.25. One of the features of X.25 is that it is very reliable; however, this reliability translates to a high latency in the X.25 cloud. Answer a is incorrect, because ISDN is a circuit-switched methodology using digital facilities. Answers c and d are incorrect, because T1/E1 and leased lines are point-to-point solutions with dedicated facilities.

Question 38

Answer d is correct. A DLCI is a data-link connection identifier, which is also commonly referred to as a "del-cee." Answers a, b, and c are incorrect, although the choices appear similar to the correct interpretation of DLCI.

Question 39

Answer b and d are correct. The DLCI can be configured for an interface, or it can obtain the DLCI from the LMI update. Answer a is incorrect because the Inverse-ARP maps the DLCI to a remote IP address, but the DLCI must be known by the router. Answer c is incorrect, because an ARP request presumes a known hardware address and is looking for a network layer address.

Question 40

Answer a is correct. The next hop is given by an interface assignment that is legal, although generally not done. Answer b is incorrect, because the network mask is 24 bits and the question calls for a 16-bit mask for the 10 network. Answer c is incorrect, because the network mask has been omitted in the statement. Answer d is incorrect. The specified administrative distance is lower than the administrative distance for IGRP; hence, the route would not float.

Question 41

Answer d is correct, **traffic-share minimum**. This type of scenario might be used when a secondary line of lower speed is added to the route table, but not used unless the primary line fails. Answer a is incorrect because **traffic-share balanced** is the default when variance is used, and the command will balance the traffic flow across the links that are within the variance limits. With the **balanced** argument, all links that are within the variance are used. Answers b and c are incorrect; although they might sound good if you were looking for a mutual fund, these commands are simply fiction.

Question 42

Answer b is correct. When a dialer interface is declared to be the backup for a primary interface, the physical interface or interfaces that the dialer is pointing to are not placed in a standby mode. In this fashion, the resources can be used for other functions as long as the backup is not needed. Answers a and c are incorrect, because they are physical interfaces. By declaring a physical interface as a backup, it is placed into a hold and can be used only for backup purposes. Answer d is incorrect, because DDR is a methodology, not a type of interface.

Question 43

Answer c is correct. The length of time before the backup link is activated depends on the link failure. If a failure is local and the DSU/CSU is lost, the backup will start in 20 seconds or the first number in the command. However, if the failure is not local, the router must miss 3 keepalives (which, by default, occur every 10 seconds), and the failover might not take place for up to 50 seconds—30 seconds to decide that the keepalives are not present (worse case), and 20 seconds before failing to the backup link. Answers a and b are incorrect because there is no absolute unless the failure is local. Answer d is incorrect, because the routing protocol does not participate in the backup decisions.

Question 44

Answer d is correct. The command is invalid. The arguments for the **backup load** are percentage values not given in a ratio to 255 as is the **threshold** command. Answers a, b, and c are incorrect, because the command is invalid. However, answer b would be correct if the command were **backup load 50 50**. It is important to remember that once the aggregation has been done, the second number declares the percentage of total bandwidth the router must be under before the second link is dropped.

Question 45

Answer a is correct. EIGRP has an administrative distance of 90. Answer b is incorrect; 100 is the default administrative distance for IGRP. Answer c is incorrect; 110 is the default administrative distance for OSPF. Answer d is incorrect; 120 is the default administrative distance for RIP.

Question 46

Answers a, c, and d are correct. This question could be very difficult, because you must know that the WFQ is not an option for X.25. Answer b is incorrect because WFQ and X.25 do not work together.

Question 47

Answer a is correct. With priority queuing, the four queues are high, normal, medium, and low. Answer b is incorrect, but it would be correct for custom queue operations where the administrator can create up to 16 custom queues. Answer c is incorrect because the number has no bearing on the question. Answer d is incorrect because four queues are created, whether they are used or not.

Question 48

Answer a is correct. Header compression was designed for Telnet traffic. A Telnet packet carries only one character as the payload; hence, the header makes up the bulk of the traffic. Answers b and d are incorrect. Using header compression for FTP or TFTP would have little or no effect, because the payload is the bulk of the traffic. Answer c is incorrect, because ATM does not support header compression at all.

Question 49

Answer b is correct. Because of the analog-to-digital conversion that must take place, the fastest speed that can be achieved with a 56Kbps modem is 33.6 in the upload direction. Answer a is incorrect; 56Kbps is the theoretical maximum speed that can be achieved if the provider is purely digital and can eliminate the need for second analog-to-digital conversion in the download direction. However, the FCC regulates that speed to 53Kbps. Answer c is incorrect because the speed was the point of the question, not the throughput based on a compression algorithm. Answer d is incorrect; 53Kbps is the maximum (limited by the FCC) for a download.

Question 50

Answer c is correct. There are 24 channels defined in a T1 span. Each channel is 64Kbps. Answers a, b, and d are incorrect because the correct answer is 24. Answer d would be correct if the question asked for the number of DS0s used in an E1 circuit.

Question 51

Answer a is correct. B8ZS allows senders and receivers to use a bit-stuffing technique so that ones density is maintained without stealing the eighth bit of every byte. This allows the entire DS0 to be used for transmission. Answer b is incorrect, because it is a maximum modem speed and not germane to a T1 link. Answer c is incorrect, because it is the wrong magnitude of speed as expressed in Mbps. Answer d is incorrect because the question declares B8ZS, and the 8K of overhead used with AMI is not needed.

Question 52

Answer c is correct. DSL, or digital subscriber line, provides a new higher speed technology for the last hop from the CO to the customer. Answer a is incorrect; it is a seemingly correct term, but it is not a provider offering. Answer b is incorrect. While VPDN (virtual private dialup network) is a provider offering, it's not a high-speed option because it uses dial technologies by definition. Answer d is incorrect because DSN is a meaningless acronym in this instance.

Question 53

Answer b is correct. The internal profile as well as the LAN and standard profiles make up the three permanent profiles that are on the device. Answer a is incorrect. Although there is a system configuration, it is not counted as a profile, per se. Instead, the system configuration (or profile) owns all the profiles. Answer c is incorrect, because *core* is not referred to anywhere within the 700 family. Answer d is incorrect, although the LAN profile is the configuration for the Ethernet interface. The profile itself is called the LAN profile not the ethernet profile.

Question 54

Answer a is correct. If a user profile calls for the routing of IP or IPX, then the protocol *must* be declared for routing in the Internal profile. If a protocol is to be routed, the Internal profile must be configured for it. However, the reverse is not true. Just because a protocol is declared for routing in the Internal profile does not mean it must be routed in a User profile. Answer b is incorrect because the statement is true.

Question 55

Answer b is correct. **Set default** is analogous to the write/erase sequence used in the customary IOS. Answer a is incorrect because the router will reboot itself when the **set default** command is issued. Answer c is incorrect because there is no system profile and **set default** will set *all* the parameters to factory default. Answer d is incorrect, because a profile does not provide a last-resort path, which is done by the routing protocol.

Question 56

Answer b is correct. The socket is the full address IP:PORT assignment. It is not answer c, the unique pool address, because overloading is obviously in use since the port number is being used. The pool address will be used again and again during the overload process. Answer a is incorrect because both the IP address and the software addressable port can be altered during the overload process. The key here is to recognize that what has been translated is the entire socket.

Question 57

Answers a and b are correct. NAT can be used when two networks overlap or when the private address space (RFC 1918) has been used and the company requires Internet access. Answer c is incorrect; if a network is not using RFC addressing, the network numbering may or may not be registered. No mention is made regarding whether the address space is registered, so it cannot be assumed that the space is invalid. Answer d is incorrect because it simply states that a network requires Internet access and does not state whether the current addressing is valid. Answer e is incorrect because the use of registered addresses does not require a NAT solution.

Question 58

Answer c is correct. Knowledge of the private network numbers is key to any installation, troubleshooting, or design issue. The private networks are:

➤ **Class A** 10.0.0.0, 1 network

➤ **Class B** 172.16.0.0 through 172.32.0.0, 16 networks

➤ **Class C** 192.168.0.0 through 192.168.255.0, 255 networks

Question 59

Answer d is correct. The end users addresses are hidden from the outside world and translated on an as-needed basis by the NAT device. This could present a security problem to an administrator who must track users' activities. Answer a is incorrect because the question is looking for disadvantages, and answer a offers an advantage of NAT. Answers b and c are incorrect because the route table size and descriptions of the routes are unaffected by NAT.

Question 60

Answer d is correct. The question asks what is an outside (device not on my network) global (address which is valid outside my network) address. Answer a is incorrect because the address may require translation to be valid inside my network—it would need to be translated to an inside global address. The term Local refers to the address being locally routable, the term Global refers to it being globally routable. Answer b is not correct because an outside global address could be selected from RFC 1918, the private address space. Remember, from my perspective (inside the network) the addresses may require translation to enter my network. If it were an outside *local* address the term local would indicate that it is routable inside my network and therefore (if it comes from the internet) it would be a registered address. However, if the scenario is such that two independent networks have merged, both the inside and outside networks could be using different private address space numbers. Answer c is not right because, by definition, a global address is globally routable. Answer d is the correct choice because it declares the global address to be globally routable and that it might be routable on the inside network. If it is invalid on the inside, then it would require translation; however the question does not declare whether the address definition is valid or invalid.

Question 61

Answer b is correct. The Link Control Protocol is used to negotiate the authentication, compression, and multilink options prior to the establishment of a link. Answer a is incorrect because NCP refers to the NetWare Control Protocol. Answer c is incorrect; even though PAP is a PPP option, it is not responsible for the negotiation of a connection. Answer d is incorrect. TCP is not part of the PPP suite—TCP is a transport layer protocol.

Question 62

Answer b is correct. A remote control solution provides near-LAN speed by allowing a remote user to "take over" the local CPU of a device. The transmissions to the remote client are the screen changes, while all the processing is performed at the central site. Answer a is incorrect because remote control is bad from the standpoint of security. The remote user cannot be sure that someone is monitoring what is being done at the central office. Answer c is incorrect because the application is being run locally and only the screen changes are being transmitted. A router can support connectivity to a local device that is providing the remote control function to the end user. Answer d is incorrect because a Cisco router cannot be the central site remote control device for COTS applications.

Glossary

AAA (Authentication, Authorization, and Accounting)—The generic reference to applications that provide security for a RAS.

administrative distance—The weight given to a routing protocol or route source that specifies the weight, or worth, of the route. If the same route destination is obtained from two sources, the source with the lowest administrative distance is kept.

a-law—ITU-T standard used to convert analog to digital signals. a-law is generally used in the European countries, whereas mu-law is used in North America.

AMI (Alternate mark inversion)—The line-code type used on T1 and E1 circuits that forces ones density by marking every eighth bit as a 1.

Amplitude—Height of an analog waveform.

analog transmission—Transmission method used to send information by varying the amplitude, frequency, and/or phase of a carrier signal.

ANSI (American National Standards Institute)—Related to the International Standardization Organization (ISO), ANSI sets standards for communications, networking, and programming languages.

AppleTalk—Communication protocols used by Apple Computer.

application layer—Layer 7 of the OSI model. This layer provides services to the network clients.

ARAP (AppleTalk Remote Access Protocol)—Provides Macintosh users RAS software unique to the AppleTalk suite.

ARP (Address Resolution Protocol)—Defined by RFC 826, ARP is the IP protocol that is used to map an IP address to a MAC address.

ASCII (American Standard Code for Information Interchange)—An 8-bit binary code for character representation.

asynchronous transmission—A method used to transmit signals without a separate clocking mechanism. Asynchronous transmissions embed the "clocking" in the signal itself by using control bits.

ATM (Asynchronous Transfer Mode)—An international standard for cell relay switching. Fixed-length cells allow cell processing to occur in hardware, which reduces switch delay.

AURP (AppleTalk Update-Based Routing Protocol)—Co-developed by Apple Computer and the IETF. AURP provides a method of encapsulating AppleTalk traffic over a WAN. AURP also uses a change-based algorithm for routing updates rather than a distance-vector method, which is used by native RTMP.

B channel—A bearer channel (or user channel) for ISDN. Each bearer channel is 64Kbps. A BRI is comprised of 2 B channels, and a PRI has 23 B channels.

B8ZS (Binary 8-zero substitution)—A line-code type used on T1 and E1 circuits. A special code is used when eight zeros are sent in sequence to maintain ones density. This line coding is needed to provide for true 64Kbps bandwidth utilization. It can be compared to AMI, which "stole" every eighth bit to ensure ones density.

baud—A basic unit of signaling speed equal to the number of discrete signals transmitted per second. Baud is the same as bits per second (bps) if each signal represents only one bit.

BCRAN (Building Cisco Remote Access Networks)—The current Cisco class dealing with remote access networking (RAS).

BECN (Backward Explicit Congestion Notification)—Frame Relay uses a discard eligible bit when a customer is transmitting above the committed information rate (CIR). When congestion is seen by the frame switches, the packets that are discard-eligible are dumped, and a BECN is sent to alert the participating stations to throttle back their transmissions.

Bisync (Binary Synchronous Communications Protocol)—Character-oriented data-link protocol for applications.

BOOTP (Bootstrap Protocol)—A protocol used by a network node to determine the IP address of its Ethernet interfaces. A BOOTP server is used to provide NIC to IP address assignments.

BRI (Basic Rate Interface)—The 2 B+D interface used in ISDN.

Briefcase—A utility that provides two-way file synchronization.

broadcast domain—A set of devices that share a common bandwidth and will receive broadcast frames originating from any device within the set. Routers provide the boundary to a broadcast domain.

carrier—Transmission signal of a single frequency, which can be modified or modulated to signal data.

Category 5 cabling—An EIA/TIA-586 standard that can transmit data at speeds up to 100Mbps.

CCITT (Consultative Committee for International Telegraph and Telephone. International organization)—The CCITT is now the ITU-T.

CD (Carrier Detect signal)—Pin 8 of the EIA/TIA-232 standard. It is generated by the modem to signal that a carrier is present and a call is connected.

channelized E1—A WAN access link that operates at 2.048Mbps and has 30 B channels and 1 D channel. E1 is the European standard.

channelized T1—A WAN access link that operates at 1.544Mbps and has 23 B channels and 1 D channel. The T1 is the North American standard.

CHAP (Challenge Handshake Authentication Protocol)—Part of the PPP suite of protocols used to provide basic security.

chat script—A text string that is sent through a modem to a remote system that defines a preset conversation. A chat-script is generally used to establish a remote login.

CIR (Committed Information Rate)—The rate that a Frame Relay customer contracts for with a carrier.

clear channel—Clear channel signaling declares that the setup and selection messages will be done out-of-band. ISDN uses clear channel, because the D channel is used to send signal information and the B channels are used only for data.

client—A network user or a computer on a network used to access resources hosted by other machines on the network.

CO (Central office)—Local telephone company office where the "last mile" to the customer originates.

collision domain—The shared bandwidth for all devices in a domain. A repeater or hub defines a collision domain.

compression—A method of reducing transmitted data by using an algorithm that reduces the number of bits needed to describe a particular data stream.

CPE (Customer premises equipment)—Equipment that is not managed by the local telco but is at the terminus end of the circuit.

CPU (Central Processing Unit)—The brains of your computer; the area where all functions are performed.

CRC (Cyclic redundancy check)—An error-checking technique. The receiver calculates, using the same algorithm as the sender, a number based on the received frame information, which should be the same as what the CRC has. If the two numbers are different, the frame has been changed since transmission and is therefore invalid.

CSMA/CD (Carrier sense multiple access collision detection)—The method that Ethernet uses to detect whether multiple devices have transmitted during the same time frame in a collision domain.

CSU (Channel service unit)—A digital interface device that connects end user equipment to the "last mile," or local loop.

CTS (Clear To Send)—The fifth pin used in the EIA/TIA-232 specification that is activated when DCE is ready to accept data from DTE.

Custom Queuing—A queuing process more complicated than Weighted Fair Queuing to configure. Custom Queuing allows an administrator to tell the router that certain types of traffic need to have more packets processed than other types of traffic.

D channel—A data channel for ISDN used for call setup and signaling. For an ISDN BRI, the D channel is 16Kbps, and for a PRI, the D channel is 64Kbps.

data-link layer—Layer 2 of the OSI reference model. Provides access to the physical media. The data-link layer specifies the physical address of a device. Within the LAN, the data-link hardware is a network interface card (NIC). The protocols are broken into parts for the media access control (MAC) and the logical link control layer (LLC).

DB connector (Data Bus connector)—Used to connect serial and parallel cables to the data bus. The DB connector is specified as a DB-#, where # is the number of pins on the connector. These connectors are defined by the EIA/TIA.

DCE (Data Circuit-Terminating Equipment)—Provides the clocking signal to a DTE device.

DDP (Datagram Delivery Protocol)—An AppleTalk network layer protocol end-to-end delivery of datagrams.

DDR (Dial-on-Demand Routing)—A technique used to create a connection on-the-fly when interesting traffic is delivered to the dialer interface. It is the responsibility of the router administrator to specify "interesting" traffic by using an access-list mechanism. DDR is generally used over ISDN or analog circuits.

default gateway—The IP address of a computer or device that serves as a router, a format translator, or a security filter for a network.

demarc—Shortened name for demarcation. Used to refer to the point where circuit responsibility transfers from the carrier to the customer.

DHCP (Dynamic Host Configuration Protocol)—A service that enables the assignment of dynamic TCP/IP network addresses, based on a specified pool of available addresses. DHCP provides a mechanism for allocating and managing IP addresses from a central device.

dial backup—The process of using a line to help out another line in the event the primary line goes down or the link becomes saturated.

dial-up networking—The application on a Microsoft operating system that allows a user to connect to a remote device.

DLCI—The locally significant data-link connection identifier used for Frame Relay. The value specifies the local circuit ID for a PVC or SVC Frame Relay circuit.

DNIC (Data Network Identification Code)—A part of an X.121 address used in an X.25 network. DNICs are comprised of two parts—country code or network code and public switched network (PSN).

DNS (Domain Name System)—The service that resolves host names into IP addresses. The Domain Name System is an application that translates network device names to IP addresses. DNS is frequently referred to as *Domain Name Server*.

DS0 (Digital signal level 0)—The framing specification used for digital signals over a single 64Kbps channel on a T1 facility.

DS1 (Digital signal level 1)—The framing specification used for digital signals over a 1.544Mbps channel on a T1 facility.

DS3 (Digital signal level 3)—The framing specification used for digital signals over a 44.736Mbps channel on a T3 facility.

DSL (Digital Subscriber Line)—Uses radio frequencies and provides dedicated point-to-point connectivity to a central office (CO) facility.

DSR (Data set ready)—Pin 6 of the EIA/TIA-232 interface standard, which is activated when DCE is powered on.

DSU (Data service unit)—A device used in digital transmission that adapts the physical interface on a DTE device to a transmission facility, such as T1 or E1. The DSU also provides signal timing to the link.

DTE (Data Terminal Equipment)—A device on the customer side of a carrier network that accepts the clocking or synchronization from the DCE device.

DTR (Data terminal ready)—Pin 20 of the EIA/TIA-232 interface standard, which is activated to alert the DCE that the DTE is ready to send and receive data.

DUN—*See* Dial-Up Networking.

E1—WAN digital transmission service offered in Europe that carries data at a rate of 2.048Mbps.

E3—WAN digital transmission service offered in Europe that carries data at a rate of 34.368Mbps.

EIA (Electronic Industries Association group)—Specifies electrical transmission standards. The EIA has worked with TIA to develop the EIA/TIA-232 standard EIA/TIA-232 Physical layer interface standard.

EIA/TIA-232 (Electronic Industries Association/Telecommunication Industry Association)—Standard for 232 signaling for a serial line.

encapsulation—The wrapping of data in a particular protocol for transmission over a network where the encapsulated protocol cannot be routed by itself.

ESF (Extended Super Frame)—The framing type used on T1 circuits that consists of 24 frames of 192 bits each, with the 193rd bit providing timing. ESF is an extended version of the original Super Frame framing type.

ethernet—Baseband LAN specification developed by DIX (Digital, Intel, and Xerox). Ethernet networks use CSMA/CD and run over a variety of cable types, such as 10Base5, 10Base2, and 10BaseT, among others.

fast ethernet—A LAN standard for transmission at 100Mbps. The 100Mbps standard includes 100BaseFX, 100BaseTX, 100BaseT, and other physical methods for transmission.

FCC (Federal Communications Commission)—Supervises, licenses, and controls electronic and electromagnetic transmission standards.

FDDI (Fiber Distributed Data Interface)—The ANSI X3T9.5 LAN standard for using a 100Mbps token-passing network using fiber-optic cable, with transmission distances of up to 2km.

FDM (Frequency-division multiplexing)—Allows multiple channels to share a larger channel by allocating a specific frequency to each participating channel.

FECN (Forward Explicit Congestion Notification)—Frame Relay uses a discard eligible bit when the customer is transmitting above the committed information rate (CIR). When congestion is seen by the frame switches, the packets that are discard eligible are dumped, and an FECN is sent to alert the participating stations to throttle back their transmissions.

FM (Frequency modulation)—A technique to represent 1s and 0s by altering the frequency from a baseline or carrier frequency.

FRAD (Frame Relay access device)—A network device that provides a connection between a customer site and a Frame Relay switch at the local central office (CO) facility.

Frame Relay—A data-link layer protocol that can handle multiple virtual circuits on a single interface. Frame Relay grew out of X.25 as a more efficient replacement.

FTP (File Transfer Protocol)—An application protocol within the TCP/IP protocol stack that is used as a reliable method for file transfer. FTP is defined in RFC 959.

full duplex—Allows both the receiver and transmitter to send data at the same time. This is compared to half duplex where only one side can transmit at a time.

GB—Gigabyte. Equivalent to 1,024 Megabytes.

Gb—Gigabit. Equivalent to one billion bits

GBps—Gigabytes per second.

Gbps—Gigabits per second.

GNS (Get Nearest Server)—Packet sent by a client on an IPX network to locate the nearest active server.

half duplex—Process by which two stations transmit data. With half duplex, only one side can transmit at a time.

HBD3—Type of line code used for E1 circuits.

HDLC (High-Level Data Link Control)— Synchronous data-link layer protocol. Derived from SDLC, HDLC specifies a data encapsulation method for synchronous serial links. HDLC, as implemented on Cisco, is proprietary to Cisco.

hello packet—Multicast packets used by link state protocols for neighbor discovery and synchronization.

hertz (HZ)—A measurement of frequency in cycles per second.

HTML (Hypertext Markup Language)—A document formatting language that uses flags to tell a viewing application how to interpret a given part of a document.

HTTP (Hypertext Transfer Protocol)—Used for Web services.

IANA (Internet Assigned Numbers Authority)—The IANA delegates authority for IP address-space allocation and domain-name assignment to the InterNIC and other organizations. IANA also maintains a database of assigned protocol identifiers used in the TCP/IP stack, including autonomous system numbers.

ICMP (Internet Control Message Protocol)—A part of the TCP/IP protocol stack. ICMP is primarily used to report errors and is defined in RFC 792.

IEEE (Institute of Electrical and Electronics Engineers)—Develops communication and LAN standards. The IEEE LAN standards are the predominant LAN standards and include 802.2, 802.3, 802.4, 802.5, and others.

IEEE 802.2—Defines the implementation of the LLC sublayer of the data-link layer, and handles errors, framing, flow control, and communications to the network layer.

IEEE 802.3—Defines the implementation of the physical layer and the MAC sublayer of the data-link layer using CSMA/CD. The 802.3 is generally referred to as Ethernet; however, it is truly 802.3.

IEEE 802.4—Defines the implementation of the physical layer and the MAC sublayer of the data-link layer using token-passing over a bus topology.

IEEE 802.5—Defines the implementation of the physical layer and MAC sublayer of the data-link layer using token passing over a ring.

IETF (Internet Engineering Task Force)—Consists of over 70 working groups that manage the development of the Internet standards.

IGRP (Interior Gateway Routing Protocol)—A Cisco proprietary routing protocol.

Internet—The collection of publicly accessible TCP/IP-based networks around the world.

intranet—An internal, private network that uses the same protocols and standards as the Internet.

Inverse ARP (Inverse Address Resolution Protocol)—A method to build dynamic routes in a network by associating an IP address with a virtual circuit ID.

IP (Internet Protocol)—A layer 3 protocol in the OSI model. This network layer protocol is used for connectionless delivery of both the TCP and UDP transport layer protocols. IP is defined by RFC 791.

IPCP—The PPP Control Protocol for IP.

IPX (Internetwork Packet Exchange)—The NetWare layer 3 protocol used for transferring data from servers to workstations.

IPXCP—The PPP Control Protocol for IPX.

ISDN (Integrated Services Digital Network)—A communications protocol that provides a higher speed connection than analog over the last mile.

ISO (International Organization for Standardization)—An organization that has developed a wide range of standards, including the OSI reference model.

ISP (Internet Service Provider)—Company that provides Internet access to other companies and individuals.

ITU-T (International Telecommunication Union Telecommunication Standardization Sector)—A standards body that develops worldwide standards for telecommunications technologies. The ITU-T is the new name for the CCITT.

KB—Kilobyte. Approximately 1,000 bytes.

Kb—Kilobit. Approximately 1,000 bits.

KBps—Kilobytes per second.

Kbps—Kilobits per second.

LAN (Local Area Network)—Generally defined as a high-speed, low-error data network that exists in a local geographic area.

LAPB (Link Access Procedure, Balanced)—The data-link layer protocol for the X.25 protocol stack. LAPB is a bit-oriented protocol derived from HDLC.

LAPD (Link Access Procedure on the D channel)—The data-link layer protocol for the ISDN D channel. LAPD was defined by the ITU-T from the LAPB protocol. LAPD is defined by the ITU-T Q.920 and Q.921 recommendations.

last mile—The physical connection between a customer and the closest central office (CO) facility.

LCP (Link Control Protocol)—Establishes, configures, and tests the data-link connection for PPP.

leased line—Transmission line reserved by a communications carrier for the private use of a customer.

LLC (Logical Link Control)—The upper sublayer of the data-link layer of the OSI reference model. LLC primarily handles error control, flow control, and MAC sublayer addressing.

LMI (Local Management Interface)—Provides the management control from the local device to the CO switch.

local loop—Line from the premises of a telephone subscriber to the telephone company CO.

MAC (Media Access Control)—The lower sublayer of the OSI data-link layer. The MAC sublayer provides access to physical media.

Manchester encoding—Digital coding scheme, used by IEEE 802.3 and Ethernet, in which a mid-bit-time transition is used for clocking, and a 1 is denoted by a high level during the first half of the bit time.

MB—Megabyte. Approximately 1,000,000 bytes.

Mb—Megabit. Approximately 1,000,000 bits.

Mbps—Megabits per second.

MLP (Multilink PPP)—The non-proprietary method of aggregating multiple links to achieve higher-speed transfers.

MMP (Multichassis Multilink PPP)—The extension to MLP that supports MLP over multiple routers and access servers.

modem—The term that stands for modulator-demodulator and is the device that converts digital and analog signals.

mu-law—North American standard used to convert between analog and digital signals in public switched networks.

Mux—A device that combines multiple signals for transmission over a single line.

NAT (Network Address Translation)—Provides a method to translate local addresses for use on the Internet.

NBMA network (Non-Broadcast Multi-Access network)—A term that describes, multi-access network that does not allow broadcasting as a mechanism for sending packets such as X.25.

NCP (Network Control Protocol)—This part of PPP serves as the go-between for the layer 3 protocol in use (IP, IPX, and so forth) and PPP. Each protocol will have a Control Protocol (CP) associated with it.

NDIS (Network Device Interface Specification)—An industry-standard specification for how protocols and adapters should be bound.

network—A collection of computers, printers, routers, switches, and other devices that are able to communicate with each other over a transmission medium.

network layer—Layer 3 of the OSI reference model. This layer provides connectivity and path selection between end systems. The network layer is the layer at which routing occurs.

NIC (Network interface card)—The PC card that provides network access.

NRZ (Nonreturn to zero)—A signal that maintains a constant voltage during a bit time interval indicating the presence of data.

NRZI (Nonreturn to zero inverted)—A signal that maintains constant voltage levels with no signal transitions or return to zero when no data is present.

NT-1 (Network termination 1)—The ISDN interface between the customer premise equipment and the CO switching equipment.

ones density—The method used to allow a CSU/DSU to synchronize to a data clock. Ones density is required for asynchronous communications that derive the clock from the data.

OSI (Open System Interconnection)—International standardization program created by ISO and ITU-T to develop standards for data networking.

OSI reference model—Open System Interconnection reference model. Network architectural model developed by ISO and ITU-T, which consists of seven layers—physical, data-link, network, transport, session, presentation, and application.

OSPF (Open Shortest Path First)—A link-state, hierarchical routing protocol.

out-of-band signaling—The method of signaling on a separate channel from the data transfer. It is contrasted with in-band signaling whereby the signaling can be affected by network problems.

PAD (Packet Assembler Disassembler)—The device used to connect devices to a network that does not support the full functionality of any particular protocol. X.25 networks use the PAD as the connection device to X.25 functionality to an end user or customer.

PAP (Password Authentication Protocol)—The PPP protocol suite. Provides minimal end user authentication for the client.

parity check—A process for checking the integrity of an 8-bit character. The parity check adds a bit that, when summed, can be even or odd. Both sides of the transmission must agree on what parity (even or odd) is to be used, and, when a word arrives, the receiver can check the parity to see if the word has been corrupted.

PBX (Private branch exchange)—The carrier switch located on the customer's premises to provide private-to-public access to a telephone network.

PDN (Public data network)—Network operated by either the government or a private entity to provide a communication path to the private sector.

phase shift—A method to allow a receiver to interpret a signal by the position of the phase in relation to the carrier phase.

physical layer—Layer 1 of the OSI model. Defines the electrical specification for the delivery of data (1s and 0s) to the media.

ping—Packet Internet groper.

POP (Point of presence)—The physical location where an ISP has installed equipment to service the customer or end user.

POTS (Plain old telephone system).

PPP (Point-to-Point Protocol)—The industry standard successor to SLIP. PPP supports CHAP and PAP for authentication and is currently the most widely used serial line protocol.

presentation layer—Layer 6 of the OSI model. This layer ensures that information sent by the application layer of one system is properly encoded to be readable by the receiver.

PRI (Primary Rate Interface)—The ISDN interface that consists of 23 B channels and 1 D channel.

Priority Queuing—Allows the administrator to tell the router to forward mission-critical traffic at the expense of non-mission-critical traffic if necessary.

PSTN (Public Switched Telephone Network)—A generic term that refers to any carrier network.

PVC (Permanent virtual circuit)—A circuit that is established by the carrier and is not "torn down." It is effectively a leased line through a PSTN.

Q.920/Q.921—ITU-T specifications for the ISDN data-link layer.

Q.931—ITU-T specifications for the ISDN network layer.

Queuing—The process where the router stores packets for processing in a specified order, not necessarily based on arrival.

RARP (Reverse Address Resolution Protocol)—A part of the TCP/IP stack that provides a method for finding IP addresses based on MAC addresses.

RAS (Remote Access Server)—A term used to describe the general concept of connecting remote users, typically using low-speed inexpensive resources like analog, DSL, or ISDN to gain access to remote resources.

RBOC (Regional Bell operating company)

Repeater—A device that regenerates an electrical signal between two network segments.

reverse Telnet—A Cisco term specifying that Telnet is being used to connect to a local port on the device. This is contrasted with Telneting to a location off the device.

RFC (Request For Comments)—Documents that provide input to the standards committees regarding Internet communication.

RIP (Routing Information Protocol)—The oldest and most common distance vector routing protocol.

Router—A network layer device that determines optimal path information to network traffic.

RS-232—Recommend Standard-232. A physical layer signaling method that has been ratified as EIA/TIA-232.

RTS (Request To Send pin)—Defined by the EIA/TIA-232 standard, the control signal that requests a data transmission on a communications line.

sampling rate—The rate at which samples of a particular waveform amplitude are taken.

SDLC (Synchronous Data Link Control)—A bit-oriented, full-duplex serial protocol. It is the basis for HDLC and LAPB.

session layer—Layer 5 of the OSI model. It establishes and manages the sessions between presentation layer connections.

SF (Super Frame)—A framing type used on T1 circuits, which has been replaced by Extended Super Frame (ESF).

SLIP (Serial Line Internet Protocol)—A standards-based protocol that has been replaced by PPP.

SMTP (Simple Mail Transfer Protocol)—Part of the TCP/IP protocol suite that provides email service.

SOHO (Small office, home office)

SPID (Service profile identifier)—Used by some North American ISDN service providers. It relates the phone number to a class of service.

SPP (Sequenced Packet Protocol)—A connection-based transmission on behalf of client processes. SPP is part of the XNS protocol suite.

SPX (Sequenced Packet Exchange)—A reliable, connection-oriented protocol that is used at the network layer (Layer 3) by Novell.

SS7 (Signaling System 7)—A standard developed by Bellcore used with ISDN.

statistical multiplexing—The method where multiple channels transmit over a physical circuit based on their need.

subinterface—One of a number of virtual interfaces on a single physical interface.

subnet—A portion or segment of a network.

subnet mask—A 32-bit address that indicates how many bits in an address are being used for the network ID.

SVC (Switched Virtual Circuit)—A circuit that is dynamically established on demand and is torn down when transmission is complete.

synchronous transmission—Describes digital signals that are transmitted with precise clocking that is maintained in the background for the circuit.

T1—Transmits at 1.544Mbps over a carrier network. The line coding in the United States is either AMI or B8ZS.

T3—Transmits at 44.736Mbps over a carrier network. A T3 consists of DS3 formatted data and is a bundle of 28 T1 circuits or 672 DS0s.

TACACS (Terminal Access Controller Access Control System)—Developed by the Defense Data Network to provide a central database for event logging and username/password authentication, to provide an easier method for administration of large numbers of dial-in users.

TACACS+ (Terminal Access Controller Access Control System)—The '+' version of this has Cisco's extensions to TACACS. These extensions include additional accounting and reporting features.

T-carrier—Time division multiplexing signaling method for carrying a DS-1 signal. T-carrier is the name given to the method of using digital signaling over T1 and T3 circuits.

TCP (Transmission Control Protocol)—Transport layer protocol in the TCP/IP protocol stack that provides reliable data transmission.

TCP/IP (Transmission Control Protocol/Internet Protocol)—Name of the protocol suite developed for the ARPANET by the Department of Defense.

TDM (Time-division multiplexing)—Allows multiple channels to share an aggregate bandwidth by giving each channel an assigned time slot.

TE (Terminal equipment)—Refers to ISDN-compatible equipment. If it is a TE1 device, it is directly compatible; if it is a TE2 device, it must be connected through a terminal adapter (TA).

TEI (Terminal endpoint identifier)—The physical address used in ISDN to identify a device. The TEI is generally assigned by the local central office switch.

telco (telephone company)—This term is used to generically reference the local provider for the area.

Telnet—Defined in RFC 854, a terminal emulation protocol that is used for remote terminal connections. It is a piece of the TCP/IP protocol stack.

TFTP (Trivial File Transfer Protocol)—A connectionless-oriented best-effort file transfer protocol, which is part of the TCP/IP protocol stack.

TIA (Telecommunications Industry Association Organization)—The standards body for telecommunications technologies.

Token Ring—LAN technology using token-passing developed by IBM. Token Ring runs at 4Mbps or 16Mbps. Token Ring was further developed and incorporated by the IEEE as the 802.5 standard.

traffic shaping—A method to regulate and prioritize the traffic that is being transmitted instead of using the first-in-first-out (FIFO) method. Traffic shaping is most used on Frame Relay networks; however, it can be used on many WAN links.

transport layer—Layer 4 of the OSI reference model. It is responsible for reliable communication between end stations. This layer is referred to as the reliable layer.

UDP (User Datagram Protocol)—A connectionless transport layer protocol in the TCP/IP protocol stack. UDP is a simple protocol that exchanges data without acknowledgments or guaranteed delivery, and is defined in RFC768.

V.32—The ITU-T standard serial line protocol for bidirectional data transmissions at speeds of 4.8Kbps or 9.6Kbps.

V.32bis—The ITU-T standard that extends V.32 to speeds up to 14.4Kbps.

V.34—The ITU-T standard that specifies a serial line protocol and offers a higher transmission rate of 28.8Kbps.

V.35—The ITU-T standard describing synchronous communications between a network access device and a packet network, and is recommended for speeds up to 48Kbps.

virtual circuit—A logical circuit created for the duration of a connection.

VPDN (Virtual Private Dial-up Network)

VPN (Virtual Private Networks)—Allow IP traffic to travel over a public TCP/IP network. A VPN uses L2TP to deliver the remote data to a central site.

WAN (Wide Area Network)—A network that spans geographically distant segments. Often, a distance of two or more miles is used to define a WAN. Microsoft, however, considers any Remote Access Service (RAS) connection as an established WAN.

Weighted Fair Queuing—A simple queuing process where the router processes packets based on the time the packet fully arrived in the router. This is the simplest method of queuing, because it is enabled by default on all interfaces not using X.25 encapsulation or compressed PPP and only if the interface bandwidth is no more than 2.048mb (E1).

WINS (Windows Internet Name Service)—A Windows network service used to resolve NetBIOS names to IP addresses.

X.25—The ITU-T standard that defines how connections between DTE and DCE are implemented and maintained for remote terminal access in X.25 PDNs.

X.121—The ITU-T standard describing an addressing scheme used in X.25 networks.

XDSL—The generic term used to refer to the many flavors of DSL, which include ADSL, HDSL, SDSL, and VDSL.

Index

. . . .

Bold page numbers indicate sample exam questions.

Look for All of the Exam Cram Brand Certification Study Systems

ALL NEW! Exam Cram Personal Trainer Systems

The Exam Cram Personal Trainer systems are an exciting new category in certification training products. These CD-ROM based systems offer extensive capabilities at a moderate price and are the first certification-specific testing product to completely link learning with testing.

This Exam Cram Study Guide turned interactive course lets you customize the way you learn.

Each system includes:

• A Personalized Practice Test engine with multiple test methods,

• A database of nearly 300 questions linked directly to the subject matter within the Exam Cram on which that question is based.

Exam Cram Audio Review Systems

Written and read by certification instructors, each set contains four cassettes jam-packed with the certification exam information you must have. Designed to be used on their own or as a complement to our Exam Cram Study Guides, Flash Cards, and Practice Tests.

Each system includes:

• Study preparation tips with an essential last-minute review for the exam

• Hours of lessons highlighting key terms and techniques

• A comprehensive overview of all exam objectives

• 45 minutes of review questions complete with answers and explanations

Exam Cram Flash Cards

These pocket-sized study tools are 100% focused on exams. Key questions appear on side one of each card and in-depth answers on side two. Each card features either a cross-reference to the appropriate Exam Cram Study Guide chapter or to another valuable resource. Comes with a CD-ROM featuring electronic versions of the flash cards and a complete practice exam.

Exam Cram Practice Tests

Our readers told us that extra practice exams were vital to certification success, so we created the perfect companion book for certification study material.

Each book contains:

• Several practice exams

• Electronic versions of practice exams on the accompanying CD-ROM presented in an interactive format enabling practice in an environment similar to that of the actual exam

• Each practice question is followed by the corresponding answer (why the right answers are right and the wrong answers are wrong)

• References to the Exam Cram Study Guide chapter or other resource for that topic

The Coriolis Exam Cram Personal Trainer
An exciting new category in certification training products

The Exam Cram Personal trainer is the first certification-specific testing product that completely links learning with testing to:

- **Increase your comprehension**
- **Decrease the time it takes you to learn**

No system blends learning content with test questions as effectively as the Exam Cram Personal Trainer.

Only the Exam Cram Personal Trainer offers this much power at this price.

Its unique Personalized Test Engine provides a real-time test environment and an authentic representation of what you will encounter during your actual certification exams.

Much More Than Just Another CBT!

Most current CBT learning systems offer simple review questions at the end of a chapter with an overall test at the end of the course, with no links back to the lessons. But Exam Cram Personal Trainer takes learning to a higher level.

Its four main components are:

- The complete text of an Exam Cram study guide in an HTML format,
- A Personalized Practice Test Engine with multiple test methods

Adaptive:	25-35 questions
Fixed-length:	Four unique exams on critical areas
Random:	Each randomly generated test is unique
Test All:	Drawn from the complete database of questions
Topic:	Organized by Exam Cram chapters
Review:	Questions with answers are presented

Scenario-based questions: Just like the real thing

- A database of nearly 300 questions linked directly to an Exam Cram chapter
- Over two hours of Exam Cram Audio Review

Plus, additional features include:

- **Hint:** Not sure of your answer? Click Hint and the software goes to the text that covers that topic.
- **Lesson:** Still not enough detail? Click Lesson and the software goes to the beginning of the chapter.
- **Update feature:** Need even more questions? Click Update to download more questions from the Coriolis Web site.
- **Notes:** Create your own memory joggers.
- **Graphic analysis:** How did you do? View your score, the required score to pass, and other information.
- **Personalized Cram Sheet:** Print unique study information just for you.

MCSE Networking Essentials Exam Cram Personal Trainer
ISBN:1-57610-644-6

MCSE NT Server 4 Exam Cram Personal Trainer
ISBN: 1-57610-645-4

MCSE NT Server 4 in the Enterprise Exam Cram Personal Trainer
ISBN: 1-57610-646-2

MCSE NT Workstation 4 Exam Cram Personal Trainer
ISBN:1-57610-647-0

A+ Exam Cram Personal Trainer
ISBN: 1-57610-658-6

$69.99 U.S. • $104.99 Canada

Available: March 2000

CORIOLIS™
Certification Insider Press

**The Smartest Way to Get Certified
Just Got Smarter**™

Better, Faster, Louder!

Get certified on the go with *EXAM CRAM™ AUDIO TAPES*

A+ Exam Cram Audio Review
ISBN: 1-57610-541-5
$39.99 U.S. • $59.99 Canada
Four hours of audio instruction
Cassettes • Available Now

Network+ Exam Cram Audio Review
ISBN: 1-57610-534-2
$39.99 U.S. • $59.99 Canada
Four hours of audio instruction
Cassettes • Available Now

MCSE Core Four Exam Cram Audio Review
ISBN: 1-57610-631-4
$39.99 U.S. • $59.99 Canada
Four hours of audio instruction
Cassettes • Available Now

AUDIO TAPES

Hear what you've been missing with Exam Cram Audio Review tapes. Each set contains four cassettes jam-packed with the certification information you must have to pass your exams. Exam Cram Audio Review tapes can be used on their own or as a complement to our Exam Cram Study Guides, Flash Cards, and Practice Tests.

FLASH CARDS

Exam Cram Flash Cards are the pocket-sized study tool that provide key questions on one side of each card and in-depth answers on the other. Each card features a cross-reference to the appropriate chapter in the corresponding Exam Cram Study Guide or other valuable resource. Each pack includes 100 cards 100% focused on exam material, along with a CD-ROM featuring electronic versions of the flash cards and a complete practice exam.

PRACTICE TESTS

Each book contains several practice exams with electronic versions on the accompanying CD-ROM. Each practice question is followed by the corresponding answer (*why the right answers are right and the wrong answers are wrong*). References to the Exam Cram Study Guide and chapter or other valuable resource in which the topic is discussed in depth are included. The CD-ROM presents exams in an interactive format, enabling you to practice in an environment similar to that of the actual exam.

CORIOLIS™

Certification Insider Press

**The <u>Smartest</u> Way to Get Certified
Just Got Smarter™**